Revolutionary Syndicalism in France

the direct action of its time

To P.F.C.R.

Revolutionary Syndicalism in France

the direct action of its time

F. F. RIDLEY

Professor of Political Theory and Institutions
University of Liverpool

CAMBRIDGE

AT THE UNIVERSITY PRESS

1970

Published by the Syndics of the Cambridge University Press
Bentley House, 200 Euston Road, London N.W.1

© Cambridge University Press 1970

Library of Congress Catalogue Card Number: 73 123663

ISBN: 0 521 07907 1

Printed in Great Britain
at the University Printing House, Cambridge
(Brooke Crutchley, University Printer)

Contents

Preface   *page* ix

Introduction   1

HISTORICAL BACKGROUND

National character and revolutionary tradition	11
From craft to industry	15
The repressive state	20
Proudhon and mutual aid	25
Blanqui and the barricades	33
Bakunin and anarchism	38
The socialist tower of babel	45
The betrayal of the politicians	53
The growth of an organised movement	63
Strength and organisation of the *C.G.T.*	72

PRINCIPLES AND PRACTICE OF THE C.G.T.

Reform and revolution: the twofold purpose	83
Political neutrality and the politics of syndicalism	88
The autonomy of labour and direct action	95
The theory of the strike	99
The strike in practice	107
The tactics of the strike	112
Subsidiary forms of direct action	120
Labour as a political pressure group	128
Antimilitarism and antipatriotism	135
Genealogy of the general strike	140
The changing picture of the general strike	147
The general strike as myth	156
Organised labour and the syndicalist utopia	165
A theory of syndicalism	170
Conflicting voices in the *C.G.T.*	176
Leaders and followers, theory and practice	182

Contents

IDEOLOGICAL CONTEXT

The revolt against reason   *page* 191
Nietzsche and the transvaluation of all values   197
Bergson and creative evolution   200
James and the pragmatic approach   204
The revolt against democracy   208
The discredit of French democracy   213
Nationalism, monarchism and the right   220
Fascism: the alternative path   230
Sorel: a moralist in search of action   239
The philosopher and the labour movement   249
The militants and the activist temper   256
Syndicalism as a philosophy of action   262

Conclusion   269

Bibliography   271

Index   277

Preface

France, May 1968. Students at the barricades, workers on general strike. Not quite a revolution, but something that might well have been a revolution had it occurred on the same scale sixty years earlier. Direct action was the slogan and direct action was what happened. More recently, a paperback by British students promising a renewal of revolutionary politics. Their struggle is against the social system as a whole; they refuse, therefore, to act according to its rules. Their revolutionary politics means the rejection of the politics of democracy as currently defined. They refuse to pin their hopes on the political parties, much less on parliament. They scorn the bourgeois passivity of a bourgeois system. Their aim is to conquer power from outside, by the extra-parliamentary opposition, a phrase already made popular by the students of Germany. The goal: power over their everyday lives exercised by the people themselves in all the particular institutions which comprise society.

Some sixty years earlier almost identical ideas had captured the French working class. Revolutionary syndicalism was the name of that movement. The syndicalists, too, rejected bourgeois parliamentary democracy and the capitalist system. Capitalism, however reformed, still meant exploitation and unfreedom. Democracy was a dead end—it could never lead to the emancipation of the proletariat. The system could not be destroyed from within, according to its own rules. They rejected political parties, election campaigns, reformist legislation, even the conquest of state power. They preached extra-parliamentary opposition, direct action and the general strike. They sought to replace the democratic state by a social order in which the workers would control their own lives through their own institutions.

Nothing is ever entirely new. Militant workers at the beginning of the century, militant students in the late sixties. There are links between what happened then and what has happened more recently, between ideas expressed then and ideas expressed more recently. They were in revolt against similar things; they advocated similar means to achieve similar ends. The syndicalist critique is echoed in later critiques, the syndicalist strategy in later strategies, the syndicalist goal in later goals. The parallels will strike the reader. It is not necessary to force them on his attention.

F.F.R.

vii

Introduction

Syndicalism is a deceptive word. It *looks* very similar to such words as marxism or anarchism and is thus often taken as the name of just another school of socialist thought. It is only too easy for the historian of political ideas to assume that he can deal with it in a chapter no different from that devoted to utopian, marxist or fabian socialism. Syndicalism, however, was not the creation of a particular writer, nor even of a group of writers. Despite the 'ism' which lends it so theoretical an air, it was originally the name given to a movement rather than a theory. Although it subsequently acquired a wider ideological significance, and was turned by some theorists into an 'ism' after all, it is not unreasonable to stay with the original use. An operational definition of this sort has the advantage of avoiding theoretical predefinitions which begin by assuming what it is intended to prove, arbitrarily limiting the scope of enquiry by reference to the critic's own conceptual framework. Syndicalism was what those who called themselves syndicalists thought and did.

Syndicalism was originally the name given by its members to the French trade-union movement during its revolutionary phase, roughly the first decade of this century or, more accurately, the name adopted by the revolutionary wing which claimed to be in a majority. Although syndicalist groups later emerged elsewhere, it was in France that the movement had its fullest development and it was from France that most of the ideas came. The English term syndicalism, indeed, was originally a straight translation from the French. It is not unreasonable, therefore, to define it in French terms and to concentrate on the French phenomenon.

The French word *syndicalisme* means no more than trade-unionism. The French described their movement as *syndicalisme révolutionnaire*. When we talk of syndicalism we really mean revolutionary syndicalism. The adjective is more easily dropped in English than in French, there being less likelihood of confusion, but it is partly upon the adjective that the definition depends. It did not simply mean that the unions were committed to revolutionary politics—that has been true at times of communist-dominated unions also. Revolution and unionism were equally important: syndicalism stood for revolutionary action by unions to establish a society based upon unions.

An account of syndicalism should therefore begin with the movement and not with some given doctrine. Syndicalism meant the sum of ideas expressed by the movement and the sum of its activities: it was the outlook shared by members and the form their action took.

Principles emerged at different times, one by one, sometimes with little reference to each other, often not supported by practice. Syndicalism lacked consistency. Principles were capable of changing almost imperceptibly as the need arose without any fundamental break ever becoming apparent. The analogy that springs to mind is the patchwork quilt—bits added now here, now there, gradually built up, but in accordance with no prearranged plan, forming no clear pattern, one patch often clashing with the next, the whole changing all the time it grows. But at least such principles can be traced. They appeared in the resolutions of trade-union congresses and in the pamphlets of its militant leaders. Syndicalism was also a mode of action and that is much harder to pin down. It is doubly difficult because such action was not necessarily rational in the sense of 'think first, act after'. The syndicalists often stressed the spontaneity of the movement. It may be, therefore, that a coherent theory did not exist at all. In so far as it did, it was implied rather than formulated and thus needs to be reconstructed by the historian of political thought.

It follows that a study of syndicalism falls between two disciplines, history and political theory. Between the two, it is hard to find a middle way. The difficulty of reconciling the analytic and the historical approaches explains the unsatisfactory nature of much that has been written on the subject. A historical study is a tedious and difficult affair. Commentators have sometimes gone to syndicalist writings rather than to the record of syndicalist action. But even that is not easy. Such material is dispersed in congress reports, newspaper articles and occasional pamphlets. As a result, they have more often followed the easier path of using material available in the book form to which they are accustomed. As far as the histories of political thought are concerned, syndicalism was put on the map by its self-appointed apostle, Georges Sorel. This was additionally unfortunate as he was quite unrepresentative of the labour movement. Those who did not fall into the Sorelian trap tended to quote a small group of militant leaders whose ideas were accepted, by and large, but who were not necessarily representative of the rank and file.

The conflict between the theoretical and the historical approach has led to another form of misrepresentation. As G. D. H. Cole put it: "it is after all with ideas that we (i.e. political theorists) are more directly concerned".[1] This has often meant a failure to draw the correct balance between theory and practice. Declarations of principle have often been taken on their face value and used to construct a theory even when they were patently unrepresentative of what the movement probably thought (if it had clear thoughts at all, itself unlikely) and even when they were obviously unrelated to how the movement actually behaved. There is another danger hidden in

[1] G. D. H. Cole, *World of Labour*, 1928, p. 6.

2

the theoretical approach. The theorist's natural desire to organise his material in logical form, with a beginning, an end and consistent argument between, may easily lead him to impose a self-made order on a subject matter quite unsuited to the purpose. To present syndicalism in this way is to treat it as something static, whereas its ideas were perpetually modified by the stress of events. It is to treat it as something unified, whereas its ideas covered a whole range of divergent shades of opinion. Over-simplification is the result. And the result of that is distortion. It is, of course, quite legitimate for the political theorist to construct a theory of syndicalism. Such a theory is valuable in its own right. It may, for example, interest the student searching for an alternative philosophy of socialism. But this must not be confused with a claim to represent the syndicalism of the French labour movement.

The central part of this study tries to bridge the gap between history and analysis. Debates, resolutions, articles and pamphlets are examined in order to extract from them, as far as possible, a number of syndicalist principles. At the same time, an attempt is made to disengage the implications of syndicalist practice. There was much unclarity, some lack of agreement; theory and practice tended to change over time; discrepancies between theory and practice can be seen. If the wood tends to disappear for the trees, it may be because it never had such clear boundaries as certain observers thought to see. There was a wood, certainly, but some of its trees were rather far apart; in some places they merged into other woods. A brief sketch of a syndicalist theory is nevertheless offered. The emphasis throughout, however, is that the underlying unity of the movement—and the key to syndicalism—lay not in theory but in the outlook of the movement, above all in the temper that inspired its action.

Revolutionary syndicalism was used by French workers to describe a particular direction in the labour movement. They used the term to distinguish their wing from other wings which were either reformist or, if revolutionary, politically oriented—i.e. from socialists and marxists. They claimed to be in a majority in the trade union movement between 1902 and 1914. Though this is open to dispute, they undoubtedly controlled the movement's central organisation, the *Confédération Générale du Travail*, during this period. As by their own definition revolutionary syndicalism was neither a preconceived theory nor an integrated doctrine but the movement itself, its principles and its practice, it is reasonable to define syndicalism as the principles and practice of the *C.G.T.* between 1902 and 1914. This definition has conceptual disadvantages but it comes close to the revolutionary syndicalist's own usage and is in line with the point made

Introduction

earlier that syndicalism should be examined in terms of the outlook and activities of those who used the label.

A working definition of syndicalism, therefore, is the principles and practice of the *C.G.T.* in the years between 1902 and 1914. 'Practice' because syndicalism was a mode of action and it was in that action, rather than books, that its expression was to be found; 'principles' because there was no official philosophy but only a series of ideas and policies pointing in a general direction. In one sense, it would have been more accurate to qualify the definition by saying majority of the *C.G.T.* and, in so far as one examines the ideas expressed by individuals, it is to the leaders of that wing one must look. But many, often conflicting, voices claimed to speak in the name of syndicalism and it is sometimes hard to see which opinion, which policy, was its authoritative expression. In so far as one can be pinned down —and this is only possible within limits—it was that of the Confederation. For this there is support from Léon Jouhaux, many years its secretary and acknowledged leader; the congresses of the *C.G.T.* played a decisive role in determining the activities of the unions; they laid down the goals to be pursued and the means to be employed; they established the principles of the movement.[1]

The choice of years is a somewhat artificial one, as any such division is bound to be. Broadly speaking, there were two fundamental principles which distinguished the trade unionism of this period from earlier and later years: revolutionary action and the autonomy of the labour movement. There was no sudden break in 1902. By then the unions had already rejected socialist party politics and state-sponsored reforms; they had already adopted the doctrine of the general strike. But 1902 saw the unification of the labour movement after a long period overshadowed by organisational questions and thus permitted a considerable increase in direct action. Nineteen fourteen marked a more definite turning point. The outbreak of war saw the end of all revolutionary pretensions. After the war, certain syndicalist ideas were reaffirmed, but as a mere formality; collaboration with the state continued and policy was essentially reformist. The *C.G.T. Unitaire*, created by the communists in 1921, was certainly revolutionary in spirit, but it was subservient to the party. A *C.G.T. Syndicaliste Révolutionnaire* was formed shortly after and survived until the outbreak of the last war, but it was very small and had no further influence on the history of the French labour movement.

The habit of political scientists has been to use syndicalism in a rather different sense. Chapters on syndicalism in histories of political thought are

[1] L. Jouhaux, *Le syndicalisme et la C.G.T.*, 1920, p. 19.

4

Introduction

likely to cover the philosophy of Georges Sorel as well as the doctrines of the *C.G.T.* Often no clear distinction is made between them. Sometimes a line of sorts is drawn. Certain writers have used the terms *militants* to describe the labour movement and *théoriciens* to describe the self-styled *nouvelle école* that gathered around Sorel.[1] Given contemporary usage, this had some advantage. The disadvantage is that it creates a misleading impression that the *C.G.T.* and the *nouvelle école* were two branches of the same movement. The relationship between them will be discussed later but the point should be made here that Sorel was at best an interpreter of the movement; he played no active part in its affairs and there were no personal contacts between him and the militants. Though he had many illuminating comments to make about syndicalism, his philosophy was really quite different from that of the workers.

Another distinction appears to be necessary, and that within the ranks of the militants. Revolutionary syndicalism owed much to a small group of men, notably Griffuelhes, Pouget, Yvetot and Delesalle. These four were the most articulate members of the revolutionary-syndicalist wing of the *C.G.T.*—they wrote most of its pamphlets. Between them they occupied the leading positions in the *C.G.T.* and one was the editor of its newspaper. In many ways they were the real force behind it. There is an obvious temptation to identify syndicalism with what they wrote. This identification is also misleading, though not as misleading as the identification with Sorel. Their doctrines were often more radical than those officially adopted by the *C.G.T.*, their tone more revolutionary, their ideas more anarchistic. Their ideas were also more sophisticated, within limits more systematised, than those of the majority. It is possible to argue, indeed, that they too were in a sense interpreters of the movement, always a step ahead of the rank and file. It would have been tempting to call Griffuelhes, Pouget, Yvetot and Delesalle the theorists of the movement and the rest the militants. As it is, it has been necessary to use the term 'militant leaders' or 'militant theorists' for the former, 'rank and file' for the latter.

Of course, such a distinction is possible only within limits. The militant theorists were after all the leaders of the Confederation and, as such, largely responsible for its activities as well as its resolutions and manifestos. The extent of their responsibility is, in fact, an important point that will have to be examined. There is no doubt that their ideas were more advanced than those of the rank and file. True, they claimed only to be crystallising ideas already at work within the movement, telling the workers what their

---

[1] Cf. Pirou, 'A propos du syndicalisme révolutionnaire: théoriciens et militants' in *Revue Politique et Parlementaire*, October 1911; and R. Goetz-Girey, *La pensée française syndicaliste: militants et théoriciens*, 1948.

instincts already told them, or would tell them were they aware of the true nature of the class war. But they also drew on other, more theoretical, traditions, on the doctrines of Blanqui and of anarchism. Evidence of a more direct nature than their own is thus necessary to understand the principles and practice of the labour movement.

A straightforward analysis of the principles and practice of syndicalism cannot do full justice to the movement, even if it takes account of all its complexities. It is the attempt of an outsider to give a rational account of something that was never intended to be translated into such words. The syndicalists were neither philosophers nor politicians but workers; they were less concerned with ideas than with the actual, everyday struggle to improve their lives. Syndicalism has often been called a philosophy of action. Sometimes this simply meant that the syndicalists were concerned with a strategy of action rather than the solution of abstract problems and that they were guided by their own experience, the lessons of life, rather than ivory-tower speculation. Sometimes, however, it meant something more: the syndicalists did not think about action but acted more or less spontaneously. In that sense, there was no consciously held syndicalist theory at all; their action *was* their philosophy. This is a little too sophisticated. More plausibly: syndicalism was a mode of action and the temper underlying that mode; syndicalist ideas formed an intuitive mind-picture not a verbal construct.

Schumpeter commented that writers who assume that everything can be described rationally inevitably emasculate syndicalism. That, for him, was the feature of syndicalism which distinguished it from all other forms of socialism.[1] Two points are involved. If the syndicalism of the workers was a composite mind-picture, it can only be grasped as a whole. Described rationally, the ideas of the movement become unrelated abstractions, their true meaning is lost. Sorel was fond of quoting Bergson in this context: to analyse is to destroy. If the picture was intuitive, it can only be grasped intuitively. The same is true if syndicalism was a particular temper: it has to be experienced to be fully understood. It is necessary to feel oneself into the movement.

To appreciate syndicalism, therefore, it is important to have a picture of the movement before one's eyes, not merely a series of facts and figures or a series of principles. Such a picture comes only with long study and the sense of familiarity created by the gradual accumulation of a host of details, minor in themselves. To recreate the spirit of syndicalism within the covers of a book, to paint the full picture, requires other gifts than those of the

[1] J. A. Schumpeter, *Capitalism, Socialism, Democracy*, 1943, p. 339.

Introduction

historian or political scientist. The problem is acute in syndicalism, though by no means special to it. It was Goethe who said: "Wird der Poet nur geboren, der Philosoph wirds nicht minder; alle Wahrheit, zuletzt, wird nur gebildet, geschaut."

A first essential is doubtless sympathy. One can take this further. According to Proudhon: "Pour juger au fond d'un système, il faut en quelque façon y croire, parce que l'on ne conçoit bien que ce que l'on étudie avec passion."[1] If, as Schumpeter claimed, there was no rationale for syndicalism, one is certainly thrown back on the somewhat paradoxical doctrine of *credo ut intellegam!*—I believe in order to understand! According to Schumpeter, of course, this is not possible for the political scientist: "Unlike marxism or fabianism, syndicalism cannot be espoused by anyone afflicted by any trace of economic or sociological training."[2] Proudhon and Schumpeter, taken together, would bar any understanding of syndicalism at all. Fortunately, both exaggerated. Sympathy may remain critical.

The first part of this study is devoted to the historical background of syndicalism. An attempt is made to trace the various forces which shaped the French labour movement and helped to form its temper, underpinning the interpretation of syndicalism as a way of thought and a mode of action. It may also help the reader to understand its character. Several strands have been picked out: political culture, economic development, the law relating to trade unions, the record of the socialist parties and the influence of certain political thinkers. The choice and arrangement of facts may appear a little arbitrary. No claim is made that this is history for its own sake. Only what seemed relevant has been discussed. The procedure is bound once more to be in some way analytic; the several strands may appear a little disjointed. To synthesise what the intellect has divided, to apprehend the multiplicity of interpenetrating causes—that, as Bergson said, is the task of intuition. Syndicalism differed from marxism or anarchism in that it never existed in isolation. It was not the product of disinterested speculation. Institutions preceded ideas and ideas reflected the character of institutions. Syndicalism was unionism, even if unionism of a special sort. The debates of the labour movement were not concerned with laws of history or blueprints of utopia but with the problems facing it. This, too, was reflected in its ideas. The final chapter of this section is therefore devoted to the history of the labour movement itself.

[1] P. J. Proudhon, *Avertissement aux propriétaires.*
[2] J. A. Schumpeter, *Capitalism, Socialism, Democracy*, 1943, p. 339.

Introduction

Syndicalism was not simply a phase in the history of the French trade unions. Syndicalist theory was not an isolated chapter in the history of political thought. The movement and its ideas together formed part of a wider current of movements and ideas. Parallel to it ran movements of right-wing revolt, first nationalist, then fascist. Both were a reaction to the same apparent failure of democracy; they had a common object of attack: the parliamentary system. Both could be seen as the expression of a similar temperament—romantic, activist, anti-intellectual—which linked them in another object of attack: bourgeois values and bourgeois life. Some attention must be paid to Sorel, the thinker, and Mussolini, the practitioner. Both stood at the crossroads where the extreme right met the extreme left; both explored the two paths. At the same time, the account of syndicalism is extended beyond the principles and practice of the labour movement as such and special attention is paid to the more sophisticated doctrines of its militant leaders. Their ideas show many points of contact with a wider movement of thought, generally described as romantic or anti-intellectual and associated with Nietzsche, Bergson and William James. The revolt against democracy on the one hand, the revolt against Reason on the other—the two were themselves interwoven. History, philosophy and temperament all conspired to relate syndicalism to this broad current of revolt. The purpose of the final section in this study is to place syndicalism against a wider background and to illustrate its deeper significance.

HISTORICAL BACKGROUND

National character and revolutionary tradition

Earlier writers often suggested that syndicalism was something especially French, born of, or reflecting, the peculiar character of the French people. Of all the influences that went to form the labour movement in France, national character is certainly the most general and may for that reason serve as a starting point. But it is well to remember John Stuart Mill's warning: of all the vulgar modes of escaping from the consideration of the effects of social and moral influences upon the human mind, the most vulgar is that of attributing the diversities of human conduct to inherent natural differences. Racial theories are now rightly discredited. National character can be defined instead as learned behaviour, shared and transmitted by the members of a particular society. This may include the Latin temperament which some claim to have observed in syndicalism itself. It is certainly possible to find passages in books about the French in general which seem to fit the syndicalists in particular. These books tend now to be out of fashion; their evidence is not very scientific. National character may be a dubious influence but it is, perhaps, the most entertaining and that alone may justify the following pages.

THE LATIN TEMPER. One Frenchman, in a book addressed to the English reader in 1925, said of his countrymen: "We are capable of impulsive, sudden and explosive action. We are easily set on fire by an idea, a cause; we abandon ourselves utterly to a spirit of exaltation that carries us away and prevents us from seeing the obstacles in our path, and as happens with enthusiasm not supported by reflection, these ardours cannot long be sustained at the same pitch. Thus we lay ourselves open to the reproach of instability."[1] Sombart had ascribed syndicalism to the Latin temperament in an almost identical passage six years earlier: "The only people who could possibly act on such a system of teaching are Frenchmen and Italians. They are generally men who do things impulsively and on the spur of the moment, men who are seized by a sudden passionate enthusiasm which moves their inmost being and forces them to act at once, and who possess a vast fund of emotion, showing itself quickly and suddenly; but they have little application, perseverance, calm or steadiness."[2]

One might conclude that the French worker, seeking an outlet for his

[1] A. Feuillerat, *French Life and Ideals*, 1925, p. 25.
[2] W. Sombart, *Socialism and The Social Movement*, 1919, p. 110.

enthusiasm in politics, would naturally incline to extremist and revolutionary doctrines. Syndicalism provided an outlet for his *élan*, an opportunity for explosive action. Such enthusiasm is difficult to sustain for long, especially in the absence of material success. The idea of the revolutionary general strike captivated the French working class, but only for a time. The brighter the fire of exaltation, the sooner it burns out; the blinder the passion, the more likely that obstacles will destroy it. The heroic age of syndicalism was necessarily shortlived. Its instability the labour movement shared with the general run of French politics.

Reason and imagination—the love of abstract ideas—is perhaps another key to the French character. "Facility is the foremost intellectual quality of the Frenchman. He unhesitatingly puts his finger on the thread which leads him to discover the essentials, keeps his eyes constantly fixed on the goal. The Englishman loves to embrace detail and often attaches more value to the details than to the whole. In submitting himself to the discipline of selection, the Frenchman acquires another intellectual quality: the capacity for generalising. To the French mind, generalisation is not only a habit, it is a need. And that is why we hold that general ideas are more important than facts."[1] The operative sentence, as far as the workers were concerned, was the last. The problems facing the labour movement, the facts to be taken into account and the ends to be achieved, could all be reduced to a simple pattern. Qualifications that would spoil the pattern were eliminated, so that only the extremes remained. One result was the syndicalist doctrine of the class war, at once crudely simplified and grossly exaggerated. Another result of this hyper-logical approach was impatience with details. In practice this showed itself in the syndicalists' professed, and often real, lack of interest in sideline reforms: 'all or nothing' was the logical consequence of their attitude. In their theoretical discussions it led to a similar unwillingness to work out the details of the revolution they advocated and the society they hoped to establish.

Although syndicalism arose largely from the experience and activity of the labour movement, the importance attached to ideas meant that, once formulated, they achieved a life of their own. By the process of simplification, they tended to become slogans, another common feature of French politics. Such slogans may have their own power to inspire action, overshadowing even the more realistic possibilities of the moment. The slogans of class war and direct action, repeated often enough, modified the policy of the labour movement in a direction that a more realistic appraisal would not necessarily have seen in its best, immediate interest. This may be linked with the love of rhetoric that has often been attributed to the French. We

[1] A. Feuillerat, *French Life and Ideals*, 1925, pp. 47/49.

have the evidence of Cato: "Duas res industrissime persequitur gens Gallorum, rem militarem et argute loqui." Combine rhetoric with a tendency to abstract ideas, and a people who are emotional to boot will be carried away by the splendour of their own phrases. Schumpeter may well have been right in saying that syndicalism could not be espoused by anyone afflicted of any trace of economic or sociological training, there being no rationale for it. Its espousal was, in part, at least, due to the witchery of its formulae.

Another French writer spoke in 1907 of the need to dream, the need for utopias, as inseparable from the national spirit of France.[1] This was taken up by Lowell: "The Frenchman is theoretical rather than practical in politics. He is inclined to pursue an ideal, striving to realize his conception of a perfect form of society, and is reluctant to give up any part of it for the sake of attaining as much as lies in his reach."[2] Utopias are plentiful in the history of French socialist thought. The goal is nothing so limited or so mundane that it could be achieved here and now; it is an absolute, a picture of perfection. Any compromise seemed a betrayal. The logic of the revolutionary arguments was thus reinforced. While eyes were fixed firmly on the goal and heads held high in the clouds, it was possible, however, to stray from the true path and enter, almost unaware, into the fields of compromise.

THE REVOLUTIONARY TRADITION. There is more to the revolutionary spirit than Latin temperament. The history of France has been dominated by revolutions: the Great Revolution itself, the *Trois Glorieuses*, the '48 and the Commune. In time, revolution became almost second nature. The point is made by Alexander Gray: "On the least provocation they visualise themselves as overturning something; there have perhaps been too many pictures of revolutionary heroes storming the barricades. The *Marseillaise* is in their blood."[3] The national anthem is a call to arms. Certainly the experience, and then the memory, of consecutive revolutions left their mark. They influenced French politics and French political thinking. David Thomson sums this up neatly: "The revolutionary tradition became a tradition of revolution as well as of the Revolution."[4] The consequences were twofold. On the one hand: a tendency to resort easily to revolutionary techniques, using that word in its widest sense to cover all forms of action involving violence and illegality, from the riot in the streets to the riotous strike.

[1] J. L. Puech, *Le proudhonisme dans l'Internationale*, 1907, p. 17.
[2] A. L. Lowell, *Government of France, Italy and Germany*, 1914, p. 161.
[3] A. Gray, *The Socialist Tradition*, 1946, p. 411.
[4] D. Thomson, *Democracy in France*, 1958, p. 11.

Historical background

'Direct action' was the slogan of syndicalism, action against, and outside, the established legal order. On the other hand: a more theoretical inclination to see in revolution the natural and fitting solution to the workers' problems.

The English Revolution of 1689 established the sovereignty of parliament; the American Revolution of 1776 created a written constitution; the French Revolution of 1789 asserted only an elusive ideal—it established no permanent institutions. "How this ideal should best be embodied in institutional form remained a matter of constant, many sided controversy throughout the nineteenth and twentieth centuries. A profound restlessness became the most conspicuous characteristic of French political life."[1] There was no finality in the institutions of the Third Republic. Another—the final and proletarian—revolution seemed logical enough.

In any case, neither the socialists nor the trade unions could escape writing Revolution somewhere on their banners. The word was almost a *cachet* of respectability: if one was not a revolutionary, one believed in *révolution évolutionnaire* or was at least loyal to the ideals of 1789. For the socialist parties this became largely a gesture: piety on the one hand, vote-catching on the other—their members were mainly drawn from the middle class and intellectuals whose revolution had already been accomplished. The syndicalist movement, however, could be described as the true heir to the revolutionary tradition of France, not only because the working class represented the unaccomplished revolution, the opposition to the existing order, but also because the revolutionary spirit itself was carried by the workers. Of course, the general strike replaced insurrection, economic weapons those of the barricades. The spirit remained the same: rejection of the existing order in its entirety, social, economic and political; rejection of reformist policies and constitutional means of action; acceptance of class conflict as war, to be fought as war; emphasis on violence and revolutionary *élan*.

[1] D. Thomson, *Democracy in France*, 1958, p. 11.

From craft to industry

The economic history of nineteenth-century France is marked by the relatively slow evolution of capitalism. Industrialisation came late and large-
scale enterprises were confined to a few centres. Workers remained on the
whole dispersed in countless small establishments and were to a large extent
employed in craft trades. There was often much poverty and unrest was
frequent in the earlier years, but the danger was political rather than economic. The labour movement as such was not a factor to be reckoned with.
Conditions were not ripe for the emergence of an industrial proletariat
until late in the century. This had important consequences for the direction
taken by the labour movement.

By the middle of the century, 70% of the population were still living on
the land. Agriculture was dominated by small farmer-owners with strong
paternalistic tendencies, a trend perpetuated by the French system of inheritance. Industry remained under the sign of the small workshop: in
63 *départements* with a total population of 32 million, there were employed
in factories with more than ten workers only 670,000 men, 245,000 women
and 130,000 children. The proportion of non-organisable labour was thus
strikingly high. Textiles were for long the country's major industry and
there the change from cottage to factory production took place only slowly
and at a very uneven rate. Workers in the important luxury and consumer
goods trades firmly upheld the traditions of their craft, the journeyman's
tour and the craft association. It was still possible for the worker eventually
to become a small, independent master himself. The labour movement was
more likely to be carried by such skilled craftsmen than by industrial
workers. The Second Empire saw a great stimulus to industry: Free Trade,
subsidies, new credit institutions, the expanding railway and transport
systems all encouraged its growth. Nevertheless, agriculture retained its
first place in the French economy. The small workshop continued to
flourish: craft and industry existed side by side. Industrialisation was held
in check by a number of factors: the widespread distribution of land meant
that there was little migration to towns and factories; the large size of the
peasantry itself meant a slow growth in the demand for mass-produced
goods; the traditional demand for quality articles ensured the survival of
craftsmanship. Cottage industry owed its resilience to the fact that the
worker could fall back on subsistence farming in times of crisis. As late as
1906, industrial workers accounted for less than a fifth of the total active
population, while the number of masters, independent or isolated workers
and white-collar employees was almost as high in industry as that of wage

15

earners. All this had its effect. André Siegfried points out that even after a century of industrial development France remained essentially a country of peasants, craftsmen and the middle class. He refers to the stubborn hostility to large-scale capitalist production found in all walks of life, preserving France as a "démocratie des petits gens".[1]

THE CRAFT SPIRIT. Many of the workers long maintained the same way of life as the small employers: their goal, by no means impossible, was one day to become masters themselves—if not as *patrons*, then at least as independent *maîtres-ouvriers*. Property, independence, craftsmanship were their ideals. They remained strongly individualistic in outlook and in that sense *petit-bourgeois*. They were not merely concerned with the problem of wage exploitation, as was the industrial proletariat, but with the problems of economic freedom and social equality. This was of considerable importance for the goals of the labour movement. Such workers were no more attracted by the vision of state ownership than by the economic system under which they lived. But it was less a negation of the existing order that they wanted than its reorientation in their favour. The anarchist and the liberal, *petit-bourgeois* pictures of society are in some ways very similar. Both emphasise individual liberty. The liberals advocated the wide distribution of property, the syndicalists proclaimed an even wider distribution of industrial control.

The syndicalist utopia clearly reflected the individualist, anarchist outlook of the craftsman as well as the familiar patterns of industry. Engaged as many workers were in small workshops, they tended naturally to think in terms of small-scale organisation. Self-regulation was not hard to visualise in a society where the factory itself was small and the worker, skilled in the techniques of production, capable of overlooking the tasks of industrial management. The same applied to the autonomy of the workshop and the local community. The ultra-federal pattern of economic organisation planned by the syndicalists was only possible in a country where large-scale industry was still relatively unimportant, the problems of co-ordinating production and distribution not overwhelming; local production—almost a subsistence economy—appeared possible for a great part of human needs. It is only in this light that one can understand the two syndicalist slogans: 'the free worker in the free workshop' and 'the workshop will replace the government'.

In a sense, syndicalism was already out of date when it became popular: industrial changes were making impossible the anarchist ideals it implied. The syndicalists themselves should have realised this, for their doctrine of

[1] A. Siegfried, *Tableau des partis politiques en France*, 1930, p. 87.

the class war recognised the changes that were taking place. Had the concepts and ideals of a previous generation left a mark on the labour movement that could not easily be changed by changing circumstances? Or was syndicalism perhaps a *cri de coeur* on the unproletarianised workman at the very moment when he saw his way of life swamped by industrial capitalism: a last struggle to safeguard the small workshop with its comparative independence, and its vision of absolute independence, from the goals of marxist collectivism?

WEAKNESS OF THE UNIONS. French trade unions long remained small, poor and unstable. The number of workers was relatively small itself; the small size of the average workshop and the dispersal of workers made organisation difficult in many cases. The tendency was towards many small, local craft unions. Except for the printers, only few could afford to pay regular strike benefits: most had barely sufficient funds for their administrative expenses, certainly not enough for any elaborate organisation. As late as 1908 regular strike assistance was assured in only 46 out of 1,073 strikes, and only in 36 in the form of cash. Their poverty was due to their small size, to the very low wages paid in most industries, and perhaps to a temperamental reluctance on the part of the French worker to pay any dues at all. This the *C.G.T.* admitted in its annual report of 1902: "Our impulsive and rebellious temperament does not lend itself to high dues, and if we are always ready for painful sacrifice of another nature, we have not yet been able to understand the enormous advantages that would follow from strong treasuries maintained by high assessment." Temperament also had something to do with union instability. Accustomed to the free-and-easy ways of the small workshop, rather than the discipline of large factories, the members were unwilling to submit to such discipline in their own organisations. Equally important was the absence of a strong class consciousness, of that sense of solidarity which comes with the crowding together of workers in large industrial units where their common interests become immediately obvious. Finally, there was the absence of benevolent payments which might have tied members to their unions. Instead, workers tended to join when some momentary interest aroused their enthusiasm and equally suddenly quit the union when their interest waned, often, indeed, joining and leaving for political rather than economic reasons.

All this helps to explain certain doctrines of the syndicalist movement, particularly that of direct action. In a sense, violence is the only path open to the weak. There is a close relationship between weak, unorganised labour movements and the outbreak of revolutionary or anarchist activity in Russia, Spain and Italy, as well as in France. The unions had little bargaining power when it came to across-the-table negotiations with employers; they had neither the membership nor the organisation with which to impress. Lack of funds, inability to pay strike benefits, meant they could not hope to achieve their ends by ordinary, peaceful strikes. They were thus forced to play for quick results: violence, intimidation and sabotage were the obvious weapons to choose. In any case, the leaders did not control the rank and file sufficiently well to organise passive strikes on any large scale or for any length of time. It was easier to maintain enthusiasm in a strike which had the appearance of battle than to maintain a peaceful withdrawal of labour.

In other words, weakness could only be counter-balanced by enthusiasm and courage, by revolutionary fervour on the part of the militants. Alexander Gray puts the situation thus: "From the higher idealism of penniless adventurousness, it is possible for the syndicalists to look down their noses across the Channel at the insipidly materialistic conception of a trade-unionism concerned solely with high wages and mutual benefits. Syndicalism, in this as in other things, is profoundly anti-rational. What is required is not foresight, planning, preparation or much goods laid up in barns. What is needed to storm the barricades is *élan*, entrainment, adventurous energy."[1] An interesting parallel can be drawn between syndicalism and the Young Turk movement in the French army. The Young Turks were a group of young officers and military theorists at the begining of the century, when France had eight million to Germany's eleven million men of military age and was armed with light, rapid-firing 75mm guns while Germany had heavy howitzers. They played on the moral superiority of the French troops and declared that French *élan* would compensate for German material and numerical advantages, just as the secretary of the *C.G.T.* thought that the *élan* of the French workers would have the advantage over the German trade unions' greater wealth and stricter organisation. The Young Turk glorification of the bayonet charge had its parallel in the syndicalists' cult of direct action.

The emphasis in syndicalist theory on direct action and *élan révolutionnaire* was quite logical, given the weakness of the labour movement. The cult of the two principles, however, reflected an unconscious rationalisation more than a logical choice. In a comparison with the Young Turks Bowditch suggests that "when French labour leaders boasted of the *élan* of their fellow workers, they were in fact fabricating myths as a means of escape from the unpleasant task of coming to terms with the hard realities of their twentieth century world. Revolutionary syndicalism seems to be little more than a rationalisation for what, in terms of the twentieth century

---

[1] A. Gray, *The Socialist Tradition*, 1946, p. 411.

industrial age, were serious weaknesses in the French labour movement."[1]
It is the words 'escape' and 'myth' that are significant here. The whole
idea of the general strike, the emancipation of the proletariat and the in-
auguration of a new society, is the type of dream theory that compensates for
ineffectuality in the world of everyday affairs.

[1] Bowditch, 'The Concept of Elan Vital' in E. M. Earle, *Modern France*, 1951, p. 33.

The repressive state

In the century following the Revolution of 1789—up to the year 1884 at least—the French worker was engaged in a long and bitter struggle with the state. Save for short periods, the state was actively hostile to the development of a trade union movement. This showed itself clearly in the laws of the time which, by their denial of the workers' right to organise permanently in professional association for the defence of common interests (*droit d'association*), the right to organise temporarily for the purpose of specific wage negotiations or strikes (*droit de coalition*), or the right to assemble for either purpose (*droit de réunion*), effectively frustrated its peaceful growth and suppressed its occasional achievements.

THE WORKER AND THE LAW. The Constituent Assembly repudiated the whole semi-feudal structure of the *ancien régime*. It dissolved both the trade guilds and the workers' own *compagnonnages*, suppressing at once the restriction placed upon labour by the former and the very real advantages gained from the latter. The free exercise of professions was proclaimed (*liberté de travail*). At the same time, the right of assembly and association was affirmed. However, hardly had the workers begun to make use of this new-found freedom than it was again abolished. The Le Chapelier law forbade the association of those engaged in the same trade of profession, or any agreement whatsoever between them. It was voted unanimously by the Assembly but various theories are possible about its significance. On the one hand, it claimed to be an application of the constitutional guarantees of liberty and the Declaration of the Rights of Man, in line with the principles of individualism introduced by the Revolution. Its sponsors saw unions as part of the restrictive mediaeval guild system they had just dissolved. They could also argue, with Rousseau, that no group loyalty must be permitted to intervene between the citizen and the state. On the other hand, economic interests were also at issue. One motive appears to have been the wage demands of a newly formed fraternal union of workers in the craft of carpentry. The bias of the legislators was shown three days later, when a special resolution exempted the Chambers of Commerce from the law. In practice, it was used only against the workers. Doubtless political theory and economic interest were closely related. The result was permanent hostility between the bourgeois-liberal state with its law and the workers with their organisations.

The Le Chapelier law was reinforced by Napoleon's Penal Code of 1810. It declared illegal any concerted action on the part of the workers, not only the strike itself but the threat of strike or any united attempt at wage negotiations. It is true that agreements between employers unjustly to lower wages were also prohibited, but the qualification 'unjust' and the difference in penalties for infringement (particularly the heavy sentences provided for the workers' leaders) again showed the bias of the state. No permanent association with more than twenty members was permitted unless official sanction had been obtained beforehand. In their various amended forms, these articles remained the basis for the prosecution of workers for the next seventy-five years.

The revolution of 1830 brought no gains. Those of 1848 were shortlived. The Provisional Government proclaimed the right to work and the right of association. National Workshops were set up and a commission, headed by Louis Blanc, was made responsible. The Constituent Assembly, when it met, was less favourably inclined towards the workers and their problems. The right to work was replaced by a right to assistance; the National Workshops were dissolved. The Legislative Assembly, in its turn, was openly hostile to the labour movement and re-enacted the provisions of the Penal Code. In the following decade, the hostility of the state showed itself in the countless prosecutions of strikers or those threatening to strike. The police searched diligently for breaches of the law on associations; leaders were prosecuted and imprisoned; organisations, unless purely benevolent or co-operative, were consistently dissolved.

After 1860 Napoleon III began to lose support and tried to win over the workers. Concessions were made with regard to the right of coalition in the defence of interests. Workers obtained the right to strike. The employment of violence, menaces or fraud was declared illegal, however, and prosecutions continued under this head. At the same time, a new crime was established: interference with the free exercise of industry and labour. The concessions were more apparent than real, in any case, as the right of assembly was still limited. Public meetings could only take place with the permission of the police. It was more or less impossible in practice to organise a strike legally. As the Empire grew more liberal, it did come to tolerate the formation of unions: the first *chambre syndicale* (that of the shoemakers) was actually formed in Paris in 1864. At first tacit, this toleration was soon made explicit. In 1868 the workers' delegates to the London exhibition of the previous year appealed to the Minister of Commerce for permission to form trade unions on the English model and their request was approved. Assemblies were permitted, provided that prior notice was given and neither politics nor religion discussed. Thus, although the Le Chapelier law and the Penal Code remained in force, the labour movement obtained official recognition of its right to organise.

Historical background

The Franco-Prussian war broke out before the workers had time to make any considerable use of the new tolerance. With defeat came the Commune; and with the suppression of the Commune the workers were back where they started. Jouhaux, the veteran trade union leader, described their situation: "The French proletariat was as if decapitated, deprived of almost all the militants who had laboured at the revival of the workers' organisations in the last years of the Second Empire; organisations dissolved, clubs dispersed, meetings prohibited, such was the situation in the years which followed the tragic Pentecost of 1871."[1] Only gradually did the workers recover. Within limits, the government continued the policy of unofficial toleration of single unions. Their existence nevertheless remained precarious: the police could, and did, dissolve them at their discretion. Any attempt at wider organisation was firmly prohibited and national associations were immediately dissolved. Affiliation with the International was specifically forbidden by a law of 1872.

Eighteen eighty-four was a turning point in the history of the labour movement. The Waldeck-Rousseau law of that year finally gave workers the permanent, legal right of association. The Le Chapelier law was repealed, as was the article of the Penal Code declaring illegal interference with the free exercise of industry and labour; trade unions were exempted from the law subjecting association to official sanction. Members of the same profession or trade could now organise freely in local unions; the exclusive purpose of such unions was to be the defence of common economic interests; unions could join together freely for this purpose, but such associations had no legal capacity nor the right to own property. From then on the labour movement grew apace. Within ten years some 400,000 workers were organised in 2,200 local unions; national federations of textile workers, miners, railwaymen, printers and other trades were formed, as were local associations of different professions.

It would be a mistake, however, to think that this ended the conflict between labour and the law. The law of 1884 was not popular with all the workers. Some opposed as a matter of principle what appeared to be a compromise with the state, the acceptance of its right to regulate the development of the labour movement. Many more specifically opposed the requirement that unions register the names of their officials, widely seen as a device for the police supervision of militants. The labour congress of 1886 actually condemned the law by an overwhelming majority, a delegate saying that it placed the workers on the same footing as prostitutes. The articles of the Penal Code relating to the use of violence and threats remained in force, moreover, and were frequently applied against the workers.

[1] L. Jouhaux, *Le syndicalisme et la C.G.T.*, 1920, p. 50.

The repressive state

There were also prosecutions for breaches of the formalities required by the law: in 1893 thirty-three Paris unions were dissolved for failing to deposit their rules with the authorities; in 1889 a Bordeaux court dissolved the local bakers' union for having admitted three restauranteurs as honorary members—and the examples could be multiplied.

During most of the nineteenth century the life of unions tended to be short; their membership could not expand, nor their funds accumulate. Lacking a peaceful atmosphere in which to grow, they also lacked solid foundations. The result was instability: unions tended to be *ad hoc* organisations, formed to meet particular crises. Political and legal suppression was a factor working in the same direction as the slow industrialisation of France.

THE WORKER AS OUTLAW. The law forced the workers into opposition to the state; in a measure, indeed, it persuaded them to reject the state altogether. Its provisions, biased heavily in favour of the employer, excluded the worker from its benefits and left him to all intents an outcast—*hors du pays légal*. The syndicalist doctrine of autonomy, the insistence that the labour movement must develop outside the state and create its own institutions to replace it, can be understood in the light of its experience. Indeed, the law forced the workers into active opposition. The narrow limits it placed on the right to organise, either in permanent unions or temporarily for peaceful wage negotiations, not to mention strikes, necessarily meant that conflicts would arise between the worker and the state. The law notwithstanding, it was inevitable that the labour movement should attempt to organise itself. Thus it automatically found itself in the field of illegality, whether it wished it or not. In that sense the law gave the movement its revolutionary character. Dolléans rightly asks whether the syndicalist outlook was not in part a hangover from the earlier period of illegality.[1] Certainly, the long outlawry of trade union organisations in France left its mark long after the law itself had been changed. The syndicalists remained outlaws from choice: they could not, or would not, readapt themselves to the society that had excluded them for so long.

This attitude was of course reinforced by the memory of the great battles they had fought with the state in 1848 and 1871. During the suppression of the Commune, with its eighteen thousand dead, Thiers declared that he would be pitiless, so that the terrible sight might serve as a lesson for the future. The lesson was remembered, though it was not exactly that which Thiers had hoped. The labour movement built on the blood of its martyrs. Equally important were the persistent 'betrayals' of the workers by the

[1] E. Dolléans, *Histoire du mouvement ouvrier*, 1936–9, vol. 2, p. 137.

leaders they helped to power in the revolutions of 1789, 1830 and 1848. The closing of the National Workshops and the insurrection which followed in June 1848 need alone be mentioned. The result was a deep-seated suspicion of all politicians, as well as of the state. Experiences seemed to show that the workers had nothing to hope from the traditional form of revolution which merely replaced one government by another—*plus ça change, plus c'est la même chose*—and could only rely on their own efforts and on their own organisations to achieve their freedom.

Proudhon and mutual aid

There can be few political thinkers whose works represent so strange, and yet so stimulating, a confusion of ideas as do those of Pierre-Joseph Proudhon (1809–65). The circles he has influenced, or that claim to be his heirs, range from the anarchists to the conservatives. There seem to be a hundred faces to Proudhon, often contradictory, depending on the aspect or period of his work examined. Given the vast extent of his publications, his polemical rather than systematic nature, his general lack of precision, and his more than occasional changes of front, this is not surprising. It is not the intention here to provide yet another interpretation of Proudhonist political theory. The purpose is simply to trace the links between Proudhon and the syndicalists: first, the similarity of ideas (selected for that purpose alone); second, his influence on members of the labour movement.

PROUDHON'S DOCTRINE. Proudhon, applying for the scholarship that was to mark the beginning of his career as a writer, said of himself that he was born in the working class and tied to it by links of common experience as well as of sentiment. He saw his role as the interpretation of the ideas of that class. Marx, who first confirmed his claim, soon attacked him as a typical *petit-bourgeois*. In fact he spent much of his youth in the country where, in Brogan's words, "he learned to know and to share their land-hunger, their rigid views of right living, their deep conservatism, all combined with a passion for equality, their class-consciousness, and their savage resolution to be each the master of his own fields and his own household".[1] When Proudhon was forced to leave school and seek a trade, he chose printing, serving his apprenticeship and becoming a compositor and proof-reader, member of an old craft which had always had intellectual and *petit-bourgeois* leanings. He was proud of his skill, proud of the trade morality learnt in the printers' chapel and proud of his independence, attempting once to set up business on his own account. He belonged neither to the bourgeoisie nor to the proletariat but to the old, still powerful class of semi-independent peasants and craftsmen.

Proudhon's work centred round two essentially moral issues. He hated the injustice of the existing order: the exercise of arbitrary power by man over man, the exploitation of man by man. And he hated the egotistic materialism of the bourgeois way of life which was spreading to other classes and threatening to destroy the traditional virtues of France. These were the virtues of the two classes he knew well: the peasant's attachment to the

---

[1] D. W. Brogan, *Proudhon*, 1936, p. 11.

25

soil, his hard labour, his strong sense of family life, his lack of sophistication or businessmen's guile; the craftsman's pride in work well done and
his sense of loyalty towards his fellows. He looked to the new working class
to re-establish them.

Justice, defined as respect for the dignity of man, was the starting point
of Proudhon's argument. It implied liberty, the right to do that which does
not injure others, as well as equality, the right of all men to equal access to
the wealth of mankind. "Whosoever places a hand on me to govern me is
a usurper and a tyrant—I declare him my enemy", he affirmed in his
Confessions d'un révolutionnaire. Liberty could only mean the complete
absence of government: anarchy in the strict sense of the word. Justice and
equality also meant order—not an arbitrary, man-made or parliament-
decreed order but a universal, moral order. His whole programme was
contained in the search for the union of anarchy and order.

In 1840 Proudhon published his first well-known pamphlet, the *Qu'est-ce
que la propriété?* The answer, *c'est le vol*, made it an immediate *succès de
scandale*. Despite the vehemence of the phrase, he did not attack property as
such but merely its abuses—the forms which are contrary to justice. Labour
alone was truly productive: unearned income could only result from the
exploitation of man by man. His attack was therefore directed against
property which gives rise to rent, interest and profits. This was also unjust
because it breaks the principle of equality. Justice demanded the reciprocity
of services, and equal sharing in the tasks of production and an equal
opportunity to share the world's wealth. Finally, under existing conditions,
it broke the principle of liberty. Property and the state were closely linked,
the one was the *raison d'être* of the other. Its unequal distribution led to the
exploitation of the weak by the strong, the tyranny of the rich over the poor.

The abolition of property—collectivisation, or nationalisation as it is
now called—was no answer to the problem of liberty, for it merely increased the power of the state, making it absolute tyrant. Communism
meant slavery. Seen from this point of view, property has the advantage of
acting as a counter-weight to the power of state, giving a measure of independence to its owners. Here Proudhon made use of Hegelian logic.
Having discovered the economic contradictions, the thesis and antithesis, he
sought a synthesis between the two. This was the abolition of property (i.e.
the unequally distributed forms that give rise to unearned income) and its
replacement by possession (i.e. the peasant's possession of the land he
cultivated, the worker's possession of the tools he employed). Widespread
ownership, individual and communal, would create a system of checks and
balances in which none could dominate.

The idea of justice led Proudhon into a more direct conflict with the state: authority is itself evil and necessarily led to injustice. The forms of authority might change but its character always remained the same. Democracy was little better than other systems of government: it meant the multiplication of masters, whereas liberty demanded their absence; it meant majority rule, while justice demanded the sovereignty of law and reason. The state was inevitably a false order of society. In practice, moreover, whatever its democratic pretensions, it was always something distinct from the people—it was the army, the police, the judiciary, the treasury—and it always created for itself an interest contrary to that of the people. At the best a parasite, it was more likely to be a tyrant. The problem was again to find the correct system of checks and balances, the correct equation that could guarantee order and make impossible the exercise of power. This equilibrium—the true order of society—was to be found in the sphere of economic rather than political organisation. The primacy of the economic was a fundamental doctrine. "Over and above the political phantoms which captivate our imagination, there are the phenomena of social economics which, by their harmony or discord, produce the good or the evil in society." This harmonious order depended upon two principles: reciprocity and mutuality. Reciprocity means society based not on authority but on free co-operation between individual and individual, group and group; it meant society based not on the rights of capital but on the free and fair exchange of services: "service for service, product for product, credit for credit". Out of this arose all the principles of mutuality: "mutual credit, mutual aid, mutual education; reciprocal guarantees of markets, exchange, work, good quality and fair price". The solution to the problem of the state was exactly the same as that to the problem of property. Proudhon advocated a system that could be described as economic federalism, one of autonomous, economic groups such as workshops and mutual credit organisations, managing their own affairs and associating with one another for the solution of purely technical problems as the need arose. The state would then be shown for the parasite it was, it would have no tasks to perform; authority would therefore disappear. Proudhon transferred the withering away of the state from the half mythical future to which Marx had consigned it into the near present: as the economic replaced the political, the administration of things would replace the government of men.

Proudhon liked to call himself a revolutionary. The word lent itself to confusion. He did not advocate revolutionary action (i.e. violence) but a revolutionary change in society (i.e. a turning upside-down of the existing order). The means were essentially reformist (i.e. peaceful) in character. This partly because he believed that no good could arise out of force, no justice out of injustice. He also turned upside-down the Jacobin formula that the political revolution was the goal, the social revolution the means. The socio-economic revolution required no *coup d'état*, no barricades, no violence; new economic institutions could be created within the existing political order: as the former expanded, the latter withered away. What were these new institutions? Here Proudhon differed from other socialist schools of thought, finding the key not in the field of production (i.e. in nationalisation) but in a reform of the system of exchange. The present order prevented the worker from acquiring sufficient capital to be really independent. It was therefore necessary to organise credit and make it freely available to all. Mutual (i.e. co-operative) credit organisations would destroy the power of capital and make possible the free and equal exchange of goods and services. The People's Bank was the solution. Industrial reform was not forgotten, however. Proudhon advocated the organisation of workers in independent producer co-operatives: the establishment of workshops without capitalists and without masters, based on mutual aid and free contract. These organisations, eminently suited to the administration of things, would replace the state.

How were these reforms to be achieved? Proudhon occasionally looked to the politicians (e.g. for the establishment of a People's Bank), but his general answer was that it could not be done by government. This would be true even if governments were not naturally hostile to any encroachments on their power. The political and the economic systems were incompatible: chaos could not create order and the lamb was not born of the lion. Reforms could not be dictated from above, they must come from the people themselves. Here one must refer to the philosophy of history which Proudhon borrowed from Hegel and amended to suit his own purpose. It lay in the laws of nature that mankind should move towards the rule of justice and equality: it was only necessary to march bravely in step with history. His role was to discover these laws and reveal them to those who were still attached to anachronistic ideas or who had become attached to false directions. Once the true facts were known, they would circulate effectively. Once the people became aware of the true laws of history and economy and thus capable of managing their own affairs—once they had attained the *capacité politique*—the new society would be created. *Démopedie*—the education of the people—was the real revolution.

Proudhon directed his appeal to the people. In his *Toast à la Révolution* of 1848 he told them that they embodied the force of revolution, of conservatism and of progress; they alone could save civilization and advance humanity. He saw them in all their diversity: peasants and craftsmen, workers and even the middle classes, all of whom he wished to reconcile. It was only gradually, as a result of the failure of the bourgeoisie to adopt

Proudhon and mutual aid

his message, that he turned definitely to the working class. His final endorsement of the workers as the torchbearers of history was most clearly expressed in his last work, *Capacité politique de la classe ouvrière*. There he asked himself three questions: Had the working class a consciousness of its own existence? Had it an idea (i.e. a philosophy) of its own? Was it capable of translating that idea into practice? His answer was not entirely affirmative. While the workers had shown themselves class-conscious (thus the revolution of 1848), they had only a very partial and unclarified knowledge of their own interest; they had shown themselves incapable of drawing the necessary, practical conclusions (thus their continued support of bourgeois governments after the revolution). If the working class was to achieve its aim, it had still to assert its autonomy, free itself from dependence on the bourgeoisie and take its affairs into its own hands. Much education was still required. It was still not the class war that he preached, merely a separation that would permit the working class to develop its own ideas and achieve its own maturity. He still insisted, moreover, that it was the peaceful revolution he desired.

PROUDHON'S INFLUENCE. Proudhon once wrote to Marx: "let us seek together the laws of society—but God forbid that, having destroyed past dogmas, we should try in turn to impose new doctrines; let us not become the heads of a new intolerance, the apostles of a new religion". He never intended to found a school and this must be remembered in any appraisal of his influence. He also remarked that the people did not read him, but heard him without reading. This was too modest. Certain workers, interested in the problems of society, began to study his work and met together to discuss his theories. Sometimes they would write to him, consulting on decisions to take or attitudes to adopt. Tolain, Limousin and other workers did so at the time of the 1864 election. The manifesto they published followed Proudhon's ideas and he, in turn, dedicated his *Capacité politique* to them. His influence was also clear in the first years of the International, which coincided with the last years of his life. Tolain and Limousin had been delegates to the founding conference in London, and with Fribourg, became the first officials of the Paris section, with a programme declaring that society must be organised according to the immutable laws of justice, the study of which is the true task of the proletariat and the key to which lay in the idea of mutuality and federation. At the first congress of the International, held in Geneva in 1866, the Paris section presented a memorandum advocating mutualism and rejected the twin policies of collectivisation and political action. Marx, whose *Communist Manifesto* had appeared a year before the *Capacité politique*, was under-

29

standably irritated. In a letter to Kugelmann he complained bitterly of the gentlemen from Paris whose heads were full of empty phrases and of the great harm done by Proudhon. Briefly, the mutualists dominated. The French delegates tried to exclude all non-workers—"les hommes politiques et bourgeois". More successfully, they forced off the agenda a proposal to study the nationalisation of land. Instead of the instrument of class warfare that Marx had intended, the French *proudhonistes* did their best to turn the International into a reformist association for the study of mutual credit societies and producer co-operatives. In a few years, however, they were submerged in the more bitter conflict between Marx and the anarchist followers of Bakunin.

The leaders of the revolution of 1871, the members of the Central Committee of the Commune, belonged to all schools: marxists, anarchists, *blanquistes*, state socialists and mutualists, the latter but a small minority. The Commune, indeed, meant the triumph of the political principle over the economic: the revolutionary barricades and the state-sponsored workshops. In *The Civil War in France* Engels called the Commune the grave of the Proudhonist school of socialism. This was wishful thinking. The French socialist movement was no longer officially Proudhonist, nor was there a group that identified itself as such, as there was an anarchist, a marxist and a *blanquiste* group, but Proudhon's reformist ideas did not disappear. More important, perhaps, was his negative influence on the following decades, the continued hostility of French workers towards marxism and state socialism. A partial explanation lies in French economic history: Proudhon's special appeal to a working class still closer in outlook to the independent craftsman than to the industrial proletariat. The conflict between Marx and Proudhon has also been ascribed to a conflict between the German and the French spirit. Proudhon appealed to the libertarianism of the French, as well as their dislike of scientific dogma. Whether or not he had a continued influence, his ideas had remained relevant. In that sense he was right when he said that the people would hear him, even if they did not read him.

The first congress of the *Fédération des Bourses du Travail* in 1892 could be seen as the beginning of an autonomous labour movement. It stood under the influence of Fernand Pelloutier who advocated a doctrine very close to that of Proudhon in at least two respects: emphasis on the role of education—both moral and technical—in the emancipation of the proletariat; replacement of political society based upon authority by a federation of workers' associations (*syndicats*) based upon free contract. The spirit of Proudhon ran like a thread through his *Histoire des Bourses du Travail*. The Pelloutier period, however, was really pre-syndicalist. It covered the years

Proudhon and mutual aid

immediately before the foundation of the *C.G.T.* and the adoption of a revolutionary programme, when *culture de soi-même* gave way to direct action. Parallels remained, particularly with regard to the autonomy of the working class and the superiority of the economic principle.

Autonomy meant the independence of the working class, a sharp distinction between it, its members and its ideas, and other classes of society. This was the message of the *Capacité politique*. Let the workers beware of the pretended leadership of politicians and intellectuals. Proudhon was convinced that the craftsman received a better training than the theorist, and he was always irritated by the claims of an intellectual elite to lead the workers for their own good. The people, with its practical instinct, was the best judge, a sentiment echoed by the syndicalists who believed that workers' common sense would tell them the direction to take better than any politician. Hence the principle of political neutrality. Autonomy meant 'ask nothing of them', as well as 'keep others out'. *Vaincre le pouvoir sans lui demander rien* was a slogan fundamental to both. It is true that the syndicalists developed a more violent notion of direct action, but both believed that the working class must build its own institutions (whether co-operatives or unions) in order to create an entirely new form of society— its own. The primacy of the economic over the political was common ground again. True, the economic action preached by the syndicalists had a revolutionary element, the general strike, quite different from the creation of mutual credit societies envisaged by Proudhon. Far closer was their vision of the new society based upon economic federalism, the free association of workshops. As late as its 1919 congress, the *C.G.T.* resolved that the union represents the retreat of politics in the face of economics and Jouhaux declared his attachment to the old Proudhonian principle that the workshop must replace the government.

Extravagant claims have been made about the relationship between Proudhon and syndicalism.[1] Parallels may be a matter of coincidence, as well as of influence. They can also be matched by divergences. Proudhon was no supporter of class war, nor indeed a committed supporter of the proletariat. The *Capacité politique* was not typical of the whole of his writing. While he offered the working class (or, more generally, the people) the prospect of building the new society, he affirmed elsewhere the revolutionary vocation of the bourgeoisie. His revolution, moreover, was a reformist one: it was the violent tone of his pamphlets and the vehemence of his attacks on the existing order that misled many of his readers. As far as his goal was concerned, the return to the simple virtues and the honest life of peasant and

---

[1] Cf. E. Droz, *Proudhon*, 1909, p. 33; Guy-Grand and Harmel in G. Bouglé, *Proudhon et notre temps*, 1920, pp. 8/38.

craftsman, his revolution was to be a reaction in the strictest sense of the word. This raises the question of Proudhon's influence on other movements. The turn of the century saw a marked *renaissance proudhonienne*. He was invoked by half a dozen superficially quite different, and in some cases entirely unconnected, movements such as the economic federalism of Paul Boncour and the reformist *solidarisme* of Léon Bourgeois. The most important for this study were the monarchist *Action Française* and the circle around the *Mouvement Socialiste* (a review published by syndicalist intellectuals) with Sorel at its centre. On the one hand the ardent defenders of tradition, on the other hand the theorists of syndicalism—both found a common ancestor in Proudhon. Both were hostile to parliamentary democracy and bourgeois values. Both wanted a society based on natural order and moral principles. For a brief spell, at least, reaction and revolution joined forces. The name they gave to their group was *Cercle Proudhon*.

Blanqui and the barricades

As a student of seventeen, Auguste Blanqui (1805–81) joined a secret republican society, the *Charbonnerie*. He participated in the riots that followed the election of 1827. In 1831 he was imprisoned for a short period for his part in a student demonstration. In 1832 he appeared on trial as a leader of the radical republican society, *Les Amis du Peuple*. Acquitted by the jury, he was sentenced to a year's imprisonment by the judges for endangering the peace during his defence. Political clubs were suppressed in 1834 and, as a result of middle-class discouragement, leadership of secret societies fell to the *déclassé* intellectuals, while the following became to an appreciable extent working class. This was true of the secret *Société des Familles*, led by Blanqui and suppressed in 1836. In that year he was arrested for his part in a conspiracy. Soon, however, he was organising again, this time the *Société des Saisons*. Though its oath was essentially republican, its philosophy—in so far as it had one—was the egalitarian communism of Babeuf and it had a larger working-class element than any other society of the time. In 1839 he tried to start an insurrection. It was a complete failure and, when he was captured some months later, he was sentenced to death, commuted to life imprisonment. Falling seriously ill, he was transferred to a hospital where he was visited daily by the workers of the district: sick and imprisoned, he inspired another secret society. In 1844 he was pardoned and lived quietly in the country for a few years.

In 1848 revolution broke out; Blanqui arrived in Paris the next day. Clubs were springing up on all sides and, in his element, he formed the *Société républicaine centrale*, known as the *Club Blanqui*. When the elections were won by the moderates, he attempted another insurrection. Crowds marched on the Assembly, only to be dispersed in a few hours: Blanqui and the other leaders were left prisoners. He was not released until ten years later, under a general amnesty. His freedom did not last: he was rearrested in 1861 as leader of an illegal society. At his trial the following dialogue took place:

"Despite your twenty years of prison, you have kept the same beliefs?"
"Exactly."
"And not only your beliefs, but also the wish to make them triumph?"
"Yes, until death."

In fact, he escaped from prison and fled the country, visiting Paris secretly to organise an underground army and then returning openly after the amnesty of 1869.

Historical background

In August 1870 he once more tried to start an insurrection. His attempt to seize a Paris arsenal was a complete failure. It was nevertheless only three weeks premature—for then the Republic itself was established. Blanqui founded a club and a paper, *La Patrie en Danger*. On 31 October, infuriated by military defeat, crowds attacked the *Hôtel de Ville* and nominated a provisional government with him as a member. It collapsed within a few hours, while Blanqui was still drafting his first decrees: he was never to get any closer to political power than this. In the elections of February 1871 he stood as a candidate on the joint list of the *Comité des vingt arrondissements*, the *Chambre fédérale des sociétés ouvrières* and the Paris section of the International. Unsuccessful, he left for the country, where he was once more arrested on 17 March—for his part in the October insurrection. Two days later the Commune was proclaimed. Although a helpless prisoner, Blanqui was in a sense its leader. Elected in two Paris districts, he was named honorary president of the first session of the Commune. Thiers refused an exchange of prisoners, although seventy-four notables were offered in return for Blanqui. Instead he was sentenced to perpetual deportation, though he was saved from this by ill health. In 1879, while still in prison, he was elected to the Assembly in Bordeaux: his election was declared void despite the defence of Clemenceau. A few months later he was granted an amnesty but was not re-elected.

Blanqui died in 1881. At his funeral the workers came into the streets for the first time since the Commune to do him honour: a vast number followed his coffin to the grave. He well deserved the name he was given, *l'insurgé*, for he fought for his ideas to the last. His life was a clear expression of his philosophy: faith in revolution and in the free will of man.

BLANQUISME. Blanqui was a revolutionary, but was he the first revolutionary socialist or the last revolutionary republican? At his trials he declared himself a republican. His following was more often than not of the lower middle class, radicals, intellectuals and students. The measures he advocated for the revolutionary provisional government were political rather than social. On the other hand, as early as the 1832 trial, he introduced a socialist note, speaking of the war between the rich and the poor and declaring himself a member of the proletariat. His writings, collected in the *Critique sociale*, are often socialist in outlook and subject matter. The society for which he fought—in so far as he stopped to consider it—was communist. In fact he was both. For him there was no contradiction: the republic was the necessary means to socialism. From a historical point of view, he stood between the republican and socialist movements, belonging equally to both. Blanqui could be seen as the link between the Jacobins and radical republicans of the middle class, who created the French revolutionary tradition, and the socialists and syndicalists, who carried it on.

A *Times* correspondent reported the following statement by Blanqui towards the end of his life: "I have no theories. I am not a professor of politics or socialism. I am a man of action. The revolutionary party will apply the necessary reforms. I have no programme."[1] Here, in a nutshell, was the key to his outlook. He was opposed to theoretical systems; he believed in action; he relied on solving problems as they arose—he was anti-intellectual, a voluntarist and a pragmatist. The same temperament was characteristic of the syndicalists. There is little trace of a consistent, worked-out theory in his writing. His vision of the future society adds up to little more than a very generalised and idealised picture of communism. Ends were greatly overshadowed by the means. *Blanquisme* was a form of action, a movement towards a goal which remains undefined. He was by temperament a man of action, more at home organising a revolt than writing a book on socialism, as were the later militants of the labour movement. Philosophic speculation was a waste of time: we can neither divine the future (the revolution alone will lift the curtain), nor even plan long-term strategy for yet unknown events. Syndicalists showed the same voluntary discretion. Theoretical quarrels, moreover, had already exhausted the efforts of several generations of socialists without positive results. That was one reason why the *C.G.T.*, in its turn, excluded socialist debates. It was action—revolutionary action—that unified Blanqui's philosophy and his life. The essence of his doctrine was summed up in that word. Deeds were more creative than ideas, examples more inspiring than words, experience a truer guide than theory. In much the same sense, its advocates later called syndicalism a philosophy of action.

It was Blanqui's tactic which influenced the labour movement. Bernstein said of it that it reflected a belief in the unlimited creative force of revolutionary action.[2] There were a number of implications. First: deeds were more effective propaganda than words, they would contribute more to preparing the revolution than any number of speeches. Usually, he thought of some act of violence, staged by a secret society in the hope of triggering off an insurrection. In one article, however, foreshadowing the syndicalists, he wrote of the strike as a flag to rally the masses; readily understood by all, it was the only truly popular weapon in the struggle against capitalism[3].

---

[1] *The Times*, 28 April 1876.
[2] E. Bernstein, *Socialisme théorique et socialdémocratie pratique*, 1912.
[3] A. Blanqui, 'Grève et coopération' in collected works, *Critique Sociale*, 1885, vol. 2, p. 13.

Second: the revolution could be provoked at more or less any time or place. Its success depended less upon objective factors (i.e. the economic factors of Marx) than upon the will of the insurgents, upon courage, enthusiasm and good tactics; only a determined effort was required to overthrow the government. Part of the syndicalist quarrel with marxism lay in their rejection of the necessary logic of history: they, too, believed in revolution born of the free will and conscious efforts of the workers themselves. Third: the revolution could be brought about by example and leadership of a small minority of conspirators who had understood the nature of the political struggle more clearly than the rest. It was their task to draw the otherwise apathetic masses into revolt. Some syndicalists shared this concept of the 'audacious minority', the class-conscious elite of militant workers whose function it was to lead the movement into the revolutionary general strike. Fourth: the proletariat must not be distracted from the real, underlying struggle by minor economic gains which leave the evils of the system intact. Blanqui opposed all Proudhonist schemes as soporifics. The militants showed the same hostility to reformist proposals that might weaken the class war.

All this must not blind one to fundamental divergences. Blanqui was perhaps the first socialist to appeal directly to the masses, but he appealed to them without regard to class. He saw the revolutionary struggle as the oppressed masses fighting against authoritarian, aristocratic government, rather than as proletariat *versus* capitalism. Thus he strongly opposed the isolation of the workers preached by Proudhon and later by the syndicalists. He believed that revolutionary leadership would be found in the enlightened *avant-garde* of the bourgeoisie, among the intellectuals and the *déclassé*— the very people against whom syndicalism was a revolt. Blanqui also believed that society could be transformed by political means. Like the marxists, he saw the conquest of power as a necessary step in the emancipation of the proletariat: the 'dictatorship of the people' alone could suppress counter-revolutionary enemies and lay the foundations of the new order. For the syndicalists this was anathema: the necessary changes in society were economic, not political and would be achieved by the workers themselves. As Blanqui's objective was political, so were his means: the battle in the streets, leading to the *coup d'état*. The syndicalists chose the economic weapon of the strike, and, in principle at least, wished to fight against the employers rather than the armed forces of the state. In fact, they adapted *blanquisme* to the possibilities of a trade union movement.

Blanqui has been called the spiritual father of modern revolutionary socialism by Max Nomad.[1] He was more than that. Towards the end of his

[1] M. Nomad, *Apostles of Revolution*, 1933, p. 13.

life he was a national figure. By his example, he taught revolution to many; by his reputation and through his disciples, he inspired many more. *Blanquisme* spread among the workers of France, especially among those of the capital. In their temper, if not in their doctrine—and in Blanqui's case temper was more important than doctrine—the militants of the syndicalist movement could be counted as his successors.

Bakunin and anarchism

Michael Bakunin (1814–76) did not participate directly in French politics, except for the brief period of the Lyons insurrection of 1831. He was, however, in large measure the founder of revolutionary anarchism, both as a philosophy and as a political movement. Bakunin was the hero of revolutionary uprisings all over Europe according to Nomad,[1] almost the embodiment of revolution itself. As with Blanqui, it was his life rather than his writing which inspired the anarchist movement, his spirit, even more than his doctrine, which he bequeathed to it. This was not surprising, as Bakunin had no really integrated system of ideas. Gray goes so far as to call him a chaotic figure—chaotic in life, chaotic in his writing, chaotic in his thought.[2] The chaos of his private life is irrelevant; it was overshadowed by the consistency of his devotion to the revolutionary cause. The chaos of his words is more apparent than real; they fall into a pattern when seen as occasional propaganda pamphlets, serving the momentary needs of the cause, rather than as philosophical dissertations written in the refuge of the British Museum. The charge of chaos could more fairly be levelled against his thought: it reflected his character: inclined to action rather than reflection, he placed relatively little weight upon the formal consistency of ideas.

Bakunin was temperamentally opposed to the rationalists, the abstract philosophers, the makers of systems and intellectuals in general. In particular, he was opposed to Marx. Bakunin was a born revolutionary and the spirit of revolution, almost for its own sake, runs like a thread through his work. Man, he declared, was distinguished from the animal by the faculty of thought and the need to revolt. E. H. Carr calls him a political romanticist[3]—he is guided by intuition rather than reason: revolution, he affirms, is a matter of instinct. Above all, like Blanqui, he was a man of action, an *insurgé* in spirit, an organiser of revolution in practice. He, too, was a firm believer in the creative value of action. Marx tended to place theory before action, he reversed the order. Although he sometimes called himself a historical materialist, he was never over-impressed by the objective conditions or historical necessity to which Marx attached so much importance. Rejecting determinism, he saw revolution as the spontaneous creation of free will, of the *élan vital* of the masses. By temperament, as well as for reasons of practical politics, he avoided committing himself to any

---

[1] M. Nomad, *Apostles of Revolution*, 1933, p. 13.
[2] A. Gray, *The Socialist Tradition*, 1946, p. 352.
[3] E. H. Carr, *Michael Bakunin*, 1937, p. 167.

specific system of ideas: no theory, no ready-made system, no book that had ever been written would save the world. The cult of action was partly the expression of an activist temper such as the militant syndicalists themselves possessed. This temper was reflected in their ideas as well as his: both voluntarist and pragmatic; both, in sum, philosophies of action.

BAKUNIN'S IDEAS. Bakunin was a passionate libertarian. "I can conceive of nothing human without liberty", he wrote, and also: "All my liberty is concentrated in just precisely that part, however small, which you cut off." He also had an unbounded faith in the capacity of man—given the opportunity—to live in peace and freedom with his fellows. To quote E. H. Carr again: "The optimism and the faith in human nature, which was inherent in the romantic creed, was the marrow of his bones. Bakunin believed as passionately as Rousseau in the innocence of an untrammelled and unperverted human nature."[1] Human nature merely required the enjoyment of freedom to achieve perfection; anarchism was the logical outcome of the romantic doctrine. He was equally optimistic in his belief that revolution could emancipate mankind—it was only necessary to destroy law, police, government in all its forms, and a free society would emerge. The syndicalists showed a similar romantic optimism in their references to society after the revolution.

For Bakunin the state meant the negation of all liberty. Government was necessarily the worker of evil, even when it would do good; for good, whenever it is enjoined, becomes evil. Liberty, morality and real human dignity consisted in men doing what is good not because they are told, but of their own free will. Only in society could men find harmonious relationships, freedom and true dignity. The state, by contrast, was repressive and artificial, by its mere existence a fatal obstacle to progress, creating only poverty, conflict, crime, hatred and frustration. This notion of state and society as opposite principles was later taken up by the theoreticians associated with syndicalism: while the state socialism of marxists and social democrats was artificial and repressive, syndicalism—the socialism of institutions, as Lagardelle was to call it—was a natural, spontaneous form of organisation. There were, of course, more concrete reasons to oppose the state. The multiplicity of states means conflict and war: under the cloak of *raison d'état*, it sacrificed the welfare, freedom, and even life, of individuals to its own selfish interests. For the labour movement, the state was also the machinery of class exploitation: its purpose was to protect property and maintain status, to perpetuate inequality and, in its latest phase, to subjugate

[1] E. H. Carr, *The Romantic Exiles*, 1949, p. 258.

39

the proletariat. Syndicalism, however, was not merely a revolt against the state as guardian of bourgeois interests but against the state as such. In that sense it was anarchist.

The destruction of the state and the future of society lay with the proletariat alone. Only the proletariat had no vested interest in its survival—nor could it have one, for its emancipation would be the emancipation of all, the end of slavery and the triumph of mankind. (Bakunin, when he took this line, was close to Marx.) The proletariat was particularly suited to the tasks of revolution and regeneration: it possessed qualities of character that other classes had lost. The superior morality of the working class, its heroism, its spirit of solidarity and justice, its willingness to make sacrifices and its uncorrupted good sense—all these, discovered also by Proudhon, were rediscovered by Sorel.

To achieve its task, the proletariat must not compromise with the state in any way, nor with other classes in society. Bakunin recognised in 1848 that there was nothing to be hoped for from the Republic. Its democratic paraphernalia was a mystification, its deceptive concessions merely weakened the struggle. Bakunin opposed all forms of democratic socialism: participation in parliamentary politics meant entering the state prison of one's own free will. He also saw that power corrupts and warned against the dangers of *embourgeoisement*. The later experience of French socialism was to prove this true: the syndicalists had even more reason to distrust collaboration with the bourgeoisie, even as opposition within the bourgeois parliamentary system. Bakunin opposed marxism with equal force. He attacked the *Communist Manifesto*'s call to capture state power. The communist state would be a state like any other; far from withering away, it would sacrifice the last remnants of liberty in its pursuit of equality, creating a barrack-like society of automatons. The actual government, passing itself off as the dictatorship of the proletariat, would be in the hands of a privileged and powerful minority—"That minority, the marxists say, will consist of workers; yes, perhaps of former workers; and these, as they become rulers, will no longer represent the people, but themselves." More likely, he thought, it would not even be workers. The term 'scientific socialism', which continuously occurs in marxist writers, showed that the alleged People's State would be ruled by a small aristocracy of intellectuals. This suspicion of the *savants* was shared by the syndicalists.

Bakunin made a sharp contrast between the scientific socialism of the intellectuals and the intuitive socialism of the workers. It was the latter he favoured. "The mass is unconsciously socialist, instinctively, through the pinch of hunger and their position, more earnestly and truly socialist than all the scientific bourgeois socialists put together." Socialism was better grounded in the necessities of life than in pure reasoning. His activist temperament, his dislike of authoritarian programme writers, the importance he placed on the *élan* of the proletariat—for all these reasons he refused to work out a detailed strategy of revolt. He rejected the marxists' assumption that such a strategy should (or even could) be imposed on the mass by an elite of socialist thinkers. "The emancipation of the proletariat is the task of the proletariat itself" ran the slogan of the International. Bakunin interpreted this as strictly as the syndicalists themselves to mean that the revolutionary method must be born within the labour movement. The function of the leaders was merely to clarify, to formulate and popularise, the revolutionary methods of the proletariat. Socialism, he declared, was not a philosophy; it was to be found in the collective will of the working class and in their organisations. While it is true that Bakunin did not always live up to this view, as a doctrine it was an early example of the pragmatic, anti-rational revolt against socialist intellectuals of which syndicalism itself was to be the extreme form.

The main difference between anarchist and syndicalist ideas about revolution was that the former emphasise the political, the latter the economic. Bakunin was a highly political figure. One could nevertheless find in his writing an emphasis on the importance of economic struggle that went beyond Marx. Thus the statement, ironical in the light of later developments, that "the founders of the International acted wisely in refusing to make philosophical or political principles the basis of their association and preferred to have the exclusively economic struggle of Labour against Capital as the sole foundation". In the same article he wrote: "It must accommodate itself to the natural instincts and ideals of the people—we mean the organisation which is founded upon the experience and results of their everyday life and the differences of their occupation, i.e. their industrial organisations." Again, of the need for propaganda by action, he said: "There is only one way out—proletarian liberation through action. And what will this action be, that will bring the masses to socialism? It is the economic struggle of the proletariat against the governing classes, carried out in solidarity." This was not far removed from the syndicalists' belief in the educative value of strikes. Bakunin, however, no more saw the strike as the beginning and end of revolution than did Blanqui. His thoughts, like those of Blanqui, were never far from the forms of revolutionary action he knew from experience: the secret society, the *attentat*, the barricades. There were links, finally, between Bakunin's ideas about the future of society and the syndicalists. For both, the question took a secondary place: sufficient unto the day the evils thereof, speculation is a diversion of energies from more profitable tasks. Despite what has been said about his character, however, Bakunin was not really an advocate of revolution for its own sake. He was voluntarily discreet about the future: the institutions of the new society must be left to their own free, spontaneous and thus unpredictable growth if they are to mirror the will of a truly free society. One clear idea did emerge, that of federalism. His plan for a free association of communes, with the delegation of limited authority from the smallest unit upwards, and with full right of secession for all, was closely parallel to the free association of producers envisaged in syndicalism. Neither was possible without a good deal of optimism about human nature and the problems of organisation. For Bakunin, an aristocrat by birth, the revolution was to usher in the age of liberty; for the syndicalists, poor workers with less lofty aspirations, it meant an end to the exploitation which kept them poor. With this qualification, there were great similarities of thought and, above all, of temperament, between them. E. H. Carr called Bakunin the last exponent of political romanticism; one may, however, incline to Elie Halévy's view that just as marxism was the continuation of the positivist tradition, so was syndicalism of the romantic.[1]

THE ANARCHIST MOVEMENT. In the International, hardly had the conflict between the French mutualists and the Central Committee, dominated by Marx, ended in the former's defeat, than a new conflict broke out, this time between the marxists and the anarchists. In a sense, one was a prolongation of the other. Both the followers of Proudhon and of Bakunin attacked the political, authoritarian outlook of the Central Committee in the name of economic organisation and labour action; both showed their suspicion of the leadership of socialist intellectuals. The division of opinion covered the structure of the International, the policy to be pursued and even the goals to be achieved. It went deeper than this and had its roots in a difference to temperament: a conflict between the right-wing realism of Marx and the left-wing romanticism of Bakunin. It also had a geographical basis: the German and English sections followed Marx, while the Latin delegates followed Proudhon, Blanqui and, above all, Bakunin. Thus the question of national character arises once more. There was a clash between the revolutionary, anarchist temper of the Latins and the logic and discipline of the Northerners. The details of the struggle between Marx and Bakunin were sordid and reflected little credit on the former. The Hague congress was so 'rigged' that the Latin delegates found themselves in a minority. Bakunin was expelled and the anarchists withdrew; the *blanquistes* had already done so. Marx gained a Pyrrhic victory: his transfer of his section of the International to America proved to be an empty gesture—

[1] E. Halévy, *Histoire du socialisme européen*, 1948.

for all practical purposes it was dead. The anarchist section survived until 1877. Its strength lay in the Jura, in Italy and in Spain, but there were French delegates at its congresses. There was considerable support for spontaneous economic action and the general strike as a means of bringing about the revolution. "The first anticipations of syndicalism" writes Lorwin, "are found in the International, and especially in the Bakuninist sections between 1872 and 1876."[1]

In the first years of the Third Republic the International was proscribed, though there were some secret groups. Gradually the militants regained confidence, anarchist propaganda increased and their influence made itself felt once more. The outrages of the years 1892 to 1894, ending with the assassination of Sadi Carnot, again drew the government's attack. Anarchist groups were broken up, their papers suppressed, their leaders exiled, and those that remained placed under police surveillance. The anarchists found themselves isolated and helpless: they had come to a blank wall where no further progress seemed possible. Their leaders recognised the futility of individual action and of the bomb as a revolutionary weapon. Eighteen ninety-five saw the first issue of the anarchist paper *Temps Nouveaux*. The name was symbolic: the anarchists, said the leading article, were entering a new phase of their struggle. At about this time, a group of exiles in London (including Kropotkin, Malatesta and Louise Michel) advised the anarchists not to wait until the workers came to them but to go out into the labour movement themselves: they should enter the unions, take an active part in union affairs, participate in all strikes and agitations—and use every opportunity for anarchist propaganda.[2] The anarchist *Groupe des étudiants socialistes révolutionnaires internationalistes* in Paris also stressed that the unions were an excellent place for propaganda.[3] Delesalle saw in the unions a ready-made field of activity; they should create an anarchist movement within the trade union movement.[4] Pouget also recognised the error of past tactics and urged the revolutionaries to enter the unions in the popular language of his anarchist paper, *Père Peinard*.[5]

The anarchists were not slow to take this advice. In the years that followed they played a role in the French labour movement out of all proportion to their number. The anarchist Tortelier was one of the first advocates of the general strike. Pouget, another veteran anarchist, rallied completely to syndicalism: in 1900 he moved to the editorial desk of the *Voix du Peuple*, the paper of the *C.G.T.* and became one of the theoreticians of the move-

---

[1] V. Lorwin, 'Syndicalism' in *Encyclopaedia of the Social Sciences*.
[2] *Cit.* J. Maitron, *Histoire du mouvement anarchiste en France*, 1952, p. 247.
[3] *G.E.S.R.I.*, *Les anarchistes et les syndicats*, 1901.
[4] P. Delesalle, *L'action syndicaliste et les anarchistes*, 1901.
[5] Cf. *Le Père Peinard*, 1 October 1894, printed in London.

ment. The infiltration of the anarchists was particularly successful in the *Bourses du Travail*; the *Fédération des Bourses* was virtually an anarchist fief, first under Pelloutier, then under Yvetot and Delesalle. It was the anarchists who led the attack on socialism and political action in the *C.G.T.* and who were largely responsible for its rejection of parties, elections and parliament in favour of direct union action (the principle of the autonomy of the labour movement). There was a striking similarity between the conflict in the International involving the followers of Marx and Bakunin and the later conflict in the French labour movement between socialists and anarcho-syndicalists—a conflict which led to a split similar to that in the International.

The anarchist movement continued in existence parallel to syndicalism and there was considerable interchange between the two. The *Temps Nouveaux*, with its column "Le mouvement ouvrier", had the collaboration of Pelloutier and then of Delesalle. The latter remained a member of the *Cercle des étudiants socialistes* while an official of the *C.G.T.* Even the *Libertaire*, which stood for the older, individualistic tradition of anarchism, became favourably inclined to syndicalism around the turn of the century. It gave a regular column on the labour movement to Yvetot. Yvetot himself, at the *C.G.T.*'s 1910 congress, stated the relationship between the two quite clearly: " I am reproached with confusing syndicalism and anarchism. It is not my fault if they have the same ends in view. Anarchism pursues the integral emancipation of the individual; syndicalism the integral emancipation of the working man. I find the whole of syndicalism in anarchism."

The socialist tower of babel

In France socialism preceded trade unionism. As a result the socialist parties were dominated by intellectuals and bourgeois radicals. Socialism became a popular, rather than a proletarian, movement. A difference of outlook and interest between parties and unions soon emerged, however, and the bourgeois monopoly of the social movement then grew irksome. As industry expanded, the unions became stronger, the workers class-conscious, a revolt against the parties inevitable. Syndicalism was the reaction against a socialism which had neglected the interests of a labour movement too weak to impose itself. Later still, when the *C.G.T.* became strong enough to play a role in national politics, the militants dropped some of their anti-political, even their revolutionary, principles in order to reap the benefits of co-operation.

DIVISIONS IN THE SOCIALIST CAMP. Jules Guesde, collaborator and representative of Marx, seemed to have won control of the French labour movement in 1879. That year's socialist congress adopted the title *Congrès ouvrier socialiste de France* in order to emphasise the union between labour and socialism supposedly achieved. Theoretically working-class in character (every delegate was to be a worker, elected by workers), it admitted collectivist study groups and isolated groups of workers, not yet organised in trade unions. The representation of purely political groups was thus strengthened; the congress was turned into a political affair. A collectivist, marxist policy was adopted and the first French socialist party founded, the *Fédération du Parti des Travailleurs socialistes*. A period marked by a confusion of parties and congresses with ever changing titles, of schisms and conflicts, was about to begin.

The situation had already changed by the following year. The organising committee of the 1880 congress refused to recognise delegates who were not themselves members of the unions they claimed to represent or who were members of study groups. After scenes of uproar and violence, the revolutionary delegates—anarchists siding with marxists—withdrew to organise their own congress. The co-operators, mutualists and reformists remained but their organisation soon disappeared through lack of support. At the revolutionary congress, there was an uneasy alliance between collectivists and anarchists. They called for the collectivisation of the means of production, but qualified this as transition to libertarian communism; a minimum reform programme was adopted, but it was to be dropped in favour of revolutionary action if it failed to win support at the coming elections. In fact, the anarchists soon separated from the *guesdistes*, though they did not form a new organisation of their own. No sooner had Guesde eliminated mutualists on the right and anarchists on the left than new conflicts arose. After the amnesty, the veteran leaders of the International and the militants of the Commune returned to France and were surprised to find new men at the head of the movement. They gradually regained their former influence. Failure at the 1881 elections was attributed to the programme the marxists had brought from London: too reformist for the revolutionaries, too revolutionary for the reformists. Guesde's influence waned.

The tenor for the 1881 congress was set by the recognition of Paul Brousse's *Prolétaire*, founded in opposition to Guesde's *Égalité*, as the party's paper. In two important debates the collectivists were defeated by Brousse and his reformist followers. One put the *guesdistes* in a minority on the central committee, the other allowed constituency committees to edit their own electoral programmes (a blow to Guesde's attachment to the orthodox party line). Soon after, a socialist candidate stood with an independent programme in Montmartre and violent polemics broke out, followed by expulsions and resignations. When the 1882 congress met, both sides were prepared for a split. The assembly decided to debate the question of party discipline and the dissident, *guesdiste* minority left the hall. They were formally excluded from the party—an empty gesture as they had already issued a manifesto declaring their independence in order to save their programme of collectivisation. The central committee accused Guesde of having broken democratic discipline (observation of a contract freely agreed) after having tried unsuccessfully to impose authoritarian discipline (defined by the caprice of one man). This was perhaps the crux of the matter. Brousse expressed the general feeling when he called the *guesdistes* authoritarian and domineering. The accusation of another delegate that they were bourgeois, attempting to exploit the working class in their own interest, foreshadowed a later and wider hostility. There were the same reactions to marxists in the French labour movement as to Marx in the International.

The majority drew up the constitution of a new party, the *Parti ouvrier socialiste révolutionnaire*. The idea of an official party line was abandoned and constituencies left free to draw up their own programmes. This reflected the absence of agreement on anything but opposition to Guesde. In so far as Brousse's influence went, however, the tendency was reformist and the party's title a misnomer. As he said: "I prefer to abandon the principle of all or nothing, which generally leads to nothing at all, and to split our demands into what is possible."[1] His followers were thereafter

---

[1] *Cit.* G. Weill, *Histoire du mouvement social en France*, 1925, p. 241.

called *possibilistes*. The collectivist minority meanwhile founded another orthodox marxist party, the *Parti ouvrier*. For a time, it appeared revolutionary, thus Guesde's dictum: in multiplying reforms, one only multiplies shames.[1] Marxist doctrine was set out: revolution was historically inevitable; the task of the party to prepare the masses; while it might participate in elections, the aim was the conquest of state power—and for that purpose it had to act alone and dictatorially. In the following years the party grew steadily, often at the expense of the *possibilistes*, largely because it alone had a clear idea of where it wanted to go and because Guesde was a man of great organising ability.

In 1883 the *possibilistes* changed the name of their party to *Fédération des Travailleurs socialistes*. Internal disagreement was not long absent and again personal conflicts appeared to be at issue. Jean Allemane founded a paper, the *Parti Ouvrier*, to rival the official *Prolétaire*. Unpleasantness arose when Brousse, as vice-president of the Paris municipal council, proposed to participate in an official welcome for officers from regiments which had taken part in the suppression of the Commune. There was an underlying difference of outlook between the moderate intellectuals led by Brousse, and the more revolutionary, working-class elements, led by Allemane. The latter resented the compromising attitude adopted by the nine Paris councillors elected in 1887, a complaint frequently to be heard later; they accused the central committee of lacking interest in such genuine labour activities as the May Day demonstrations. The *allemaniste* group grew stronger, particularly in Paris, and tended to concern itself with questions of trade-union organisation: in many ways, they were the forerunners of syndicalism. By the time of the party's 1890 congress, a split was inevitable. The *allemanistes* withdrew almost immediately. Bitter personal attacks followed. The party became markedly conservative, with a moderate programme of parliamentary reform and state socialism, but its influence waned and its organisation disintegrated.

The *allemanistes* held the first congress of their own in 1891, where they took over the old name: *Parti ouvrier socialiste révolutionnaire*. Antiauthoritarian, they adopted a very decentralised form of party organisation: the central body, reduced in title to secretariat, consisted of six revocable delegates whose task was correspondence between the regional sections. The party accepted the revolutionary class struggle, the subordination of political to economic action, the importance of trade-union organisation. Its proletarian character was stressed and all members were bound to join a union; politicians (deputies and councillors) were excluded from the secretariat. The principle of the general strike was adopted. The electoral pro-

---

[1] *Cit.* H. W. Laidler, *Social-Economic Movements*, 1946, p. 285.

gramme, which was qualified by the statement that the conquest of political office was only to be pursued as a means of propaganda, showed strong anarchist influences: communal self-government, direct legislation, suppression of the army and the courts. In 1892 a report entitled 'The revolution and the immediate steps necessary to assure its success' assigned leadership to the unions, in sharp contrast to the marxists who still advocated the leadership of the party. In 1894 it was decided to place the general strike on the agenda every year, a resolution introduced by a member of the trade unions' general strike committee.

Other groups added their voice to the confusion on the socialist scene. In 1896 the *allemaniste* party excluded a number of deputies and councillors who had refused to contribute part of their salary to party funds, as well as certain candidates who had entered unauthorised electoral alliances: they formed their own *Alliance communiste internationale.* The followers of Blanqui, returning to France, after the amnesty of 1880, founded a Revolutionary Central Committee under the leadership of Eduard Vaillant. Although few in number, they managed to play a certain role in the politics of the capital. Their platform was the conquest of political power by all possible means; to that end they adopted the doctrine of double autonomy: independent economic action by the unions and independent political action by the parties. To that extent, they too were favourable to the development of syndicalism. In 1898 they changed their name to *Parti socialiste révolutionnaire.* Although the anarchists had no national organisation of their own, they were active in Paris and throughout the country; their influence was far from negligible. Finally there were the Independents. In 1886 a dozen of the more radical of the radical deputies formed the first socialist group in the Chamber. Gradually they increased in number. Millerand and Jaurès were important members. Jaurès effectively described their outlook: "It is necessary to annexe the economic programme of socialism to the political programme of the radicals."[1] There was little agreement between them; what they had in common—so their opponents could claim—was their bourgeois background and attitudes. From a purely electoral point of view the group soon became the most important of the socialist parties, though it had no organisation beyond constituency and parliamentary committees until 1898. In the year the *Confédération des socialistes indépendants* was formed. Towards the end of the century, therefore, numerous socialist organisations were competing for the attention of the workers: *guesdistes, broussistes, allemanistes, blanquistes,* anarchists and moderate independents.

There was an increasing demand for unity in the socialist camp. After the

[1] In Millerand's *Petite République,* 12 February 1893.

electoral successes of 1893, the socialist deputies of various persuasions formed a loose group in the Chamber. It was an uncertain process, with frequent reversals and numerous disputes. A serious conflict was caused by the Dreyfus affair: while *allemanistes*, *broussistes* and independents sided with the radicals in his defence, *guesdistes* and *blanquistes* declared the matter of no concern to the proletariat and remained neutral—as they had done in the Boulanger crises. This, however, only brought home the need for some more organised common front. The attempted *coup d'état* by Déroulède in 1899 led to the formation of a *comité d'entente* on which all parties were equally represented. Dissension returned almost immediately. Waldeck-Rousseau formed a government of republican defence and called upon both Millerand and General de Gallifet, whose name was associated with the suppression of the Commune, to serve in his cabinet. Some of the parliamentary group supported the new government, others did not: the *comité d'entente* was incapable of dealing with the situation. Jaurès appealed for a national congress of socialism and all parties agreed.

A congress of socialist parties met the same year. A *guesdiste* motion that the class struggle precluded the entry of socialists into a bourgeois government was carried, though with a rider that the question might be reconsidered under special circumstances. On the question 'ways and means for the conquest of power', a compromise resolution was adopted: all means of propaganda, all forms of action should be employed—electoral, economic and revolutionary, including the general strike. A new organisation was to be created, consisting of parties, regional associations and trade unions; there was to be an annual congress, a central committee and a single parliamentary group. For a moment it seemed as if unity had been reached and the congress closed with enthusiasm. The hope was premature. The central committee was often divided and was itself in conflict with the parliamentary group, which declared itself free from any party supervision. The 1900 congress, in which the large majority of unions failed to participate, began with a long dispute over the validity of mandates and ended with blows. The *guesdistes* finally left to hold their own meeting. In their separate halls, both groups then voted once more for the principle of unification. Another joint congress was held in 1901 and the question of socialist participation in bourgeois governments was again at issue. The syndicalist theoretician, Lagardelle, introduced a motion declaring Millerand 'outside the party': it was amended by Briand to read 'outside the control of the party' and carried. The *guesdistes*, *blanquistes* and their revolutionary allies thereupon once more declared themselves unwilling to co-operate.

For the next years the ministerial question was to divide the socialist camp. The *Parti ouvrier*, the *Parti socialiste révolutionnaire* and the *Alliance communiste* combined to form a *Parti socialiste de France*. Predominantly marxist, it advocated the class struggle, the conquest of state power and the collectivisation of the means of production; it opposed participation in bourgeois coalitions. The *Fédération des Travailleurs socialistes*, the *Parti ouvrier socialiste révolutionnaire* and the *Confédération des Indépendants* formed a rival *Parti socialiste français*. This was a moderate, reformist group, largely under the influence of its deputies, preaching essentially the extension of the Republic to labour; it had its left wing, however, in Gustave Hervé, whose antimilitarist agitation caused a number of clashes.

Representatives of all the French groups attended the international socialist congress held in 1904 at Amsterdam. Here the so-called Dresden resolution was voted, framed originally to combat Bernstein's revisionist policy in Germany: socialists were to decline all political responsibility under existing conditions and, specifically, office in bourgeois governments. Bebel then introduced a motion calling for socialist unity and this was accepted by Jaurès and Vaillant in the name of the two French parties—an acceptance, by implication, of the Dresden resolution also. Later that year a French commission laid down the principles on which a unified party could be organised. Fundamental divisions were covered by neat phrases: "While pursuing reforms, the socialist party is not a party of reform but of class war and revolution" (revolution, in this context, of course, could be evolutionary as well as violent); "The deputies must refuse the government any support which would prolong bourgeois domination" (here too, the qualification introduced an ambiguity). On this note agreement was reached and, in 1905, the *Parti socialiste unifié—Section française de l'Internationale ouvrier* was formed, today's *S.F.I.O.* Unity of organisation was achieved. Not unity of outlook, however, for the party included all shades of opinion, ranging from Hervé on the extreme left to supporters of the parliamentary republican bloc on the extreme right, and taking in such diverse figures as Jaurès, Vaillant and Guesde. Meanwhile, numerous independents remained on the scene, earning the particular hostility of the unified socialists. After the election of 1910 the majority of these—independent socialists, reformist socialists, republican socialists and all the other titles they had chosen— joined to form a *Parti republicain socialiste*. The declaration of principles began with the words 'Resolutely and exclusively reformist' and ended with 'the duty never to forget the superior interests of the Republic'. Lacking organisation, the party had no strength in the country; in the Chamber, however, it had thirty-three deputies to the seventy-five of the *Parti unifié*.

THE WORKERS' REACTION. The schisms that followed one another so closely undermined French socialism. The movement remained divided too long, its forces scattered among too many bitterly rival, jealously independent groups. Conflict, both of men and of ideas, had become so ingrained that it could neither cede to political expediency nor be eradicated by compromise resolutions. The search for agreement was long and difficult, almost a full-time occupation: the energy dissipated in fighting about socialism might have been better spent in fighting for it. Even when formal unity was achieved, so occupied were the leaders with smoothing over personal disputes and doctrinal differences, with permanent questions of organisation and reorganisation, that they found little time to reap the advantage. Weakness, instability, preoccupation with internal affairs—these were the characteristics of the socialist movement. Alliance with socialism seemed to have little political advantage to offer at the time—except, of course, to prospective deputies. Thus when the socialists tried to forge closer links between the unified party and the labour movement, the unions were not very impressed. There appeared little to gain and much to lose.

The spectacle of personal and doctrinal rivalries, often carried to the bitterest extreme, brought the socialists into disrepute. Ceaseless polemics filled their press, virulent accusations dominated their congresses, endless manoeuvres occupied their leaders. Socialism appeared to many workers as just a long, theoretical, usually violent argument between middle-class intellectuals. These debates, indeed much of the history of socialism, seemed irrelevant to the mass of workers who were, by the nature of things, less interested in fixing the true doctrine than in positive steps to improve their lot. Despite the enthusiasm of a few argumentative militants, these discussions soon began to tire, then to exasperate the less theoretically-minded of the rank and file who did not wish to see their organisations develop into political debating clubs run by intellectuals. One purpose of the political neutrality rule adopted by the *C.G.T.* was to restore peace in the unions and make time for the discussion of trade-union affairs. The role of personalities had a particularly bad effect. Disputes seemed not differences of opinion about how best to serve the interests of the working class but struggles for power in which the rank and file were used as pawns, usually by socialist intellectuals of bourgeois origin. This aroused resentment and ended in the distrust of socialists of whatever tendency, in hostility to their intrusion into the labour movement. The marxists aroused an especially strong reaction. For a while it appeared as if they had the labour movement in their grasp. This, however, carried with itself the seeds of its own destruction: the authoritarian character of Guesde and the strict discipline of his party organisation proved intolerable. Marxist doctrine, moreover, was almost calculated to repulse the workers: its language was too intellectual; its fatalism frustrated those who believed with Blanqui and Bakunin in revolutionary free will, were impatient for results and eager to strike a blow for themselves.

The most serious reaction came when the disruptive influence of socialist disputes began to make itself felt within the organisations of labour movement. From the start, the parties had regarded the unions as a coveted prize, and had made every effort to win control over them. Infiltration of the unions was tried by all; all consistently enjoined their members to enter the unions for the purpose of political propaganda, even to create new unions where it would serve their purpose. Even during the period in which the *guesdistes* had control of the national labour organisation and its congress, this never extended down to the local unions. There, all tendencies were represented and, in Paris, other parties had greater influence: *possibilistes, blanquistes, allemanistes* and anarchist elements were active from the start. The division between marxists and others finally reached a national level in a conflict between the national federation of trade unions and the national federation of trades councils (i.e. the *Bourses du Travail*): the labour movement was effectively split and many disorganised years of weakness followed. If political dissension prevented the organisation from having a strong labour movement at national level, the effect of political rivalry was equally grave lower down. Many unions became houses divided against themselves, undermined, weakened and split for political causes. The adherence of a union to any one of the socialist parties would usually enrage the supporters of other tendencies, quite apart from repelling non-socialists. In the extreme case, it would end in the disruption of the union or in the establishment of a rival union in the same town. At best, it led to frictions which sapped its authority and diminished its fighting power.

The autonomy of the labour movement, as proclaimed by the *C.G.T.*, was the expression of workers' hostility to politicians, political doctrines and political parties, to politics in general. In self-defence, all politics was excluded. Officially, there was no judgement for or against any party: the *C.G.T.* was to be strictly neutral ground, based on the economic interests that united the working class and excluding the political elements that divided it. It was neutrality the mass of workers probably wanted, not the formation of yet another group, that of the anti-politicals, to compete with the existing parties. The militant syndicalists, however, were more anti-political than neutral. The automony of the labour movement worked to their advantage, as did the fact that they themselves were union leaders, not parliamentarians. The acceptance of syndicalism can be explained, negatively at least, by the rejection of socialism.

The betrayal of the politicians

The evolution of the French socialist movement after 1873 has been described by one of its historians in the following terms: A persecuted minority, facing a government of reaction, excluded from the republican party, from the Republic itself, all socialists declared themselves revolutionary; the subsequent history of the socialist parties shows them moving steadily away from this position; in order to reap the benefits of universal suffrage, they turned more and more towards political and parliamentary action.[1] As the memories of the Commune faded, the socialists re-entered the Republic by the door of parliament; at the same time, their interest in revolution vanished. The word itself remained in their vocabulary—for sentimental reasons perhaps, perhaps as a matter of habit but empty of meaning. As Robert de Jouvenel remarked, there was more in common between two deputies, one of whom was a revolutionary and the other was not, than between two revolutionaries, one of whom was a deputy and the other was not.[2] The socialists—*embourgeoisés*—became largely identified with the bourgeoisie in the eyes of the labour movement. Socialist leaders in any case usually had a bourgeois background, a cause for distrust in itself, whatever their protestations of sympathy with the working class. Their behaviour only confirmed that distrust.

THE PARLIAMENTARY REVOLUTIONISTS. The municipal elections of 1892 and the general election of 1893 were a success for the socialist parties. This influenced their policies. Guesde, in particular, was overwhelmed. A simple calculation sufficed to change his outlook: "In the old Chamber we were less than ten; now we are forty; at that rate we shall be a hundred and sixty in 1897."[3] In 1883 Guesde had written that the *Parti ouvrier* did not enter elections to win seats—those they willingly left to the bourgeoisie—but to make propaganda.[4] At their congress, that year, the *guesdistes* had resolved that the gradual conquest of power and the parliamentarisation of the party was a betrayal of the working class; revolutionary action alone could lead to the emancipation of the proletariat. The *Communist Manifesto* was itself very clear on this point: "The Communists disdain to conceal their ideas. They openly declare that their ends can be attained only by the forcible overthrow of all existing social institutions. Let the ruling class tremble at a Communist revolution." After the elec-

---

[1] A. Zévaès, *Le socialisme en 1912*, 1913, p. 5.
[2] R. de Jouvenel, *République des Camarades*, 1934.
[3] *Cit.* E. Halévy, *Histoire du socialisme européen*, 1948, p. 223.
[4] *Programme du parti ouvrier*, 1883.

tions, however, there was a marked change of tone. Guesde stated categorically from the rostrum of the Chamber that his party had had enough of fighting and would in future rely on the bourgeois constitution to overthrow the bourgeoisie itself. There was little in the subsequent behaviour of his party to belie this statement.

The *possibilistes* had already dropped the word 'revolutionary' from their title in 1883 in order to make their position clear. Brousse later refused to be associated with May Day celebrations because of the revolutionary sentiments expressed by the organising committee. The independents, who formed more than half the socialist group in parliament around this time, had, of course, been reformist parliamentarians from the start. The *blanquistes* and the *allemanistes* remained attached to the principle of revolution, but in practice they too preferred to seek electoral victories, rather than plan a *coup d'état*, an insurrection or a general strike.

THE REFORMIST EMANCIPATORS. It was in the field of local government that reformist ideas first overtook the *guesdiste* party. In the 1883 programme, Guesde had declared that the party did not under any circumstances believe in the possibility of achieving reforms through municipal government. In 1892, however, the socialists captured many towns, including the important industrial centres of Lille, Roubaix and Marseilles. Thereupon Lafargue wrote in the party's yearbook that the immediate task was the conquest of municipal councils as their powers were sufficiently wide to make useful reforms possible. Guesde had also said earlier that in multiplying reforms one only multiplied shames, for the rights granted to workers in a capitalist regime would always remain dead letters. Programmes of reform, however, were an essential element in election propaganda and the promise of an immediate reform was more likely to win support for parliamentary candidates than talk of an eventual revolution. A series of programmes followed, clearly designed as vote-catchers: when the small farmers and farm workers were promised that land would not be nationalised, Engels himself was led to protest at this betrayal of marxist doctrine. If these programmes were originally electoral stratagems, they soon lost that character. Deputies were not prepared to sit quietly in their seats until they had a majority; they were soon drawn into the process of legislation, with the compromises and partial reforms which they had professed to despise while mere theoreticians in the wilderness. The minimum programme (the minimum reforms which the party would accept as the price of its collaboration in parliament) soon became a maximum programme, covering all the party's real intentions, each item subject to compromise meanwhile. Except in congresses and manifestos, the emancipation of the proletariat was forgotten. Perhaps the

54

marxists were too busy in parliament, perhaps too realistic—in any case, their reliance on parliamentary reforms and the constitutional conquest of power went a long way. Enjoined by the *Communist Manifesto* to "support every revolutionary movement directed against the existing social and political order", they actually opposed the revolutionary action of the workers. At its 1894 congress, the *Parti ouvrier* resolved that, while strikes must necessarily be supported if they occurred, neither they nor the general strike should be in any way encouraged.

It was equally surprising to see a disciple of Blanqui leading the life of a devoted parliamentarian. Yet that was what Vaillant became, taking part in the most routine parliamentary work and collaborating on the most modest reforms. The programme of the independents had, of course, always been restricted to limited reforms. The *possibilistes* had got their name by adopting the same policy. As a result, the *Parti socialiste français* reached the stage in 1902 when it could discuss whether the word 'revolutionary' should not be dropped entirely from its programme. Jaurès justified its retention—in the sense of *évolution révolutionnaire*: a gradual series of reforms would, in the end, seen as a whole, add up to a revolution in the social order. When the *Parti unifié* was formed, it affirmed its attachment to the revolutionary principle in a phrase that could mean almost anything; while pursuing the reforms demanded by the working class, the socialist party was a party of class struggle and revolution. In practice, this was interpreted after the fashion of Jaurès. At its 1908 congress, after the usual revolutionary protestations, the party claimed to be 'the most essentially, the most actively, reformist'. Hervé not surprisingly called this resolution the finest reformist and electoral *bouillabaisse* ever cooked up at a socialist congress.

THE INTERNATIONAL PATRIOTS. Patriotism was to be expected of the independents. It was not surprising to find Jaurès writing that a strong France was vital to humanity and that, in the case of danger, the socialists would be the first to rally to the defence of the country whose blood ran in their veins.[1] The opposite sentiment might have been expected from the marxists. Did not the *Communist Manifesto* state that the proletariat had no fatherland and that socialism was international? Yet, in its 1893 manifesto, the *Parti ouvrier* declared that the socialists were patriots who desired to see a powerful France because, so ran the argument, France was one of the most important factors in the evolution of mankind. The claim that France would have no more ardent defenders than the socialists was maintained thereafter. It is true that, replying to an attack by Hervé, Guesde

[1] In the *Dépêche de Toulouse*, 3 January 1893.

55

later explained his patriotism in the following terms: pacifism means the victory of the country with the fewest socialists, the defeat of the country with the most.[1] Perhaps this was an assessment of the long-term interests of workers everywhere. Or perhaps the socialist deputies had discovered a stake in the country sufficient to make it their own. To quote Guesde again: "Since 1848 the proletariat has had a fatherland—it is its fault if it makes no use of it."[2] Some workers, on the other hand, continued to regard property, rather than parliamentary seats, as the valid criterion of interest.

THE ELECTORAL DEALERS. The search for votes led from the watering down of programmes to direct collaboration with bourgeois parties during elections. The electoral system required a second ballot if no candidate obtained an absolute majority on the first, and it was customary for the weakest candidates to retire in favour of those better placed. Partly as a result of the numerous crises which shook the Third Republic, largely to gain seats, the principle of republican solidarity was evolved: socialists and radicals systematically retired in each other's favour. This principle was adopted unanimously at the first congress of the unified party, but there was a significant exception: candidates were never to withdraw for an independent socialist or any other candidate 'claiming to be a socialist'. There may have been good reasons why radicals should be preferred to unco-operative socialists, but the impression given was that the party was prepared to ally itself with the bourgeoisie in order to defeat its closer rivals. Republican discipline broke down periodically: it often functioned where the candidates of the right were strong; other alliances, some very strange, were made where they were weak. The principle itself was questionable for a party committed to the class war and was bound to raise doubts in the minds of the workers; the spectacle of horse-dealing, *la cuisine électorale*, which it involved was far more discreditable, raising suspicion about the candidates' and their parties' integrity.

THE REPUBLIC'S DEFENDERS. The principle of republican discipline at elections was matched by that of republican defence in the Chamber. The Republic had not been established very securely in 1875; it seemed seriously threatened on a number of occasions. The Boulanger crisis of 1889 led to a government of republican concentration of the right-centre. Although the socialists did not support the government, many rallied to the defence of the Republic. Even the *Parti ouvrier* issued a manifesto declaring that the

---

[1] At the socialist congress of 1907.
[2] At the socialist congress of 1893.

republican form of government was necessary for the emancipation of the proletariat and that it should be preserved at all costs. Failure to maintain the right-centre coalition forced Léon Bourgeois to form a purely radical government in 1895, based, however, on the support of the socialists, who thus entered the parliamentary majority for the first time. The strength of the opposition frustrated whatever reforms this government might have achieved—it had plans of income tax reform and the Minister of Commerce spoke of *un socialisme sage, pratique*. The socialists had nevertheless been forced into a major compromise. Some years earlier they had bitterly opposed legislation excluding incitement to revolt from trial by jury. In 1895 Bourgeois opposed a motion to repeal the law: the socialists, including Guesde and Vaillant, unwilling to embarrass the government, thereupon voted for a motion approving his stand. This was the first of a long series of such tactical betrayals of principle.

After the encyclical *Immortale Dei* of 1892, the monarchists and catholics rallied to the Republic. The danger thereafter was less to its survival than to the principles for which it stood. "You accept the Republic, but do you accept the Revolution?" was the question asked. In face of the possibility of a right-wing clerical majority in parliament, the 'parties of the Revolution' joined in defence of the Republic *égalitaire, laïque et sociale*. The Dreyfus affair brought the issue to a head. Agitation grew and riots became serious. In 1899 Waldeck-Rousseau formed a government of republican defence. A moderate conservative with an anti-socialist reputation, his ministry included Millerand and had the support of the independent socialists. Agreement between socialists, radicals and moderate conservatives (the so-called 'left republicans') was impossible in the longer run except on one question: anti-clericalism. Waldeck-Rousseau made this the major political issue in the Chamber and such it was to remain for many years. Defence of the lay Republic forced socialists into many compromises on the social and economic front. Even worse was to come. The extreme right tried to use the 'massacre' of strikers at Chalon-sur-Sôane to engineer a defeat of the government with the votes of the left. The socialists voted instead for the motion approving its action; many socialists even voted against the demand for an enquiry introduced jointly by Guesde and the right. This seemed rank betrayal to the labour movement outside Parliament.

The Combes government of 1902 moved considerably to the right. The struggle against the Church, however, was in full swing: anticlerical legislation overshadowed all other political questions and the republic bloc remained secure. Indeed, it was strengthened by an inter-party steering committee, the *délégation des gauches* (a title comprehensible only in terms

57

of French parliamentary conventions). Only the *guesdistes* abstained from membership, and even they voted for the government. Jaurès was elected a vice-president of the Chamber. Again there were betrayals. Many socialists voted confidence in the government after it had proceeded against the pacifist *Manuel du Soldat*, written by Yvetot and distributed by the *C.G.T.*

The founding congress of the *Parti unifié* opposed participation in bourgeois governments. In 1905, therefore, the *délégation des gauches* was abandoned, though not until after some dispute between the parliamentary group and the party executive. As a result, the right-wing independent socialists finally separated from the party. This group, which later formed the *Parti républicain socialiste*, was really no more socialist than the radicals (who, indeed, called themselves radical-socialists), but its actions tended to reflect on those with whom they had once been identified.

THE CAREERISTS IN OFFICE. Participation had, of course, already occurred as the inevitable second step to the support of bourgeois governments. Millerand, who entered the Waldeck-Rousseau cabinet in 1899, was the first socialist member of any European government. Acceptance of office caused much confusion in socialist ranks: the so-called 'ministerial question' dominated party discussions long after. When Millerand first informed the parliamentary group of Waldeck-Rousseau's invitation, their reaction was favourable, though with the proviso that he should act on his own responsibility and not in the name of the party. The announcement that General de Gallifet was also a member of the cabinet came as a considerable shock. Many then blamed him for not having withdrawn. The parliamentary group split and a similar split divided the socialist movement. That year's congress of socialist parties decided that the class struggle did not permit membership of bourgeois governments, though with the escape clause that the matter might be re-examined if necessary. The issue was not settled, however. Compromise about the ministerial question proved impossible and the only unity the socialists could achieve in 1901 was the reduction of their many parties to two.

While this argument went on, Millerand remained Minister of Commerce. His behaviour was indistinguishable from that of a bourgeois minister. The workers may well have wondered why a *soi-disant* socialist should present decorations to their employers or make after-dinner speeches in the company of men like the steel magnate Schneider. The two major laws he introduced in 1900, moreover, were both unfortunate. The first provided for a ten-hour day in establishments employing women as well as men (to be extended everywhere by 1904)—at a time when the *C.G.T.* was campaigning for the eight-hour day for all. The second provided for compulsory arbitration in

industrial disputes and a secret ballot of all workers before strike action—
its application was prevented by the opposition of the employers as well as
of the workers. His positive achievements, some minor reforms, were wholly
offset by the unpopularity of these measures. The advantages to be gained
from participation showed themselves negligible. Thereafter, until the
outbreak of war, no member of the unified party joined the government.
Millerand, Viviani and Briand, however, were consistently in office; although elected under the *Parti républicain socialiste* label, they had previously been socialists, Briand a left-wing militant. *Les arrivistes arrivés*
was the bitter comment.

The one major reform of the period, the weekly day of rest, was achieved
not by socialist ministers, nor even by socialist deputies, but by the direct
action of the *C.G.T.* Social legislation was limited to assistance for the aged
and sick (1906) and a contributory pensions scheme (1910), strongly opposed by the *C.G.T.* and used by only a small fraction of the workers. As
far as the law was concerned, the relationship between workers and employers hardly changed in the half century between 1848 and 1914. The
bourgeois democracy had showed itself either uninterested in, or incapable
of, dealing with the social problem.

GOVERNMENT OF ASSASSINS! The years after 1906 were ones of continuous industrial unrest. Workers came into direct conflict with the state,
in the shape of the Clemenceau government with the ex-socialist Viviani as
Minister of Labour. Clemenceau was determined to act firmly. A state of
siege was declared during the great miners' strike of 1906 which followed
the Lens disaster: some 40,000 soldiers were called out. When an electricians' strike plunged Paris into darkness in 1907, military engineers were
called in as replacements. Strikes in the vineyards around Narbonne led to
collisions with the troops and blood was shed. The reaction of the workers
was expressed in a *C.G.T.* poster—'Gouvernement d'Assassins!'—
bitterly attacking the 'sinister trio'. The government retaliated by trying
to prosecute all members of the *C.G.T.* council who had been present at its
drafting. The same year, a strike at Raon-l'Etape left one dead and thirty-
two wounded. 'Encore du Sang' declared the posters. In 1908 striking
builders were involved in clashes at Draveil-Vignoux and Villeneuve
Saint-Georges in which three workers lost their lives. This time, the posters
—'Réponse aux Massacres!'—led to the imprisonment of *C.G.T.* leaders.
The word 'massacre' remained on many lips, however; the labour movement could not forget that in two years nineteen workers had lost their
lives, while an estimated seven hundred were injured.

Historical background

THE RENEGADE. In 1910, when the ex-socialist Briand was President of the Council and Minister of the Interior, Viviani still Minister of Labour, a general strike of railwaymen was declared. It was Briand's oratory which had originally persuaded the labour movement to vote the principle of the general strike. Boasting of this achievement at the socialist congress of 1899, he had claimed the duties of paternity. These duties he saw very differently ten years later. His intervention was as forcible as any that might have been expected from a conservative government: he declared a state of military emergency, mobilised all railwaymen, forced them to resume work on pain of court martial, and arrested the strike committee. Within a week, he had broken the strike. The rights and wrongs of his action could be argued; the *volte-face* was spectacular.

THE WORKERS' REACTION. There had always been a gap between the intellectuals and middle-class politicians, who formed the vocal element of the socialist parties, and the labour rank and file. Many leaders had never belonged to the working class; others—*arrivistes*—cut themselves loose after their election. Socialist deputies and councillors were eminently respectable, law-abiding citizens, undistinguishable in appearance from the representatives of the bourgeoisie. Syndicalist hostility to the 'politicians' was caused as much by what they were as by what they did: it reflected a class conflict within the left. Syndicalism was a reaction of the workers against the domination of the socialist movement by elements foreign to the working class—intellectuals, journalists, lawyers and professional politicians.[1] Measured by its achievements, moreover, socialism appeared at best the vanguard of liberal democracy. Its overriding concern had been the preservation of the parliamentary Republic.[2] Association with other parties had brought the workers few material gains, certainly less than those they had achieved through their own trade-union activities. The socialists had shown themselves to be not the revolutionaries of their doctrine but merely the left wing of the radical-republican party.[3] Meagre achievements on the one hand, an obvious anxiety to enter parliament on the other: the workers naturally became suspicious of their motives. It appeared as if the politicians were simply climbing into power on their shoulders. The sharpest reaction, no doubt, was caused by the spectacular betrayals: Millerand sat in a cabinet with the butcher of the Paris Commune; Briand later broke a general strike by the mobilisation of workers and threats of court martial. More generally, the workers could watch the manoeuvres of 'their'

[1] Cf. G. Yvetot, *Les intellectuels et la C.G.T.*, n.d.
[2] Cf. Szabó in *Mouvement Socialiste*, No. 25, p. 114.
[3] Cf. Lagardelle in *Mouvement Socialiste*, November 1904, p. 1.

representatives in parliament: quite apart from the obvious turncoats, all seemed to compromise their principles, making peace with the existing order to further their own or their party's cause.

The conclusion seemed obvious: the system was essentially bourgeois: those drawn into its orbit inevitably succumbed to its spell and became bourgeois themselves. Disillusioned with the parliamentary system in general, the socialist parties in particular, many workers came to reject both. Pirou summed up the situation: experience showed that the presence of a socialist in the government brought little change in the life of the working class, that the political arena, with its bargains and compromises, tended to dissolve the purity of doctrine and undermine the resolution of individuals; the result was a widespread demand for a return to the revolutionary spirit of earlier days.[1] The syndicalists repudiated parliamentary reform. The revolutionary class struggle was inevitably emasculated in parliament; it could only be carried on in the unions, where the clarity of conflict between capitalists and proletariat was maintained and from which the bourgeois socialists were rigorously excluded. They claimed to be the true heirs of the socialist tradition. Socialism having degenerated into mere parliamentarianism, its original goals could only be achieved by the direct action of the labour movement.

A linked, and equally obvious conclusion, was the rejection of the state. The proletariat must emancipate itself without trying to capture state power. Consistent intervention in strikes, and the use of armed forces to defend the interests of the employers, showed that the existing state was simply the executive committee of the bourgeoisie. Bloodshed brought emotion to this belief. A change in rulers could only profit self-styled socialist politicians whose ambitions politics alone served. Experience strengthened the anarchist tradition; the existing state was hostile to the interests of the working class; the state as such would always be a force of repression. The tradition of Proudhon pointed the same way, though from a slightly different angle. The Republic, permanently engaged in defending itself against monarchists and clericals, had failed to cope with the pressing socio-economic problems which were being created by the industrialisation of France. Despite the presence of socialists, no serious measures of reform had passed through parliament. The capacity of the democratic system came to be challenged, quite apart from the motives of its rulers. Parliamentary democracy was discredited for two reasons: its failure to achieve tangible reforms; its patently bourgeois (liberal-intellectual) character. The labour movement sought to achieve its aims not only by direct action but also through its own institutions. The state was to be replaced by economic

[1] G. Pirou, *Les doctrines économiques en France*, 1925, p. 26.

61

organisations. It is significant that democracy was attacked at much the same time, and on much the same grounds, from the extreme right as well as from the extreme left. The attack on the bourgeois-intellectual character of the parliamentary Republic was echoed by Sorel, the *Action française* and the fascists; advocates of an alternative order included the syndicalist theoretician Lagardelle (later a supporter of the Vichy regime), the supporters of the corporate state and the guild socialists.

The growth of an organised movement

Unlike anarchism or socialism, syndicalism began from existing organisations and developed the ideas appropriate to them. It is thus relevant to trace the path followed by the labour movement in its attempt to organise itself. This was a laborious process, organisations gradually taking form, slowly growing stronger, often changing, until the pattern of the *C.G.T.* finally emerged.

MARXIST DOMINATION. The defeat of the Commune left the labour movement shattered, its leaders imprisoned or exiled, its organisations cowed or dispersed. The first step towards reconstruction thus came from a republican journalist, Barberet, who saw in the unions a means of eliminating the strikes which he regarded as dangerous to the Republic. An attempt was made in 1872 to associate such unions as were still tolerated in a *Cercle de l'union amicale ouvrière* but this was dissolved by the government almost immediately. The first national congress of labour organisations was called in 1876 as an alternative step. Some 360 delegates of unions, co-operatives and mutual-aid societies met in Paris. Moderation marked their congress. The demand was for limited reforms: higher wages and shorter working hours plus the political programme of the radicals. The strike was pronounced an unsatisfactory weapon and the peaceful solution of all industrial questions favoured. An anti-political sentiment was apparent in the rule that only representatives of labour organisations should have the right to speak. It was also shown in the mutualist ideas expressed, notably in the workers' determination to rely upon themselves to improve their condition, only demanding of the state the right to associate freely for this purpose.

The second congress was held in Lyons in 1878, still under the influence of the moderates, and the conservative press was full of praise for the wisdom of the delegates. Meanwhile, however, veteran socialists had returned to France. Jules Guesde had a clear programme and the gift of leadership; his influence grew rapidly. It was decided to call an international labour congress in connection with the International Exhibition of that year and the socialists associated themselves with that move. When the government decided to ban the gathering, indignation threw the two groups together. The moderates obeyed; Guesde seized the opportunity and called the congress himself. It was dispersed at the first session and he was arrested: martyrdom assured his popularity. The result was a triumph for marxism at the third labour congress, held in Marseilles in 1879. A collectivist resolution was passed by 73 votes to 27 (in the previous year it had obtained only 8 votes out of 177). Guesde appeared to have gained control of the labour movement. At the same time, he founded the first socialist party. As the official history of the *C.G.T.* later declared, these events had serious consequences. The introduction of politics (the subordination of economic action to political propaganda and electoral campaigns) reduced the trade-union movement to an auxiliary of the party. This led to the establishment of rival labour organisations later and the postponement of labour unity for some twenty years.

The French unions—the *syndicats*—were local units, organising workers of the same trade or industry within a particular area (town or region). Although still weak, they did manage to form some national federations in the following years, associating unions of the same trade. With the passing of the Waldeck-Rousseau law (1884), the number of unions and federations increased rapidly. Demand grew for a wider organisation that would associate all sectors of industry. The weavers of Lyons took the initiative and a congress was called there in 1886. The intention was moderate and apolitical, just as it had been ten years earlier. Official support was obtained and delegates had their travel expenses paid from public funds. The *guesdistes* again captured the congress, however, although many of them represented small unions that were little more than political fronts. A collectivist resolution was voted almost unanimously; hostility to reform through state action was shown in the rejection of the Waldeck-Rousseau law. At the same time, a new organisation was created: the *Fédération nationale des syndicats*. It was something of a sham: the member unions were generally small and frequently inactive, day-to-day links between them and the centre almost non-existent. The Federation was run by marxists who showed little interest in the development of labour organisations as such; their interest centred on the annual congress which could be used as demonstrations of political strength and platforms for political propaganda.

The 1887 congress was in fact held at Montluçon, where the *Parti ouvrier* was strong. There were only fifty delegates, mostly party members who in no way represented the labour movement as a whole. The tone was revolutionary but no important decisions were taken. In 1888 the display of red flags at Bordeaux led the police to close the meeting after a minor brawl. The congress moved to a small town nearby, Le Bouscat, where the mayor offered hospitality. Briefly, almost by the way, the general strike came up for discussion. In the absence of the marxist leaders, the workers were taken by a sudden enthusiasm and voted two resolutions which clearly contradicted the party line. The first declared that only the general strike could lead to the emancipation of the proletariat; the second called on the workers to separate themselves from the politicians and concentrate on the organisation of their unions, the sole Grand Army of the revolution.

The politicians learnt their lesson and tightened their control. In 1890 the *Parti ouvrier* met just before the *Fédération des Syndicats*, so that delegates could be instructed in the party line. The *guesdistes* resolved that the general strike presupposed levels of awareness and organisation which the workers had yet reached. The delegates then went on to the trade union congress at Calais. The two groups, their agenda and resolutions, were almost identical. At Marseilles, in 1892, the collectivists were strengthened by the presence of Guesde, Lafargue and Liebknecht. A tactical error had been made, however: the unions had been allowed to meet before the party. A report on the general strike was presented by Briand and, partly because of his eloquence, partly because the idea was very much in the air, the principle was voted once more. The party congress passed over the question in silence. It was obvious, however, that the contradiction could only lead to a split—not in the party, for that was too well organised, but either within the Federation or between the Federation and the party. In fact, the Federation was already beginning to disintegrate. A second federation had been established in 1892 and was ready to receive dissidents —as indeed was another political party, that of the *allemanistes*, who had voted the general strike at their first congress in 1891.

THE PERIOD OF DIVISION. The Paris municipal council had inaugurated the first *Bourse du Travail* in 1887. Others were established in the following years throughout the country. The *Bourses* were intended to act as labour exchanges and general meeting places for the unions of the town: they acquired something of the character of trades councils, associating different trades within a particular area. The strength of the *guesdistes* had lain in the provinces: in Paris the more revolutionary *allemanistes*, anarchists and non-party militants gained control of the *Bourse*. The provincial *Bourses* proved to be similar rallying points. By the turn of the century the majority of the fifty *Bourses* then in existence had repudiated all links with political parties, largely as a result of anarchist influences; three were more or less dominated by *blanquistes*, five by *guesdistes* and ten by *allemanistes*.[1] Those hostile to the marxist leadership saw the opportunity for organising a rival federation and in 1892 the delegates of ten *Bourses* met at Saint-Etienne to form the *Fédération nationale des Bourses du Travail*, led by Pelloutier. It remained under the influence of the more revolutionary, anti-political militants of Paris, an influence maintained by keeping the central committee in that city, rather than allowing it to move around the provinces

[1] Cf. Pelloutier in *Mouvement Socialiste*, 1 November 1899.

with each congress as the *Fédération des syndicats* had done. There was, from the start, little doubt that it would come out victorious, for it had two considerable advantages over its rival: it had the more active working-class membership and it was more solidly founded. The *Bourses* were well organised. Stability was assured in early days by municipal subsidies: the less militant workers were attracted by the services offered; the provision of offices and halls made them the centre of all labour activity in their towns. The links between the *Bourses* and their constituent unions were personal, direct and continuous. Their small number made their Federation a relatively homogeneous and close-knit organisation. By comparison, the *Fédération des syndicats*, with its many small unions scattered throughout the country and its lack of contact except at annual congresses, was largely a paper organisation.

In 1893 the *Bourses* resolved to call a congress of unions jointly with the *Fédération des syndicats*. Paris was to be the venue. It seemed as if the *guesdistes* would reject the idea, but when the Minister of the Interior closed the Paris *Bourse* it took on the character of a united labour protest and a large number of unions sent their delegates. Claiming to represent over 300,000 organised workers, the Paris congress voted for the principle of unification: all unions were to join (or, where necessary, form) national industrial federations and local inter-industry federations (i.e. *Bourses*); the two groups were then to form a confederation with representatives of both sides on its central committee. The congress took another decision, however, which was to make this impossible. It voted the principle of the general strike and set up a commission to prepare for it. Finally, it was decided to hold another joint congress at Nantes the following year. The Nantes *Bourse*, which had already been instructed by the *Fédération des syndicats* to organise its own congress for 1894, was asked to organise the joint congress at the same time.

This decision was seen by the *guesdistes* as an attempt to steal their movement. The *Fédération des syndicats* sent a letter to its members telling them that it would not allow its name to be used in conjunction with any other. If Guesde was willing to sacrifice labour unity in order to maintain the independence of his own organisation, the *Bourses* were more conciliatory. They decided at their own meeting, that as the congress of the *Fédération des syndicats* would be open to all, they would support it rather than try to organise another joint venture. At the same time, they reaffirmed the principle of the general strike. The *guesdistes* saw the danger. Wishing to fix their line in advance, they held their political congress in Nantes first. Their rejection of the general strike was more categoric than ever. They proclaimed it a blind alley, self-organised defeat: only political action could emancipate the proletariat. There followed what was in effect another joint labour congress: delegates represented 21 *Bourses* (with 776 affiliated unions), 30 industrial or trade federations (with 682 unions) and 204 otherwise unaffiliated unions. The meeting began in uproar and continued in bitter conflict. The second item on the agenda split the congress wide open. Briand made another persuasive speech: he was not asking for the immediate application of the general strike, he declared, but simply asking the delegates whether they were afraid to vote for the principle. The leading marxist spokesman replied by ridiculing the general strike as a lawyer's sword. After three days of heated debate, the principle was accepted by 65 delegates against 37, with 9 abstaining. Blows were exchanged and the *guesdiste* minority left the hall. The *Fédération des syndicats* was thus split in two: an unco-operative *guesdiste* minority and a majority in favour of collaboration within the labour movement. Pelloutier and the *Bourses* had clearly drawn ahead of Guesde and the *Parti ouvrier* in the battle for leadership.

The congress of the *guesdiste* faction of the *Fédération des syndicats* was held in 1895 at Troyes. It systematically repudiated the Nantes resolution of the previous year, voting unanimously against the general strike and against fusion. It advocated instead the conquest of public powers (state and local) by political means and adopted the reformist electoral programmes of the *Parti ouvrier*. Only a small minority of the original membership was represented. Thereafter the Federation had no more than a nominal existence: the name was retained for a while but no further congresses were held, nor did it show any other signs of life. Its death was due to an excess of politics. At Limoges, a few weeks later, the majority held another joint congress where they were strongly supported by the *Fédération des Bourses* and the *Parti ouvrier socialiste révolutionnaire*, whose leader, Allemane, was present. This sealed the victory of the revolutionaries over the politicals: while only some 300 unions had been represented at Troyes, delegates at Limoges represented 18 *Bourses*, 18 federations, 126 unaffiliated unions—altogether 1,662 unions.

THE PERIOD OF CO-OPERATION. At Limoges, in 1895, a new organisation was founded, the *Confédération Générale du Travail*, with its seat in Paris. The general strike was reaffirmed. Workers were urged to vote at elections only for other workers, members of trade unions; a minimum programme was adopted as a condition of support for candidates at the forthcoming municipal elections (eight-hour day, employers' liability for industrial injuries, closing of private employment bureaux). The *Fédération des Bourses* was invited to join the Confederation. Léon Blum later called the Limoges congress a true Constituent Assembly.[1] Discussion was devoted almost entirely to questions of organisation and a detailed constitution was drawn up. The exclusive aim of the *C.G.T.* was to be the unification—in the economic field—of all workers struggling for their emancipation. Constituent groups were bound to remain outside all political parties. A whole range of labour organisations qualified for membership: unions (*syndicats*) and their national federations, *Bourses* and their national federation, other local or regional associations (in French, *unions*) of *syndicats* represented similar of different trades. The national council was to consist of delegates. It was to be responsible for co-ordinating the policy of the movement, the organisation of campaigns such as those for the eight-hour day and the weekly day of rest, as well as for the general strike. All labour organisations, whether members of the *C.G.T.* or not, were to be invited to annual congresses.

The labour movement had finally freed itself from the politicians and could develop along its own lines. Unity, however, was not yet achieved. Though the *C.G.T.* and the *Bourses* tended to co-operate, they remained independent of each other: rivalries still showed. Unions were often weak, their existence precarious, their links with the *C.G.T.* were still not strong. The *Bourses* remained an important element of stability and cohesion. With the *guesdistes* eliminated, they tended to act as leaders of the labour movement: until 1900 they followed the precedent of the *Parti ouvrier*, holding their own congresses in the same town just before the *C.G.T.* In 1896 they met in Tours. Discussion centred round the future relationship of the two organisations. On the advice of its secretary, Pelloutier, the *Fédération des Bourses* decided not to join the *C.G.T.*, the main reason being given as the *C.G.T.*'s lack of vitality. It was agreed, however, that the Federation might affiliate if the *C.G.T.* amended its constitution to turn itself into a mere co-ordinating body between *Bourses* and industrial federations (i.e. if it dropped its claim to organise the entire labour movement). The *C.G.T.*'s congress opened a few days later. The secretary, Lagailse, admitted the weakness of the new organisation. The change proposed by the *Bourses* was not accepted, however, and the new organisation remained impotent a while longer.

In 1897 the congresses were held in Toulouse. The *Bourses* again discussed their relationship with the *C.G.T.* and were again unwilling to join. Personal rivalry between Pelloutier and Lagailse played a considerable role. There were other reasons, however. The *C.G.T.* was still weak, thus not an attractive proposition. Its structure was still in dispute, the *Bourses* wanting no more than a top-level link between two quite distinct forms of organi-

---

[1] L. Blum, *Les congrès ouvriers et socialistes français*, 1901, p. 154.

sation: the industrial and the regional, the vertical and the horizontal. Friction was also caused by conflicts of function: the *Bourses* tended to take on the tasks of general propaganda which the *C.G.T.* could not organise effectively, and this the latter resented. It was obvious, however, that the Confederation could never hope to be viable alone. It therefore made concessions. Direct membership was restricted to national organisations. Its national council was to become a confederal committee, composed of two separate bodies: a national council of industrial federations and the federal committee of the *Fédération des Bourses*—each with full administrative and financial autonomy, independent in all matters except the organisation of national campaigns.

Rennes was the seat of the 1898 congresses. The *Bourses* were still unwilling. Their annual report claimed that the reason was not petty rivalries but differences in their degree of development, but the debate was largely devoted to the unfriendly relations between the two. At the *C.G.T.* congress, the report also dealt with the many incidents that had arisen between Lagailse and Pelloutier, claiming that the sole cause of trouble was the latter's fear that the Confederation would absorb the dues paid by members of the *Bourses*—'a grave danger to the salary of their secretary'. There was a sharp debate about whether the ultimatum of the *Bourses* should be accepted in its entirety or whether the Confederation should go its own way alone. The path of separation was followed. The industrial federations, with their national council, and the *Bourses*, with their confederal committee, were to remain entirely independent of one another, both adding the letters *C.G.T.* as a formal prefix to their own title. The possibility of occasional meetings between the two organisations was suggested, but not very enthusiastically, and no specific provisions were made. There was talk, indeed, of positive advantage in two parallel systems. The advent of a unified movement seemed further off than before. The Paris congress of 1900 brought no change.

UNITY ACHIEVED. Accused of weakness during the railway strike, Lagailse resigned the secretaryship of the *C.G.T.* in 1898. His successor, Griffuelhes, brought a new vigour to the Confederation. In 1901 Pelloutier died. Thus the old quarrels gradually dropped into the background, while differences in strength between the two organisations also disappeared. The way was open for another attempt at unification. The *Bourses* held their 1901 congress in Nice. Niel, one of the delegates, became the chief advocate of fusion and it was partly due to his efforts that this was later achieved. The labour movement had two heads, he declared, and one must give way to the other: it was time for the *Fédération des Bourses* to renounce, not its identity, but its independence and its leadership in favour of the *C.G.T.* Yvetot, the new secretary of the Bourses, replied by pointing to the growing strength of his federation and obtained the postponement of any decision; delegates going on to Lyons for the *C.G.T.* congress were nevertheless invited to support the principle of unification there. Nothing came of it that year. At Lyons, indeed, the statutes of the *C.G.T.* were modified in a way that apparently shut the door on the *Bourses*. Membership of the *C.G.T.* was to be restricted to national federations of trade or industry and unions not yet federated nationally; attendance at congresses, previously open to all labour organisations in the country, was to be limited to affiliated bodies.

The last congress of the independent *Fédération des Bourses* was held in Algiers in 1902. Niel again took up the theme of unity and urged once more that the Federation should merge with the *C.G.T.* A committee was appointed to draft a new constitution which could be presented to the *C.G.T.*; Niel was to act as *rapporteur* at both congresses. The committee recommended that the *C.G.T.* should become the *force unitaire et agissante* of the labour movement but that the Federation should retain a measure of autonomy within the Confederation. The principle of unity was generally accepted, its success seemed a foregone conclusion. And, indeed, it was also accepted by the *C.G.T.* at Montpellier that year. Only groups actually affiliated to the *C.G.T.* were admitted at that congress but the *C.G.T.* had not yet in fact excluded the *Bourses* from membership. 165 delegates thus represented 458 organisations, including 56 *Bourses* and 29 federations. The only major question was that of unification; there was not even time to discuss the general strike, although it was on the agenda. Another committee was appointed, with ten representatives of the federations, five of the *Bourses* and ten authors of various constitutional projects. After much discussion, it proposed a plan based largely on proposals submitted by the *Bourse d'Alger* and the *Fédération de la Metallurgie*. The *rapporteur* introduced it by saying that immediate action had been expected of them and that, after fifteen hours of often heated debate, they had only been able to agree as a result of compromise on all sides.

The new Confederation was to have two sections: that of the *Bourses* and that of the federations. Individual unions were supposed to affiliate with both a federation and a *Bourse* and could only join the *C.G.T.* indirectly. The latter could thus claim to be a 'federation of federations'. Each section was to have its own federal committee, executive bureau and budget. A joint confederal committee was to meet every two months; the general secretary of the *C.G.T.* was to double as secretary of the section of federations; both were to have the same treasurer, though separate accounts were

Growth of an organised movement

to be kept; the *Bourses* could hold their own conferences for administrative questions immediately after the biennial congresses. Three permanent committees were to be set up for the *C.G.T.* newspaper, financial control and the general strike. The idea of establishing a parliamentary committee was rejected without division. On this, the *rapporteur* was emphatic: "We ask the state, the parliamentarians and the politicians to let the unions get on with their own business themselves for we cannot forget that it is to politics that the workers owe the divisions which have weakened them." The non-political character of the *C.G.T.* was entrenched.

This constitution was adopted by 440 votes to 1, with 44 abstentions—almost without disagreement. It remained in force for the rest of the period of syndicalism. The *C.G.T.* was now more than a name. The movement towards unity and independence had reached its end.

Strength and organisation
of the C.G.T.

THE SYNDICAT. The *syndicat* was the basic unit of trade union organisation. It united workers of the same profession, or employed in the same industry, in a particular town or some not much larger district. Its size would typically run somewhere between 100 and 300 members. The average membership of the *syndicats* affiliated to the *C.G.T.* rose from 100 in 1902 to 200 in 1914. Even the *syndicats* of the relatively powerful *Fédération du Bâtiment* had an average membership of only 120 in 1908, of 200 in 1910. Such *syndicats* obviously differed a great deal from the much larger English trade unions, usually organised on a national basis. They were small, local and homogeneous, in a real sense cells of the labour movement. This fact clearly influenced the picture the syndicalists had of the way in which society might be organised after the revolution, a point to be considered later in the chapter on the syndicalist utopia. It is true that the growth of industry meant the emergence of the factory as an even more basic cell, often with its own works committee, but this remained dependent on the *syndicat* and was in any case a slow and late development in France. The important point is that the *syndicats* and, to an extent, the *Bourses* were the only really integrated, really live organisations in the movement; the federations and the Confederation were relatively formal organisations, representing the collaboration of *syndicats* at committee level. The movement was essentially pluralist.

The *syndicat* was an autonomous body; its independence was guaranteed by the statutes of the *C.G.T.* It established, directed and controlled its own administrative machinery. Within wide limits, it could formulate its own policy and choose the line of action to be pursued at any moment. Two examples will suffice to show the extent of this autonomy: internally, the wide and bewildering variety of constitutions, of services offered and of contributions demanded, even in *syndicats* of the same trade; externally, the fact that, although the federation concerned might attempt to enforce prior consultation, the *syndicat* declared strikes on its own initiative.

Statutes varied greatly and ranged from the elaborately detailed to the merest skeletons. In their fundamental provisions, however, they were all fairly similar. Each *syndicat* had three organs. The sovereign body was the general assembly or meeting of all members; it decided all matters of principle. The administrative council was responsible for the execution of policy and could decide on everyday questions. Administration was the

72

responsibility of a bureau, consisting typically of the *syndicat's* secretary and treasurer. Given the large number of *syndicats*, one would expect to find variations in the distribution of power between these three organs. At one extreme, the rules might provide for direct government by the assembly; others, though there were fewer of these, were more authoritarian and vested considerable powers in their councils or bureaux. The actual, as distinct from the formal, distribution of power was of course, more important. The small size and homogeneous character of the *syndicats* often made it possible for all members to participate in minor decisions as well as major policy. Whether they did so depended largely on the character of those concerned. The militants undoubtedly had considerable influence over the rank and file. The nature of the *syndicats*, on the other hand, made difficult the emergence of professional leaders, at least at this key level.

THE FEDERATION. The federation united at the national level all the *syndicats* of either the same industry or the same profession. There were only a few exceptions where the syndicat itself was national, for example the *Syndicat national des chemins de fer* which had non-autonomous local sections. The federations were organised on lines similar to the *syndicats*, each with its own congress, council and bureau. In general, each *syndicat* sent one delegate to the federal congress, regardless of size, though again there were a few exceptions to this rule, allowing for representation proportionate to membership (e.g. the *Fédération du Livre*). The principle of federalism was thus emphasised: each *syndicat* adhered to its federation as an autonomous and indivisible unit (i.e. casting a single vote), equal in status to all other units.

The function of the federation was largely confined to co-ordination and propaganda. In its activities—even where a common policy was obviously required or decisions had to be taken at national level—it was bound by the autonomy guaranteed to member *syndicats*. In many cases even the federal congress could only take important decisions subject to approval on reporting back. Use was also made quite often of the referendum: the principle of direct government was extended to the federation and the dangers of remote control (i.e. the delegation of powers to a parliament) lessened. In any case, the independence of the *syndicats* was such that there was never any guarantee that they would act in accordance with federal decisions, even when these were reached by the most democratic procedures possible. This was particularly true in the case of strikes. In matters of major policy, however, persistent refusal to keep in step sometimes finally led to expulsion.

Historical background

THE BOURSE DU TRAVAIL. The *Bourse du Travail* was an institution peculiar to France. As the name implies, the original idea was simply to establish a labour exchange, a place where workers seeking employment could meet (a 'vast glass rotunda' according to one project). The first such proposal was submitted to the Paris municipality as early as 1790. In 1886 a project of much wider scope was presented by Mesureur. He visualised a *Bourse* which would provide the unions with permanent offices and meeting halls; for the workers there would be a library so that they could inform themselves about economic matters and rooms in which they could discuss their problems—they would then be able to play a more intelligent part in the affairs of society. The scheme was accepted and the Paris *Bourse* inaugurated the following year. Other municipalities followed suit, providing accommodation and subsidies, so that the number of *Bourses* grew quite rapidly. Typically, they provided permanent offices for the unions of the town and meeting rooms, as well as libraries and other facilities.

As an employment exchange the *Bourse* was not all that important. Instead, it became the obvious meeting place for militant workers. It became the centre of union activities and a rallying point in times of strike. Legally, however, it remained a municipal building in which the local authority merely lent rooms to the unions; use of the building was the responsibility of a committee representing the unions, the local authority and the Ministry of Commerce. This often led to conflict. The *syndicats* soon felt the need for a home of their own, as, indeed, for an independent association (i.e. a trades council). Such an organisation was formed by the *syndicats* of the area—the *Union des syndicats de la Seine*—and, some time later, it moved its headquarters from the municipal *Bourse* to the headquarters of the C.G.T., for which building it made itself responsible. This example was followed in the provinces, often as the result of interference by the local authority; where the *syndicats* continued to use the municipal building, they formed their own local associations. It was these purely labour organisations which were affiliated to the C.G.T. The use of the term *Bourse du Travail* was somewhat misleading therefore; in C.G.T. parlance it referred not to the institution but to the local union of *syndicats*, a federation of different *syndicats*, usually within a town and its environs.

The smaller towns were too small to be an effective basis for co-ordinated action. It was necessary, moreover, to bring rural areas into the system. This led to the creation of larger *unions* on a departmental (i.e. county), or even regional, basis. These grew in importance and in 1912 the departmental *unions* replaced the *Bourses* as directly affiliated members of the *section des Bourses* of the C.G.T. If the larger associations resembled the

74

federations, in that they were essentially formal organisations, the old *Bourses* resembled the *syndicats*: they were based on the everyday meeting of rank and file rather than on the annual congress of delegates and a council composed of near full-time union officials. The administration of the *Bourses* followed the usual pattern of the federations. There was a general assembly of all members, a council consisting of one delegate from each affiliated *syndicat*, and a bureau of permanent officials. The *syndicats* retained the same autonomy.

Fernand Pelloutier, in large measure their creator, saw the functions of the *Bourse* under four heads. The first was mutual aid (e.g. employment bureau, unemployment and sickness benefits); the second, education (e.g. general culture, economic research, information service); the third, propaganda (e.g. encouragement to form new *syndicats*); the fourth, resistance (e.g. organisation of strikes and strike funds, agitation against laws hostile to the labour interest). On the whole, this plan was followed. It was more or less agreed, when the *C.G.T.* was unified, that the *syndicats* and the federations were to be the fighting units, concerned primarily with strikes, while the *Bourses* were to devote themselves to the general welfare of the working class. In a sense, they were the creative arm of the labour movement. Interesting in this respect was the emphasis placed on education. Pelloutier had attached the greatest importance to this aspect of their work and—theoretically at least—the educational aim was maintained. The 1908 congress, for example, called on them to establish courses for the study of the writings of 'all those thinkers who honour humanity' as well as courses to give primary and technical education to workers who had missed out on the state system. *Culture de soi-même* was a natural corollary of the slogan *le syndicat suffit à tout*. The real importance of the *Bourse*, however, lay in the sense of solidarity it established in its district. It united in common action workers of different trades, with different interests, who might otherwise have remained divided in their various *syndicats*.

THE CONFEDERATION. The Confederation had two sections, that of the *Bourses* and that of the federations. Other trades councils were originally excluded by a rule against duplication; in 1912, however, it was decided that county associations, the *unions départementales*, should replace the more locally based *Bourses* as direct members of the first section. The question of industrial *versus* craft organisation was raised at the founding congress but freedom of choice was left to the unions until 1906, when it was decided that only industrial federations should be admitted as *new* members into the second section. Individual *syndicats* could not adhere directly to the *C.G.T.* (with the exception of a few national *syndicats* and some *syndicats* not yet nationally federated). All *syndicats*, on the other hand, were required to affiliate with both a federation and a *Bourse*, though this dual membership was never fully achieved.

At the biennial congresses, however, all *syndicats* were represented directly, each with one vote, regardless of size. This was a continuous source of conflict, with periodic demands for proportional representation based upon membership. The rule adopted by the *C.G.T.* reflected its confederal character. Delegates represented autonomous and equal *syndicats*. The equality of voting rights meant that it was not individual interests which were represented but group interests; implied was something of an organic theory of the *syndicat*. The doctrine of the *mandat impératif* was officially rejected but many delegates were in fact mandated on important issues, and some preferred to abstain from voting in the absence of such instructions. In that sense the *syndicats* participated directly in the congresses, thus further enhancing the confederal character of the *C.G.T.* The decisions taken were furthermore not necessarily binding on the *syndicats*; according to Delesalle they had only an indicative or educational value.[1] One cannot tell how far the freedom left to the *syndicats* reflected a genuine respect for their autonomy and how far fear of splitting the *C.G.T.* on disputed issues. When the *Fédération du Livre* defied the decision of the congress of *Bourses* to campaign for an eight-hour day, voting instead for a nine-hour day at its own congress the following year, no formal steps were taken against it. Less important *syndicats*, on the other hand, were expelled on occasion, though usually for breaches of the *C.G.T.* statutes, the acceptance of which was a condition of membership.

The council of the *C.G.T.* consisted of delegates of the federations and *Bourses*. It was in no sense an independent body for its members often came with instructions from their own organisations. Nor did the council have much power to direct the policy of the movement: the federations, like the *syndicats*, retained their independence and often pursued policies contrary to those adopted by the Confederation. The bureau, with the general secretary at its head, was theoretically no more than the servant of council and congress. In practice, of course, things looked rather different and the militant officials of the *C.G.T.* played a predominant role in policy making. The implications of this will be considered later, particularly with reference to the question whether syndicalist doctrine really expressed the ideas of the rank and file of the movement. In the last analysis it nevertheless remained true that the *C.G.T.* was a federation of federations. One observer described it as a committee or a system of committees;[2] it existed for

[1] P. Delesalle, *La C.G.T.*, 1907.
[2] M. Leroy, *La coutume ouvrière*, 1913, p. 479.

Strength of the C.G.T.

the purpose of discussion and co-ordination. Most of the real activity, the real life of the movement, was to be found in the cells of the movement, not in the central organisation.

THE STRENGTH OF THE C.G.T. According to the census of 1901, out of a total population of approximately 39,000,000 there were some 11,400,000 persons who came under the broad heading of wage and salary earners. The last figure included a large number of women and some children, isolated workers (e.g. in domestic service or in village shops), another large group of white-collar workers (i.e. clerical staff), some supervisory and even managerial employees and others of professional standing, none of whom one would expect to find organised in trade unions at that time. One can reckon with a total of about 3,800,000 male workers in industry and transport as potential union members.[1] To this might be added a share of the large number of agricultural workers in view of the fact that the *C.G.T.* claimed also to represent this section of the working population.

The number of persons of all descriptions organised in some form of *syndicat* was given officially as follows:

1902	3,679 syndicats	614,000 members
1906	4,857 syndicats	836,000 members
1912	5,217 syndicats	1,027,000 members.

A better picture of the situation, perhaps, was given by the official figures for the extent of unionisation within certain industries in 1912: Mining 32%, Building 30%, Transport 27%, Paper and Printing 15%, Furniture and Woodwork 14%, Textiles 13%. They were lower in all other industries, usually well under 10% (except in the case of a few small trades such as match-making where it rose as high as 70%). All were substantially lower in the earlier years.[2]

These figures are deceptive. They included many unions outside the *C.G.T.* and with an entirely different outlook. Some were bourgeois in composition, independent professional organisations. Many more were bourgeois in sympathy, at least in the eyes of the *C.G.T.* These fell into two main groups. There were the so-called *jaune* unions, generally sponsored by employers and often limited in membership to one enterprise. Often established deliberately to counter the militants, their doctrine could at best be described as liberal unionism, collaboration with the employer and perhaps some share in the profits. A national federation was formed in 1902 with the title *Union fédérative des ouvriers et syndicats professionels.* At the first congress a membership of 200,000 was claimed; in 1907 it claimed

[1] Cf. E. Levasseur, *Questions ouvrières et industrielles en France*, 1907, pp. 271/929.
[2] Cf. Ministère du Travail, *Annuaire des syndicats professionnels 1897–1914.*

77

to have 439 workers' *syndicats*, 76 agricultural *syndicats*, 87 employers' *syndicats* and a large number of other groups. Exaggerated though this was, the movement was important in some areas, especially in the textile industry of the north. There were also Catholic unions. Christian unionism, based on the encyclical *Rerum Novarum*, also preached collaboration between labour and capital, though with rather a different concept of the social order. These *syndicats* included some mixed employer-employee groups and some white-collar organisations, as well as a number of unions for female employees. In addition, there were some Church-sponsored *syndicats* rather more hostile to the employers. In the textile industry, as a result, Catholic *verts* competed against syndicalist *rouges* and collaborationist *jaunes*. Christian unionism did not become much of a force until later, however, and it was not until 1913 that the *Fédération française des syndicats d'employés catholiques* was formed.

Even when these *syndicats* are excluded, the great majority of the remainder stayed outside the *C.G.T.* There were numerous reasons why so many *syndicats* chose to remain either entirely independent or to affiliate with independent federations. Apathy in one form or another was sometimes a factor, e.g. purely local interest or unwillingness to pay subscriptions. Doctrinal differences were another factor, often political, though sometimes a matter of disagreement about some immediate tactical issue. Personal conflicts were not without their influence. Civil service unions (e.g. postal workers) were not permitted to affiliate.

It is difficult to determine the actual membership of the *C.G.T.* The following figures are based on its own congress reports:[1]

1902	1,043 syndicats	100,000 members
1906	2,399 syndicats	300,000 members
1912	2,837 syndicats	600,000 members.

A number of qualifications are necessary. The statutes of the *C.G.T.* required double affiliation but there were many limping *syndicats* in both sections which failed to meet this condition. The *section des Bourses*, originally the stronger, was not able to expand so rapidly as the *section des Fédérations*:

| 1902 | 1,112 syndicats affiliated to Bourses |
| 1906 | 1,609 syndicats affiliated to Bourses. |

The number of *syndicats* entitled to a vote at *C.G.T.* congresses could never be higher than this. A distinction must also be made between nominal (quoted above) and paid-up members. The financial report presented in 1912 gave the following:

---

[1] Cf. M. Leroy, *La coutume ouvrière*, 1913, p. 477; and H. Montreuil, *Histoire du mouvement ouvrier*, 1947, p. 226.

Strength of the C.G.T.

1906   203,273 contributing members

1912   400,000 contributing members (estimate).

Turnover was always high. Many workers joined a *syndicat* at a moment of conflict, only to drop out again afterwards. Many failed to renew their subscriptions after the first payment. Others paid grudgingly to a union official who collected dues at the place of work but never attended union meetings. Even these figures were thus swollen by passengers whose sole formal link with the *C.G.T.* was that they had at one time or another paid a few *centimes* to their local *syndicat*.

It is clear that the *C.G.T.* never officially represented more than half the organised workers in France and at best one tenth of the industrial wage-earners (to say nothing of the agricultural workers). This, however, was not the true indication of its strength. It often provided leadership. In periods of strike or agitation, the *C.G.T.* was able to rally the unorganised workers and draw them into action under its flag. At such times, as Leroy noted, the workers came to the *syndicats* which led the struggle; these *syndicats*, a small elite in relation to the newcomers, hosts for a few days or months, crystallised the amorphous mass of wage-earners.[1] At the same time, the influence of the *C.G.T.* made itself felt more widely. Its ideas spread throughout the working class. It was the militant wing of the labour movement, the most active in everyday industrial disputes, the most extreme in its long-term demands on society. Almost permanently in the news, it was seen by both sides as the protagonist of the revolutionary labour cause against capitalism and bourgeoisie.

[1] M. Leroy, *La coutume ouvrière*, 1913, p. 33.

PRINCIPLES AND PRACTICE
OF THE C.G.T.

Reform and revolution:
the twofold purpose

The purpose of the Confederation was set down in a number of authoritative documents: the statutes of the *C.G.T.* adopted in 1902 at Montpellier; the model statutes prepared for individual *syndicats*; the report presented to the international labour congress at Dublin in 1903; and the famous statement of principles adopted in 1906 and known as the *Charte d'Amiens.* All stressed the *double besogne*: the dual nature of its task. The *C.G.T.* had to defend the workers' immediate interests and to pursue the final emancipation of the proletariat—it had thus a short and a long term programme, an economic and a political function, a reformist and a revolutionary character.

ANTITHESIS: PRESENT AND FUTURE TASKS. The first, and indeed natural, aim of the *C.G.T.* was the defence of the immediate 'economic, moral and professional' interests of the workers. Wage rates, hours and conditions of work, trade practices, terms of employment—such matters were of course the everyday concerns of the *syndicats*. They arose naturally from the worker's position in the wage economy, requiring of the syndicalists merely a statement of existing practice. Focussed on his job and his relationship with the employer, it sought improvements within the capitalist system; it was the reformist—the trade union—aspect of syndicalism, no different from the goals of trade-union movements elsewhere. The second aim of the *C.G.T.* was the final emancipation of the proletariat by the destruction of the capitalist system and the overthrow of the state itself. Referring as it did to the more or less distant future, this was a consciously formulated principle of syndicalism. Concerned with the structure of society as a whole, it was—despite syndicalists' objection to the word—a political aim, closer to the aim of socialist parties than of most trade unions. Involving the abolition of the existing order, it was also revolutionary.

In the early, really pre-syndicalist, days the militants tended to draw a fairly sharp distinction between the two functions. It was in the revolutionary task, the *besogne d'avenir*, that they saw the essence of syndicalism. In their view, the final emancipation of the proletariat could only be achieved by the general strike, the once-for-all revolution, an entirely different level of action from the everyday conflicts of industry. They tended, as a result, to belittle the ordinary strike: the concessions to be gained were trivial at best and more than likely to distract from the revolution ahead.

6-2

Principles and practice of the C.G.T.

In its first issues, the *C.G.T.* paper—the *Voix du Peuple*—warned the workers of the ephemeral character of their immediate gains and urged that efforts should be directed instead to preparing the proletariat for the great battle to come.[1] This early concentration on the future was later described by Griffuelhes, writing in 1908 and wise in hindsight, as 'revolutionary romanticism'—all interest focussed on the coming revolution, politics considered a distraction, the reformist strike a mere waste of time and energy.[2] To some extent it was a form of sublimation, compensating for weakness that made major present gains unlikely.

As the *C.G.T.* grew in strength and confidence, it found itself capable of organising effective national campaigns directed against the government as well as the employers, for immediate but limited concessions to the working class as a whole. The reformist task, earlier the province of the *syndicat* (the strike limited to one sector of industry or even a single town), thus became more and more a pre-occupation of the *C.G.T.* Given the possibility of a substantial gain in the present, and the enforcement of the eight-hour day or the weekly day of rest would have appeared as such to the rank and file, interest in the general strike and the hypothetical revolution was bound to diminish. Romanticism gave way to a more practical approach and to more practical forms of action. Griffuelhes attributed the change of heart to an expansion of trade-union activities which filled the time of the Confederation, detached the worker from his earlier habit of relying on a mystically providential revolution to solve all his problems, and absorbed him in everyday matters and everyday struggles.[3] The complete emancipation of the proletariat remained the goal. Increasingly, however, the *C.G.T.* tended to ignore this half of its twofold task: instead of preparations for the revolutionary general strike (a task limited to propaganda in any case), it emphasised the organisation of mass movements for immediate reform.

The theorists of the *C.G.T.* reflected this changing interest and adapted their doctrines. The *besogne d'avenir* gradually became absorbed in the *besogne quotidienne*. A synthesis was achieved, however: everyday activities were seen in a more revolutionary light than before. Pouget, for example, described as partial expropriations the concessions gained from employers and state which had previously been dismissed as ephemeral.[4] He came near to suggesting thereby that the expropriation of the capitalists, which, after all, was to be the core of the revolution, would take place as the gradual

---

[1] *Voix du Peuple*, December 1900.
[2] Griffuelhes in *Action Directe*, 23 April 1908.
[3] Griffuelhes in *Action Directe*, 23 April 1908.
[4] E. Pouget, *Le syndicat*, 1907.

84

Reform and revolution

by-product of everyday union activities—a doctrine not far removed from the *évolution révolutionnaire* of the reformist socialists such as Jaurès. It is true that the syndicalists had earlier been willing to admit that the everyday strike could be a *champs d'exercice*, a training ground for the coming struggle. But the distinction vanished almost completely. Pouget spoke in terms of a permanent revolution, carried on in the present as well as in the future.[1] Griffuelhes made the same point when he wrote that true revolutionary action was that which, practised every day, unified the proletariat and strengthened its position.[2] Lagardelle, although more of an outsider, could explain by 1912 that the everyday action of the labour movement differed from the final only in character (i.e. consequence) and not in form (i.e. intensity); that the two were part of a chain of events, the links of which were continuous and homogeneous; that movement and goal were thus merged into one.[3] It was this sort of view, not unrepresentative of the militants, that allowed one commentator to call syndicalist action at once reformist and revolutionary.[4]

A distinction must however be drawn between this interpretation, put forward by the militant theorists of the movement, and the attitude of the rank and file. While the idea of complete emancipation unquestionably remained alive, it was probably not a major force of inspiration behind the activities of the *C.G.T.* once that had become a widely-based organisation. Although the most pressing demands of the *syndicats*, such as the agitation for the eight-hour day, were always advertised as steps towards liberation, they were in fact pursued for their own sake, as ends in themselves, rather than as episodes in a permanent revolution. Roughly speaking, the revolutionary militants were the original members of the *C.G.T.*—as membership grew, it came to include a less adventurous majority, attracted by the hope of some immediate improvement in their conditions of work. The attention of the *C.G.T.* was thus directed to the pursuit of reforms. The militant theorists, unwilling to sacrifice their revolutionary ideal, were forced to interpret the reformist part of the *C.G.T.*'s programme so that it fitted into their own philosophy. Levine makes this point very well: "The struggle for immediate gains is a necessity which they must make a virtue of while waiting for the hoped for final struggle; and when they theoretize about the continuity of the struggles today with the great struggles of tomorrow, when they interpret their everyday activities as part of a continuous social warfare, they are merely creating a theory which in turn justifies their practice

[1] E. Pouget, *Le parti du travail*, 1905.
[2] Griffuelhes in *Action Directe*, 23 April 1908.
[3] Lagardelle in *Mouvement Socialiste*, February 1912, p. 134.
[4] Challayé, 'Le syndicalisme révolutionnaire' in *Revue de Métaphysique et de Morale*, January/March 1908, p. 114.

and preserves their revolutionary fire from extinction."[1] The syndicalists, when pushed, could find their own dialectic.

This argument must not be driven too far. The idea of permanent revolution was not simply a rationalisation. The revolutionary goal—the final emancipation of the proletariat—did not disappear; nor, indeed, did the picture of a final, once-for-all revolution, different in character from preceding struggles. The respective importance of the two goals of the C.G.T. is not easy to determine. Formally: statutes and declarations of principle gave equal weight to the reformist and the revolutionary tasks. Theoretically: the militants were able to evade the problem by dissolving the distinction. What, however, did the rank-and-file majority think? Or, to look at it another way, what motivated them when they took part in the everyday struggles of the labour movement? A clear answer is impossible. Behind most of the strikes organised by the C.G.T. lay the demand for specific reforms, valued for their own sake. At the same time, the revolutionary ideal survived; the 'myth' of final emancipation remained part of many workers' *idées reçues*. Most of the time it was probably no more than a hazy picture at the back of their minds, receding as their attention turned to questions of more immediate interest, until almost forgotten, but occasionally, at the height of battle, in the great nation-wide movements of strike and agitation, when the class war was seen most sharply, the picture grew bright and clear again, suddenly giving a wider revolutionary significance to a campaign that was perhaps reformist in intention, stimulating the participants to carry it beyond the limits of action associated with merely reformist demands.

SYNTHESIS: PERMANENT REVOLUTION. At such moments of great tension, revolutionary ardour flared up and, while the excitement lasted, the revolutionary ideals of the C.G.T. came to the fore. On several occasions there was a widespread feeling, both among workers and the bourgeoisie, that revolution or something very similar was about to occur. May Day 1906 was such a time: both right- and left-wing press seemed prepared for dramatic events. This feeling reoccurred during the public service strikes of 1909. *The Times* correspondent reported a member of the barber's union as saying that he could detect from the expressions of the bourgeois customers he shaved that they were in utter terror of revolution.[2] In London cooler heads naturally prevailed. The *Spectator* confirmed the atmosphere of panic but commented more soberly: "Englishmen lately returned from Paris tell us that respectable French people are alarmed at the frequency and

[1] L. Levine, *The Labour Movement in France*, 1912, p. 201.
[2] *The Times*, 17 May 1909.

Reform and revolution

viciousness of labour riots, shake their heads at the signs of the times, and speak of another revolution. We cannot help feeling that there will be no revolution. Paris would not be Paris if it were not on the verge of one; it generally has been; and we have come to understand that in the clear atmosphere of quick and vivid thought there things seem much nearer than they are."[1] It was right, of course. Pataud, one of the leaders and certainly the firebrand of the 1909 strike, claimed at a mass meeting that there was not a single member of the C.G.T. who was not in revolt and ready to do anything to overthrow the regime, so rotten that it could be toppled at any moment.[2] In fact, however, the workers were not ready for anything of the sort. They had entered neither the 1906 nor the 1909 strikes with any such intention. The picture of revolution may have been vivid enough, even stimulating, but in the last resort it was not seriously believed. Even in those apparently revolutionary situations, there was little revolutionary purpose, in the strict sense of the word, behind the actions of the labour movement.

This does not mean that syndicalism was not a revolutionary movement. In its earlier, romantic period the goal had been revolutionary; later, when the task was seen primarily as the defence of immediate interests, the C.G.T. remained revolutionary in its practice, in the tactics it employed, in the sense that its policy of direct action was outside the law (by-passing the electoral and parliamentary, i.e. constitutional, procedure) and often against the law. Indeed, there was a marked increase in direct action after the turn of the century as the C.G.T. began to mobilise the labour movement more effectively. To that extent, the movement was more revolutionary during the later period than it had been in earlier years, when its revolutionary goal was matched by relative inactivity. "We need another fifty years of struggle to reach the final hour", a leading syndicalist is reported to have said in 1901.[3] This was probably the general belief among all but the Patauds of the movement towards the end of the period of syndicalism. Meanwhile, despite the ingenious synthesis advanced by the theorists, the labour movement was reformist in purpose but revolutionary in character: it pursued reformist ends by revolutionary means.

[1] *The Spectator*, 26 June 1909.
[2] *Cit. The Times*, 17 May 1909.
[3] *Cit.* A. Pawlowski, *La C.G.T.*, 1910, p. 130.

Political neutrality and the politics of syndicalism

The C.G.T. proclaimed itself the association of all class-conscious workers, regardless of their political beliefs, in the very first sentence of its statutes. It stated firmly that the C.G.T. was to stand outside the world of politics, politicians and political parties. This was the principle of political neutrality.

THE APOLITICAL PRINCIPLE. Broadly, neutrality had two aspects. First: the C.G.T., the Bourses, federations and syndicats, were bound to remain neutral vis-à-vis political organisations. No labour organisation was to give official support to either a party or a politician. This rule was clearly stated in the model statutes for syndicats which forbade political affiliation or even participation in a political congress. No section of the C.G.T. was to appear even temporarily associated with a party. The C.G.T. thus rejected a socialist proposal for a joint protest against the visit of the King of Spain in 1905. A similar rule applied to individuals: they could not use the name of the C.G.T., or of an affiliated labour organisation to which they belonged, in connection with any political activities in which they might be engaged personally. The C.G.T. statutes referred specifically to election campaigns; the model statutes to the use of their titles by union officials outside union functions. Second: the C.G.T. and the other labour organisations were themselves to remain neutral ground. No political controversy, propaganda or proselytization was to take place within the unions. The C.G.T. statutes declared that the lectures and discussions it organised were to limit themselves to economic questions or education in union affairs. The model statutes were even more specific; they forbad any political discussions at all at meetings of the syndicat.

The official principle, then, was this, and no more than this: the political neutrality of the labour movement. Political parties and their activities were nowhere explicitly condemned in the statutes. Members of the C.G.T. were not forbidden to join parties or take part in political activities as private individuals; indeed, their complete freedom was assured in this respect. A guarantee of toleration was to be found in the Amiens Charter: any member, individually and outside his labour organisation, might participate freely in whatever form of activity corresponded to his own political or philosophical beliefs—all the C.G.T. asked in return was that he should not introduce such beliefs into the Confederation; the labour organisations, for their part, were not to concern themselves with the

88

Political neutrality

activities of parties or sects—these could pursue social reform unhindered, side by side with the *C.G.T.* The only exception to this rule was the case of union officials. The hope had been expressed at the 1901 congress that delegates and members of the committee, as well as officials of affiliated unions, would not engage in politics as deputies or local councillors. Nothing was decided then, however, and in the following years several members of the confederal committee sat in the Chamber of Deputies as members of the socialist party. The question of incompatibility was debated again and the statutes of the *C.G.T.* were amended in 1911 to forbid the candidature of any officials. Many of the federations and *syndicats* had similar rules.

THE ANTIPOLITICAL PRACTICE. The rule of neutrality was more formal than real. The *C.G.T.* did not remain outside politics. The idea that workers should lay aside their political, philosophical or religious differences within labour organisations, standing united on the basis of their common non-controversial economic interest, was wishful thinking. The highly political, sectarian and argumentative character of French militants made it unlikely. So did the fact that economic questions had obvious political implications and were, in any case, not as uncontroversial as the syndicalists like to maintain. Members brought their political beliefs into the *C.G.T.* with them. Its meetings never remained neutral ground. Every opportunity was taken—and there were many—to raise political issues and the question of the unions' relationship with the socialist party; the opponents of political socialism were as vociferous as its supporters.

In practice, the *C.G.T.* made but the merest pretext of remaining uncommitted *vis-à-vis* the socialist party: the hostility of its leaders was clear and outspoken. It is true that they claimed to be adhering strictly to the rules. In 1911, for example, a statement appeared in the *Bataille Syndicaliste* over the signatures of the *C.G.T.* secretaries Griffuelhes and Jouhaux, that no attack on the party could be found in any resolution passed by the labour congresses; the unions, proud of their independence, had always respected the independence of the socialist party. But this was only half the truth. Congress resolutions may well have respected the party, but syndicalist leaders, speaking to all intents in the name of the Confederation, showed little of that respect themselves. They made use of the positions they held to propagate their own ideas. The official newspaper, *Voix du Peuple*, was a regular forum for anti-socialist propaganda; socialist leaders were attacked in almost every issue as traitors to the working class; every opportunity was taken to undermine the party's reputation; abstention was counselled at elections. The same bias was shown by speakers at lecture

Principles and practice of the C.G.T.

meetings organised by the *C.G.T.*, ostensibly a form of trade-union education. These articles and speeches were widely interpreted as representing an official view.

RIVAL IDEOLOGIES. Looked at formally, the Charter of Amiens was based on the principles of distinction (i.e. separation of the labour and socialist movements) and parallel action (i.e. no condemnation of the one by the other). The recognition of two possible spheres of activity—party and union, political and economic—was also implied in the statutes of the *C.G.T.* Some union leaders were compromisers and were prepared to interpret neutrality in this way. In the first issue of the *Voix du Peuple*, for example, Guérard argued, under the title *Chacun chez soi!*, that both forms of action could be pursued with advantage by the workers, though it was necessary that they remained distinct.[1] From this point of view, Niel was equally correct when he argued at the Amiens congress that, as there was no official syndicalist doctrine, men of all political tendencies could be accommodated in its ranks, while continuing their political activities outside the *C.G.T.* In fact, however, political neutrality was basically incompatible with the spirit of syndicalism, whatever the letter of the rules may have said.

Both Guérard's and Niel's claims were based on a very narrow interpretation of syndicalism: they saw it as the everyday action of unions in defence of the everyday interests of the workers, a fairly uncontroversial matter, requiring little in the way of theory. As the revolutionary syndicalists understood it, on the other hand, syndicalism was a political doctrine, containing an analysis of the social situation, a goal to be achieved, the complete transformation of society, and a comprehensive strategy of action. The delegate Latapie was nearer the truth when he answered Niel at Amiens that syndicalism was an entirely new theory, a doctrine distinct from all others. Thus, even if the same broad ends were to be pursued, syndicalism and socialism were necessarily rivals in exactly the same way as communism and socialism or anarchism and socialism. If syndicalism was right, the others must be wrong.

Another fundamental principle of syndicalism implied in the Amiens Charter, was the self-sufficiency of the labour movement. *Le syndicat suffit à tout!* was the slogan. That was another answer to the doctrine of parallel action. Syndicalism was a rival to socialism, not simply as an alternative ideology, but because of its all-embracing claims. At best, the party was unnecessary for the emancipation of the proletariat, for this did not depend on the conquest of state powers, either by constitutional means

[1] *Voix du Peuple*, December 1900.

or on the barricades; in fact, the party was a positive hindrance: it misled the workers, wasted their energy in the *cul-de-sac* of parliamentary intrigue and distracted them from the real struggle. Leroy rightly asked how, in rivalry with the parties, syndicalism could fail to acquire the character of a party itself.[1] The answer was given by the syndicalists in their frequent use of the term *Parti du Travail*. Pouget, for example, actually described the Amiens Charter as the baptismal certificate of the party of labour.[2]

THE AMBIGUITY OF 'POLITICS'. The word 'politics' itself introduced much confusion into the rule of political neutrality. The debates on this question, that dominated the congresses of Bourges (1904) and Amiens (1906), turned essentially on what the different groups considered to be its proper interpretation. Many apparent contradictions arose from a linguistic difficulty: the use of a term that was never clearly defined and was capable of bearing at least two quite different meanings.

'Politics' was often used in the French labour movement in a sense derived from Proudhon and the anarchists: it referred to the activities of government (or, more broadly, the state). The syndicalists, like the anarchists and unlike the communists or socialists, rejected government as an instrument through which to achieve their ends. Opposed to government in principle, refusing to make use of its institutions, determined, indeed, to overthrow it entirely, they could with some show of logic refuse to call their activities 'political'. Government meant parliament and parliament meant the parliamentary parties which were thus equally marked with its stigma, even when they opposed the bourgeois-capitalist regime. The syndicalists could therefore interpet the rule 'No politics in the C.G.T.!' as no parliamentary-party-politics. This was made quite clear in a statement of policy in the first issue of the *Voix du Peuple* which specifically coupled politics with participation in the parliamentary system; the paper's promise to remain unpolitical was defined as refusal to participate in election campaigns.[3]

This restriction was arbitrary, however, and did not correspond to the more common use of the term. Politics normally covers all that is concerned with the organisation of the community or, more broadly, though one must draw a line somewhere, with public affairs (politics are the affairs of the *polis*). This was recognised by Niel who compared economic activity, the purpose of which was to alleviate the immediate hardships of the working

[1] M. Leroy, *La coutume ouvrière*, 1913, p. 355.
[2] Pouget in *Mouvement Socialiste*, No. 179, 1906, p. 27.
[3] *Voix du Peuple*, December 1900.

class, with political activity, which had a moral basis and tried to change the social order. As syndicalism was concerned with a fundamental change in the structure of society, it was inescapably political in this sense.[1] Latapie, a syndicalist himself, also recognised this, though with the opposite intention to Niel, when he declared that as union activities were concerned with more than reform, but sought the transformation of society, they were necessarily political in the wider sense of the term.[2] The opponents of the syndicalism within the *C.G.T.* were therefore justified when they accused its leaders of committing the Confederation to an obviously political line of action behind a cloak of political neutrality.

The idea that the *C.G.T.* was a non-political organisation could be argued in another way. Whatever its goals, whatever the scope of its concern, its action, the means employed, were economic in character and therefore on an entirely different plan from all the forms of action associated with politics in the past; it was important not to confuse them. The complement of the neutrality rule is the principle that the *syndicat* is concerned only with economic activities. The Amiens Charter made this point when it explained the *C.G.T.*'s claim to unite all workers, regardless of their political beliefs, as a recognition of the fact that the class struggle took place in the economic field.

The distinction between an economic and a political conflict, again a Proudhonian idea, was equally unrealistic. The class struggle was necessarily both, as Marx was not slow to point out. It was true that the charter declared that, in order to achieve maximum effect, the labour movement should direct its action against the employers. But the syndicalists, on their own theory, knew quite well that the conflict could not be limited to one between workers and employers; the whole basis of their attack on the state was the belief, shared with Marx, that the state was the executive committee of the bougeoisie.[3] In any extensive strike movement, not to speak of a general strike, the syndicalists were bound to come into conflict with the forces of the state, acting as the defenders of capital. The revolutionary character of the direct action they propagated made this all the more inevitable. Whether they wished it or not, the workers were thus drawn into a form of action which, even if economic in origin and purpose (i.e. concerned with relations between employers and employees), could not but break those bounds and become political (i.e. involve relations between government and governed). The antimilitarist campaigns of the *C.G.T.* showed their understanding of this very clearly: they were as much con-

---

[1] At the 1906 congress of the *C.G.T.*
[2] At the 1906 congress of the *C.G.T.*
[3] Cf. E. Pouget, *Les bases du syndicalisme*, 1906.

cerned with preventing the use of troops as strike-breakers as with the international solidarity of the proletariat.

On a number of occasions, in any case, the *C.G.T.* chose to organise campaigns directed specifically at the government, e.g. to support their demand for legislation to close private employment bureaux and to establish the weekly day of rest. On such occasions it left of its own accord the field of conflict with employers for that of conflict with the state. As a last resort, it might be argued that even these campaigns were non-political in so far as economic means were employed that were not dissimilar from those used against employers. This argument is difficult to maintain, however. Such campaigns went well beyond the organisation of strikes. Even when their hand was not forced by the armed intervention of the state, the syndicalists often chose to give them an essentially political character. Street demonstrations, riots and violence— these were much the same whether organised by the syndicalists or some more politically-minded group. Griffuelhes himself likened the agitation against private employment bureaux to that for the release of Dreyfus. If the one was political, then so was the other.

At the time of the public service strikes of 1908, Guesde sensibly commented: "If once it is maintained that trade-unionism is sufficient unto itself, it becomes absolutely necessary for it to indulge in politics; as it desires to become the rival of the socialist party, or even to take its place, the *C.G.T.* is condemned constantly to compromise its economic action by continued intervention in politics."[1] It was obvious that the more non-political syndicalists tried to be, the more they tried to avoid parliamentary politics, the more they were bound to involve themselves in the wider field of political action, in rivalry with the party and in conflict with the state. To that extent, there was an internal contradication in syndicalist doctrine.

A SYNDICALIST PRESERVE. This contradiction could nevertheless be resolved, partially at least, by distinguishing between the formal rule laid down in statutes and charter and the spirit of syndicalism as a whole. The principle of neutrality was not to be taken on its face value. While its apparent intention was to guarantee the neutrality of the *C.G.T.*, its real purpose was to restrict the influence of politicians within the labour movement. This was made quite plain by the *rapporteur* at the Montpellier congress of 1902: "We demand of the state, of the deputies and the politicians, that they leave us to manage our own affairs." In other words, the rule was intended to do little more than keep the rival party out of the

Cit. *The Times*, 8 August 1908.

Principles and practice of the C.G.T.

C.G.T. Chacun chez soi! Guérard entitled his article—but he might better have written *Les socialistes chez eux!* Political neutrality ensured, if anything at all, that the syndicalists were left free to impress their own politics on the labour movement while being relieved of the stigma that the word bore.

The autonomy of labour
and direct action

The significance of the neutrality rule lay in the autonomy of the labour movement it proclaimed. This idea of autonomy lay at the very heart of syndicalism. Carrying the doctrine of the class war to its extreme, but logical, conclusion, the syndicalists drew the line between the proletariat and the rest of society more sharply than any other socialist theoreticians. Not only did syndicalism deny 'outsiders' the right to intervene in its affairs, it also refused (theoretically, at least) to be associated with members of another class or institutions not its own. The proletariat, as one syndicalist put it, was no longer part of the nation. The doctrine of separation has been called a form of isolationism.[1] Parallel to the idea of autonomy ran that of the self-sufficiency of the labour movement. The proletariat could achieve its ends entirely by its own efforts and through its own resources; it required neither the aid of other classes nor the help of institutions other than its own. It could 'conquer power without demanding anything of it'; it could replace the institutions of power by a system of its own creation. Syndicalism as the syndicalists said, was sufficient unto itself.

AUTONOMY IN THEORY AND PRACTICE. However, theory and practice were not wholly consistent. This applied particularly to the principle of self-sufficiency. From the beginning, the C.G.T. organised campaigns which really belied the assumption that they could rely entirely on their own efforts. The campaigns referred to earlier, for example, demanded reforms from one intermediary (parliament), to be enforced by another (labour inspectorate, the courts). The whole notion of absolute independence, of a new society created entirely within the labour movement, was taken from Proudhon and developed while labour was weak. The inevitable result of growing strength was a shift from the theoretical to the practical; with it came a willingness to compromise for the sake of immediate concessions, regardless of the purity of doctrine.

The principle of autonomy was more consistently respected, though its meaning was somewhat widened in the process. In pursuit of reforms, the syndicalist movement did not collaborate with employers or government but limited itself to exercising pressure from outside; it thus remained a closed, autonomous and independent bloc facing the bourgeoisie and its institutions. The syndicalists relied on their own strength, not on the good

[1] R. Goetz-Girey, *La pensée française syndicaliste: militants et théoriciens*, 1948.

95

will of others. It was resolved at Bourges in 1904, with reference to the eight-hour day campaign, that the workers could obtain concessions only if they relied on their own action. This statement could be interpreted in two slightly different ways. The workers might personally enforce their demands against the employers by such unilateral action as walking out after eight hours' work. They might, on the other hand, rely on their own strength to force others to grant their demands. In the latter case, it was a secondary matter whether the employer himself gave way or parliament made the decision for him. At first sight, at least, it seemed as if no co-operation with the bourgeoisie was necessary in either case: the autonomy of the labour movement was not impaired.

It was only at first sight, however, that no collaboration with capital or state appeared necessary. If one looked closer, one saw that almost every strike ended with some sort of negotiation between strike-leaders and employers and that more strikes were settled by compromise than by unilateral victory. Nor were the syndicalists as unprepared to collaborate with the institutions of government as they might have been. Once a reform such as the weekly day of rest had been obtained, the revolutionaries naturally became ardent defenders of the law and appealed to the authorities to enforce it. Often even convinced syndicalists appealed to legal procedures for the settlement of industrial disputes; sometimes they went further, as in 1906 when the radical building workers' union called on the Minister of the Interior to intervene in a strike to protect their rights. Collaboration with the sponsors of reformist legislation was also necessary and, towards the end of the period, in the discussions of the pension law of 1910 for example, syndicalists and socialist deputies worked together. Strictly speaking, the only really autonomous action the *C.G.T.* ever proposed was the plan to down tools after eight hours.

These objections did not alter the character of the movement as a whole. What was important was that the workers were prepared to take the law into their own hands: by creating their own forms of struggle, they bypassed the constitutional (i.e. electoral-parliamentary) system even when it was legislation they wanted; by strikes and other forms of agitation, they coerced employers and state into meeting their demands. In that sense, the movement was autonomous and revolutionary. It was this that Griffuelhes meant when he declared roundly at Le Havre in 1912 that the *C.G.T.* was permanent illegality.

THE DOCTRINE OF DIRECT ACTION. Autonomy, as such, was a negative principle; its positive side was the syndicalist proclamation of the worker's duty to act for himself. Of course, the workers did not need anyone to tell them this, for the will to act was the very basis of the syndicalist movement; it was upon their readiness to act that a great part of syndicalist doctrine was built. From the point of view of theory, the principle of action was the logical corollary of the principle of autonomy; in fact, it preceded all other principles.

Autonomous action was called 'direct action' and this became the most popular of all syndicalist slogans. The practice of direct action was spontaneous and concrete—it was what the workers did. Formulated as a theory, however, it tended to lose content and became something of an abstraction. Pouget defined it as action by the working class, drawing upon its own strength, acting independently and through its own organisations, relying on the help of no intermediary, expecting nothing from men or forces outside itself, creating its own conditions of struggle, its own means of resistance and aggression, bringing into everyday life the formula 'the emancipation of the proletariat is the task of the proletariat itself'.[1] The idea of direct action, as such, was a more or less artificial concept created by the militant theorists. It existed on the level of theory and, on that level, it followed logically from the idea of the class war and the autonomy of the proletariat. Union activities, on the other hand, were relatively spontaneous, arising out of the worker's situation in a capitalist economy but reflecting also his experience of politics and the state. Preceding theory, action was in the main pursued without reference to theory. While much could be described as 'direct' in the sense of Pouget's definition, this explains why a principle of direct action was never formally adopted by the *C.G.T.* in the way that political neutrality or the general strike were. Direct action, from one point of view a link in the chain in syndicalist theory, was from another simply the name given by the observer to various forms of labour activity in order to bring out their common characteristic. But here again, though the procedure was empirical rather than deductive, one was at the level of the theorists.

The forms of action pursued by the *C.G.T.* will be discussed later. The point to stress here is that they were not consciously chosen by the workers as fitting into a doctrine of direct action: they arose naturally and without much reflection. The strike apart, indeed, they never really acquired a theoretical content sufficient to build them into a comprehensive theory of syndicalism. And a warning is necessary even as regards the strike. It was advocated by the militant leaders, the theorists of the movement, as an ideal form of direct action. The workers, however, usually struck because of the immediate pressure of economic conditions. One must not fall into the trap of treating their action—the practice of the *C.G.T.*—as a consequence

[1] Pouget in V. Griffuelhes and L. Jouhaux, *L'encyclopédie du mouvement syndicaliste*, 1912.

of syndicalist theory. Which is not to say that it did not have a theoretical importance. The workers, whether consciously or unconsciously, were acting in a manner that syndicalists believed would contribute to the emancipation of the proletariat.

Nor do these qualifications belie the fact that the slogan of direct action obtained wide currency in the labour movement as a result of the militants' propaganda. It has been claimed that the French are susceptible to fine phrases. Bearing in mind the revolutionary tradition of France, it is not surprising that it should have been so popular. What effect it had is another question. Many members of the *C.G.T.* undoubtedly spoke of direct action and many of their actions were undoubtedly direct. Did the principle, once extracted from practice, formulated and launched by the theorists, in turn affect practice? Did it stimulate the workers to further action and to less compromising attitudes than they would otherwise have shown? There seems to be evidence for this, though, on the whole, it probably remained a slogan, a magic formula like the general strike, unconnected in the minds of the rank and file with their everyday activities.

The theory of the strike

The idea of the strike was fundamental to syndicalism. Writers about the movement often went further, describing syndicalism itself as a philosophy of the strike.[1] The title was apt, but it was too apt. Little attempt was made to explore its meaning or even define the sense in which it was used. It was, in fact, an ambiguous phrase and those who used it did well not to look too closely at its implications. Was syndicalism a philosophy *about* the strike, a theory of its significance? Or was the strike itself the philosophy, a philosophy *in action*, not of minds but of arms? In a sense it was both: about the strike for the militants, the strike itself for the rank and file. This was really the problem of 'syndicalism and metasyndicalism' which will be taken up again later. Either way, the question of the strike was of central importance but more complicated than most writers would lead one to suppose.

THE STRIKE AS SPONTANEOUS ACTION. The strike was the most common form of action organised by unions. Beside it, other forms of industrial action such as boycott or sabotage were insignificant; political agitation took up a very small part of the workers' time by comparison. It was a form of action, moreover, that lay at the very root of the unions' existence. The labour movement, after all, had organised itself very largely in order to make strikes more effective. They remained its primary concern.

This raises two points. First: the strike was everyday action and as such taken for granted by the workers. It was not often a subject of debate at the *C.G.T.* congresses and no declaration of principles was ever adopted. Attention was naturally reserved for rarer and more exciting forms of action such as sabotage, or for the more theoretical and more inspiring question of the general strike itself. For the *C.G.T.* as a whole, therefore, the idea of the strike remained unformulated. One can only speak of a rank-and-file syndicalist attitude.

Second: strikes obviously occurred before syndicalism and were thus not a specifically syndicalist form of action. They were, indeed, a spontaneous form of action (i.e. a natural reaction to the pressures of circumstance rather than the result of a considered, long-term strategy) and thus often had no theoretical content at all. Delesalle, for example, admitting in 1900 that the workers were acting according to the necessities of the moment, complained of the fragmentary nature of the strikes that occurred and hoped that a

[1] E.g. Challayé, 'Le syndicalisme révolutionnaire' in *Revue de Métaphysique et de Morale*, January/March 1908, p. 103.

Principles and practice of the C.G.T.

wider, more class-conscious, revolutionary approach would develop in time.[1]

Syndicalism has been defined as the outlook and practice of the labour movement. The theory of the strike, however, was formulated by a number of militant leaders, more philosophically inclined than the rest. Any discussion of the subject involves quotation from the articles of a small minority rather than an analysis of principles adopted by the majority of the C.G.T. True, they claimed that their theory was based on observation; true also, it filtered back to the rank and file. But one must be cautious in saying that syndicalism was a philosophy of the strike, whether one means that there was a philosophy behind strikes (i.e. a deliberate purpose) or a philosophy implied in them (i.e. an unconscious function).

MARX AND CLASS WAR. The theory of the strike depended upon the theory of the class war. If syndicalism was a philosophy of the strike, the corollary was Lagardelle's claim that the idea of the class war was the beginning and the end of syndicalism.[2] The idea that society split into two classes, proletariat and bourgeoisie, labour and capital, and that the conflict between them was the dynamic force of history, above all the dynamic behind the labour movement, was of course closely associated with Marx. Stripped of its dialectical implications, however, it was the common heritage of all socialist movements, belonging as much to syndicalism as to marxism or European social democracy. The direct influence of Marx on the French labour movement was in fact very small. Marxism was never absorbed by French workers, at least until later, in the same way as the ideas of Proudhon, Blanqui and the anarchists. The notion of the class war, however, had achieved the status of common knowledge in labour ranks. Though in rather crude terms, almost in slogan form, it was accepted by the syndicalists as self-evident.[3] Rather than elaborate the obvious, they preferred to deal with the more important, because more pressing, questions of action.

Capitalist society was based on the exploitation of labour. Conflict between employers and employees was inherent in the system: employers tried to push wages down in order to increase their profits or, which came to the same thing, refused to increase wages when prices rose. The worker was thus continually forced to defend his standard of living. The opposing interests were irreconcilable: agreement was impossible; an improvement could only be achieved by force. When the pressures became too great, the

[1] P. Delesalle, *Aux Travailleurs—la Grève!*, 1900.
[2] Lagardelle in H. Lagardelle *et al.*, *Syndicalisme et socialisme*, 1908.
[3] Cf. E. Pouget, *Le syndicat*, 1907.

workers broke out in revolt against their employers. This revolt was the strike.[1]

The workers combined to defend their interests. This was the origin of trade unions. Marx made the point: "Industry masses together in a single place a crowd of people unknown to each other. Competition divides their interests. But the maintenance of their wages, this common interest which they have against their employer, binds them in the same idea of resistance —combination. Thus combination always has a double end, that of eliminating competition amongst themselves while enabling them to make a general competition against the capitalist. If the first object of resistance has been merely to maintain wages, in proportion as the capitalists in their turn have combined for the purpose of repression, the combinations, at first isolated, have formed groups and, in face of constantly united capital, the maintenance of the association becomes more important and necessary for them than the maintenance of wages."[2] Thus Griffuelhes and Pouget could argue, in a statement published by *L'Humanité*, that the union was the primary organisation to which the workers were led by the logic of facts and where the class struggle was seen at its sharpest.[3]

CLASS WAR AND REVOLUTION. With the development of capitalism, society splits up more and more into two great hostile camps, the bourgeoisie and the proletariat. In the ensuing struggle the workers realise that the power of the bourgeoisie rests on the ownership of the means of production and that economic exploitation can only be ended through the establishment of a socialist society based upon collective ownership. The conflict was thus gradually seen to be wider than that between industrial employers and employees: it was a conflict between labour and capital that grew into a war between two classes. Marx described this development: "The economic conditions have in the first place transformed the mass of the people of a country into wage-earners. The domination of capital has created for this mass of people a common situation with common interests. Thus this mass is already a class, as opposed to capital, but not yet for itself. In the struggle this mass united, it is constituted into a class for itself."[4] The cumulative effect of strikes was to create a class awareness among the workers. This changed the nature of the strike: formerly a symptom of conflict between employer and employee, it became a symptom of war between a class-conscious proletariat and the bourgeoisie.

In so far as the strike was felt to have a significance wider than the im-

[1] Cf. G. Yvetot, *A.B.C. syndicaliste*, 1906.
[2] K. Marx, *The Poverty of Philosophy*, 1909, p. 157.
[3] *L'Humanité*, 12 August 1906.
[4] K. Marx, *The Poverty of Philosophy*, 1909, p. 158.

mediate readjustment of wages, seen, that is to say, as an episode in the class war, it could be regarded as part of the revolutionary movement. Recognition of the strike as part of the class war could change the striker's attitude to it, even if strike methods remained superficially unchanged. This enables one to distinguish between the revolutionary and the spontaneous (i.e. not class-conscious) as well as between the revolutionary and the reformist strike.

The article on *Strikes* in the *Encyclopaedia of Social Science* says: "It is in the settlement of strikes rather than in the direction that the social and political philosophy of the labour organisation is apt to manifest itself. Unions proclaiming a radical or revolutionary philosophy are not especially addicted to violence in strikes, since the weapon of violence is reserved for definitely revolutionary purposes. There is no strike method known to the organisations of a left-wing tendency that is not employed by the conservative unions as well. But a revolutionary union, while endeavouring to secure improvements in the conditions of its workers, utilizes the labour conflicts for the additional purpose of attacking the institutions of capitalism. Consequently it avoids as far as possible all compromises (arbitration, agreements, etc.) preferring to retain its freedom to renew the attack whenever circumstances warrant."

Behind every strike of a revolutionary union lurked the spectre of revolution itself; the agreement on the basis of which its members returned to work was no peace treaty but a temporary armistice; the strike was not an isolated skirmish but a battle in a long war. By contrast, the reformist strike was a once-for-all affair, its settlement regarded (at the time, at least) as a lasting one. The extreme of this argument was advanced by a French syndicalist in a pamphlet published in America: "The new unionists no longer consider what material advantages were achieved when they estimate the results of a given strike. The new unionist strikes are mere incidents in the class war; they are tests of strength, periodical drills in the course of which the workers train themselves for concerted action."[1]

This dismissal of interest in immediate gains hardly reflected the views of the rank and file. French strikes nevertheless tended to lose their isolated character. The facts of the class struggle forced themselves upon the consciousness of a large section of the working class and the wider significance of strikes was recognised. A sympathetic historian said: "Originally accidental, over the last twenty years the strike has become systematic; once simply economic, it has become revolutionary—the workers have made of it a weapon of war."[2] A hostile witness said exactly the same thing: "The

[1] A. Tridon, *The New Unionism*, 1917.
[2] M. Leroy, *La coutume ouvrière*, 1913, p. 634.

Theory of the strike

syndicat is a military formation organised for the class struggle; whatever the aims it pursues, the class struggle is certainly the principal and the strike the most common weapon."[1]

REVOLUTIONARY FREE WILL. Though the syndicalists took from Marx the concept of class war, they borrowed little more than the phrase itself. They rejected (or ignored) the whole philosophy of history which, under the name of dialectical materialism, claimed to predict the inevitable victory of the proletariat. This doctrine was too theoretical to be digested by the workers. Even edited in the simplest language, moreover, its implications would have been unacceptable. The marxist promise of a revolution at some unspecified future date was unlikely to satisfy those who wanted to participate in a revolution themselves or who preferred to believe that they were masters of their own fate. Martin Buber has distinguished between the apocalyptic and the messianic revolution.[2] The former is predestined, imposed upon man by forces beyond his control; the latter is contingent, depending upon his own free will. The marxist doctrine of revolution could be described as apocalyptic, the syndicalist as messianic. In syndicalist eyes the strike (and ultimately the revolutionary general strike) depended upon the workers themselves, upon their will to act. This view came naturally to the militant leaders who were activists at heart. It was reinforced by Bernstein's revision of marxism: the class war, far from leading to an inevitable revolution, was being undermined by the extension of democratic institutions—to reaffirm it, thus making revolution possible, required a positive act of will.

ISOLATION OF THE CLASS. While the syndicalists agreed with Marx in seeing the strikes as the primary expression of the class war, they went far beyond him in the importance they attached to it. The point is made by Gray: "Syndicalism is almost exclusively a theory of the class war and of the place of the strike (and ultimately of the general strike) as a weapon of warfare. The class struggle is not, however, the particular property of the syndicalists. But the glorification of the strike is their undisputed glory."[3] When Marx wrote "in this struggle the mass is constituted as a class for itself", he added "but the struggle between class and class is a political struggle".[4] When the proletariat became aware of itself, the struggle reached a higher level and was carried into the political (in the later context

[1] E. Levasseur, *Questions ouvrières et industrielles en France*, 1907, pp. 736/8.
[2] M. Buber, *Paths in Utopia*, 1949.
[3] A. Gray, *The Socialist Tradition*, 1946, p. 427.
[4] K. Marx, *The Poverty of Philosophy*, 1909.

of French marxists: parliamentary) arena. There the syndicalists refused to follow.

There were theoretical reasons for this refusal. Some were taken from the anarchist criticisms of the state. It was possible to see the syndicalists and the marxists as starting along the path of class warfare in agreement, only to be divided by the anarchists. It was equally possible, however, to see the refusal to transfer the class struggle into the parliamentary-political field as the result of an extreme interpretation of the theory of the class war itself. Total war meant sealed frontiers between the proletariat and the bourgeoisie. Sorel and his followers presented the isolation of the proletariat as a return to the purity of marxist doctrine. Raléa, in a study of the idea of revolution in socialist doctrines, was perhaps nearer the truth when he labelled the extremist doctrine 'hypermarxism'.[1] The view, briefly stated, was that the parliamentary-political conflict did not involve the worker as a worker (i.e. as a unionist) but as a citizen (i.e. as a member of a party, where he rubs shoulders with bourgeois socialists and intellectuals, or at least as a voter, where he is likely to cast his ballot with others). Thus Lagardelle wrote that if the whole of socialism was comprised in the class war, then the whole of socialism was also comprised in syndicalism (because outside the latter there was no class war). He meant that outside the fight waged by the *syndicats* there could be no organised proletarian struggle against the capitalist class. The truth, he declared, was that parliamentary socialism had not only failed to open any unbridgeable gap between proletariat and bourgeoisie but had in fact become one of the constituent factors of the state, one of the agents of the *solidariste* force of democracy.[2]

For the syndicalists, however, the refusal to accept the marxist conclusion that the class war must become political could be explained in large measure by the fact that they belonged to a trade-union, and not to a political, movement. It was economic exploitation, rather than political domination, which spurred them to action. As a result, they saw the class war in economic, rather than political, terms. Conflict with the employer was an immediate, everyday issue. Strictly political questions, on the other hand, had a much weaker claim to their attention—politics was often something distant, abstract, entering their life on rarer occasions. It must be remembered, moreover, that the workers had good reasons to distrust the socialist parties and parliamentary politics.

THE STRIKE AS A NATURAL WEAPON. The strike was seen as the most practical expression and as the most vivid symbol of class war. It involved

---

[1] M. Raléa, *L'idée de révolution dans les doctrines socialistes*, 1923.
[2] H. Lagardelle in *Mouvement Socialiste*, February 1912, p. 134.

Theory of the strike

the direct confrontation of the antagonists. This gave it a double advantage over other possible forms of direct action. First: the fact that the material interests of the workers were directly involved made it the ideal ground to fight on. Participation was ensured by the immediate issues (e.g. wage demands); the energy thus aroused could be canalised into the less immediate, thus less stimulating, revolutionary purpose. Political conflict lacked this direct appeal: the political system was, after all, as Marx himself said, only a superstructure; political issues often seemed to represent only disagreement on abstract questions of no obvious direct interest to the working class. Second: the strike, whatever its cause, made crystal clear the fundamental conflict between labour and capital (illuminating it, in Sorel's phrase, as if by a flash of lightning), increasing the class awareness of the workers, deepening the chasm between them and their opponents, and spurring them on to further action. It thus had a cumulative effect and a revolutionary value.

The strike was also the most effective weapon the proletariat had. In face of the capitalists, the workers possessed nothing but their own labour-power. The strike, basically no more than the withdrawal of that power, was thus their natural remedy. It was argued, though more often in earlier days, that the simple cessation of work was enough to hit at the heart of the capitalist system. The flaw in this, the fact that loss of wages was almost always more serious than loss of profits, seems to have struck the labour movement relatively late. The syndicalists then advocated violence to compensate for their lack of funds. The more practical point was that the worker spent the great part of his day in the factory, where links of solidarity could be established, so that in a strike he was fighting on home ground.[1] On his own terrain he had a good chance of success; elsewhere he was almost certain to lose. If he participated in election campaigns, he was likely to be duped by the bourgeois politicians; if he took part in an insurrection, he was certain to be overwhelmed by the armed forces of the bourgeois state.

THE WIDER SIGNIFICANCE. The theorists of the movement saw these facts, formulated them and worked them into their philosophy. In Pouget's phrase, syndicalism was the *interpretation clairvoyante* of the experience of the labour movement.[2] They advocated the strike as the natural weapon of the proletariat, arousing the most enthusiasm, the most easily organised and the most likely to succeed; they saw it as the clearest expression of the class war and, of course, as an expression *par excellence* of direct action. To this

[1] Cf. V. Griffuelhes and L. Niel, *Les objectifs de nos luttes de classe*, 1908.
[2] E. Pouget, *Les bases du syndicalisme*, 1906.

105

simple confirmation of the facts, however, they added two further ideas to produce an integrated theory of the strike.

The strike, they maintained, had an educative value. It created new ideas, peculiar to the workers and in opposition to those of the existing social order: solidarity, responsibility, the autonomous organisation of the working class, the negation of capitalist property. Here there was a clear link with Sorel who wrote in his *Reflections on Violence* that strikes had engendered the noblest, deepest and most moving sentiments of the working class. The more sober, and less moralistic, view taken by the syndicalists was that the strike prepared the workers for the coming revolution: it was the vital training-ground (*champs d'exercice*), the revolutionary drill (*gymnastique révolutionnaire*), the preview of tactics for the great day itself (*manoeuvre préparatoire*). The report of the confederal committee to the Amiens congress of 1906, for example, made the point that the proletariat still required much training before it could hope to succeed—but that every conflict the workers entered, every battle they fought, added to their experience as well as to their initiative and vigour.

The strike also led (or could lead) to immediate gains by the proletariat at the expense of the capitalists. The successful strike was, in effect, a partial expropriation. Even an unsuccessful strike, one leading to no material gain, could undermine the power of the capitalists if it proved the independence, strength and solidarity of the workers, and their determination to pursue their goal without reference to parliamentary reform. Jouhaux was thus able to claim that every strike robbed the employers of a little of their authority, while the workers at the same time became more confident in themselves.[1] Just as revolution had come to be seen as a permanent activity, so there was sometimes a tendency to see the expropriation of the expropriators as a permanent process, though the syndicalists never quite believed that either, alone, could achieve the final solution.

Taking these two lines of thought together, one could see the strike as revolutionary and reformist at one and the same time; it fulfilled simultaneously the *double besogne* of the C.G.T. It achieved immediate results which were at least a step towards the expropriation of the capitalists; it was an expression of permanent revolt against the bourgeoisie, an episode in the class war, and thus another step towards the emancipation of the proletariat.

[1] L. Jouhaux, *Le syndicalisme et la C.G.T.*, 1920, p. 39.

The strike in practice

Members of the *C.G.T.* do not philosophise, they act!—this typically syndicalist view[1] led Leroy to comment that the theory of direct action was 'concrete, the expression of a manner of being'.[2] Syndicalism could be described as a philosophy of the strike in the sense that the strike was an essential part of the syndicalists' manner of being. In that sense, too, no very conscious attitudes were necessary on their part. It was possible to argue that every strike automatically had a double purpose, the one reformist, the other revolutionary. The *Encyclopaedia of the Social Sciences* says that even where the aim appeared to lie solely in the field of reformist bargaining, there was usually something more, "whether clearly understood by the strikers or not". This point is made in a study of the strike published in 1928, not so long after the period of syndicalism: "Every individual strike may (also) be regarded as a single episode in a larger revolutionary movement, a movement of which the participants are perhaps only dimly conscious."[3] The character of the syndicalist strike, then, did not depend entirely upon the conscious value that workers placed upon it. The *C.G.T.* had clearly expressed revolutionary aims, the complete transformation of society. Even when the apparent motive was immediate reforms within the capitalist system, the strike acquired a revolutionary function because of those aims and because of the exclusion of all other forms of action to achieve them. Even when the *besogne quotidienne* alone was explicit, the *besogne d'avenir* was necessarily implicit. To that extent, the strike was necessarily revolutionary, almost despite itself, in fact as well as in theory.

THE AWARENESS OF THE RANK AND FILE. The following claim was made in a contemporary analysis of the theoretical foundations of syndicalism. "The idea of absolute class war lay at the centre of syndicalism; it was the touchstone by which it measured all problems, all events and all institutions which it met in daily life. The whole of syndicalism was actually based on this one principle. All other principles were deduced from it by means of logic."[4] This view of syndicalism as a logical construction was only partly true of the militant theorists who claimed a far more pragmatic character for their doctrines; it was quite false as far as the rank and file were con-

[1] A. Pawlowski, *La C.G.T.*, 1910, p. 56.
[2] M. Leroy, *La coutume ouvrière*, 1913, p. 588.
[3] E. T. Hiller, *The Strike*, 1928.
[4] Harpuder, 'Theoretische Basis des Syndikalismus' in *Sozialistische Monatshefte*, October 1908, p. 1329.

Principles and practice of the C.G.T.

cerned. It is impossible to give that sort of logical explanation of syndicalism. On the other hand, the syndicalists as a whole did, of course, have some sort of attitude towards the strike, some consciously held ideas on the subject. The point has rightly been made that "the class struggle was a fact, not a theory in need of proof; a fact manifested every day in the relations between employers and wage-earners; a fact inherent in the economic organisation of existing society".[1] This fact forced itself upon the consciousness of the workers: it was not held as a theory; it was an experience. The same could be said of the significance of the strike. It was not a rational mode of conduct to further the class war, if rational meant a deliberate choice of means to achieve desired ends.

The revolutionary significance of the strike was realised only after it had been practised for some time. The idea of the strike as an episode in the class war and as the weapon *par excellence* of the proletariat grew spontaneously out of the strikers' experience—it was experience. One could use the language of Bergson in this context and say that it was the result of instinct which worked organically rather than mechanically, which lived knowledge and did not think it. Their attitude was not formulated; it existed, as Sorel would have said, in the form of mind pictures.

This, however, was only half the truth. The rank and file did appear to hold some fairly clear revolutionary ideas, not that these always had much connection with what they actually did. Levels of thought and action were not necessarily identical. Nor must one overrate their sophistication. The leaders of the *C.G.T.*—good propagandists—conveyed many of their ideas to the rank and file or, if one is prepared to accept their own claim, made the latter aware of ideas that were already there subconsciously. Like the communist party, vanguard of the proletariat (or, indeed, like Rousseau's legislators), they simply interpreted the real will of the working class, telling it what it would have known itself, had it reached their own level of class-consciousness. The militant theorists drew on the experience of the labour movement, clarified what they discovered, formulated it and sent back the resultant doctrine to the rank and file. What was received at this third stage was another matter. Sombart, for example, seemed sceptical whether it was understood as intended: "The syndicalist leaders are mistaken if they imagine that the masses understand the new teaching as they themselves do. The masses regard it as a revival of the old ideas of revolution, so dear to their hearts. No matter what the leaders of the movement may say, syndicalism has taken the place of antiquated *blanquisme* in the hearts of impatient Frenchmen."[2]

[1] L. Levine, *The Labour Movement in France*, 1912, p. 119.
[2] W. Sombart, *Socialism and the Social Movement*, 1919, p. 237.

The strike in practice

This was an exaggeration, but it was certainly true that the ideas bandied around were elementary in form, simple formulae and rousing slogans. These slogans were not necessarily the motive force behind strikes, perhaps not even an integral part of strike action. The traditional eloquence and verbal ardour of Frenchmen has already been mentioned. Revolutionary phrases came easily to the tongue in moments of tension and when tempers were frayed, as during prolonged strikes. That did not prove they had a practical influence on affairs but only that "for a Frenchman it was not sufficient to act under necessity: the act had to be generalised into a principle, the principles systematised, and the system compressed into concise and catching formulae".[1] These formulae had their place at mass meetings, in newspaper articles or in talk about the strike rather than in the everyday action of the strike itself.

THE WORKERS STRIKE-PRONE. It has been pointed out that there was no strike method known to the organisations of a left-wing tendency which was not employed by the conservative unions as well. As the *Encyclopaedia* adds, it was in the settlement of strikes rather than in their direction that the philosophy of labour organisations was apt to manifest itself. It is in this context that one can most easily recognise the syndicalist character of many of the strikes that occurred during the period in question. Another observation has already been quoted: the strike became systematic, the workers made of it a weapon of war. Unlike the reformists, they did not see it as a once-for-all affair, an isolated conflict, designed to achieve a limited improvement of the workers' position within the existing order and terminated by an agreement accepted by both sides. The general hostility of the *C.G.T.* towards the whole idea of collective agreements was evidence of this. There was little feeling in France at the time that the settlement ending a strike restored social peace, even if it was to the workers' advantage. On the contrary, the more radical unions, such as those of the building industry, showed a permanent tendency to declare strikes for the most trivial of reasons. André Philip wrote of the period that if results were not obtained quickly, the unions accepted compromise or simply went back to work, ready to try again as soon as circumstances permitted: these short but frequent strikes had the added advantage of keeping the working class in a state of alert.[2]

Several reasons could be given for this strike-prone character of the labour movement. One, clearly, was that belief in the class war had developed to such an extent that no more than a temporary truce was possible

---

[1] L. Levine, *The Labour Movement in France*, 1912, p. 199.
[2] A. Philip, *Trade-unionisme et syndicalisme*, 1936, p. 254.

at any time. Another was psychological: certain workers found in the strike an outlet for their naturally combatative temperament—in earlier times they would have run to the barricades at every call. This explanation obviously contradicts the previous one for it requires no developed class-consciousness; it seems most apt, perhaps, for such relatively militant unskilled workers as builders and navvies. Finally, there was an economic explanation: a policy of sporadic strikes was the only one possible given limited funds and the inability to pay much in the way of strike benefits; the unions could not afford long, but few and decisive, strikes.

THE USE OF FORCE. The reformist unions within the *C.G.T.*, such as the miners and printers, were often willing to negotiate with employers, even to accept arbitration. In contrast to these diplomats, the militant syndicalists preferred to rely on their own strength. 'Deeds, not words!' was their motto. As one student of the movement put it, the *C.G.T.* advocated *la manière force.*[1] This, again, was an ambiguous phrase. Any strike meant action rather than words, meant the use of 'force'—at least to the extent that strikes were an attempt to bring pressure on the employers. In general, however, it meant more than this. Etienne Buisson, writing in 1907, saw the distinction between the syndicalist and the reformist strike in terms of the tactics employed, rather than of the ends pursued. He claimed that despite much talk of direct action, no new tactics had appeared that could really intimidate employers or bourgeoisie except for the use of violence: the only contribution of the syndicalist theory of direct action, in other words, the only distinguishing mark of syndicalism, therefore, was the principle of violence.[2]

Buisson in fact denied that violence was often used by the unions and thus implied that there were few really syndicalist strikes. This was an oversimplification. The temper of strikes was probably more radical in France than elsewhere, the use of radical means more consistent and their justification certainly more outspoken. Violence—*la manière force*—was no syndicalist monopoly. "It is obvious that violence in the form of physical assault or destruction of property may easily arise in the course of a strike, particularly if it be prolonged or if bitter feeling is engendered."[3] But it was a common feature of French strikes during this period.

[1] G. Serbos, *Une philosophie de la production*, 1913, p. 199.
[2] Buisson, 'Die beiden Tendenzen der französischen Gewerkschaftsbewegung' in *Sozialistische Monatshefte*, July 1907, p. 525.
[3] 'Strikes' in *Encyclopaedia of the Social Sciences*.

The strike in practice

THE SYNDICALIST INFLUENCE. Refusal to negotiate and the tendency to violence were evidence of syndicalist influence. Evidence, too, was the fact that, over the years, an increasing proportion of strikes were not a spontaneous reaction to economic pressures. It seems likely that these were actually inspired by the *C.G.T.*, though the aims were not always especially syndicalist. The number of strikes for a reduction in hours of work, for example, rose sharply as the *C.G.T.* campaign for the eight-hour day got under way (reaching 30% of all strikes by 1906). There was also a steady rise in the number of strikes for the discharge of unpopular foremen or non-union workers, or for the reinstatement of unfairly dismissed workers (reaching 30% in 1905). "The influence of the *syndicats* is shown here very distinctly", commented *The Times* in 1909.[1] There was some controversy, however, whether the growing number of strikes could be attributed to syndicalism. Charles Rist started the discussion with an article in the *Revue d'économie politique* in 1904. He demonstrated by ingenious figures and diagrams that a direct relationship existed between prosperity and strikes: the more prosperous the country, the more strikes there were. This correlation he took as evidence that strikes were the result of economic factors. If there was a causal relationship at all between strikes and revolutionary attitudes, it was the opposite of that claimed by syndicalists: prosperity stimulated strikes and strikes in turn stimulated a revolutionary spirit in the labour movement.[2] The employers tended to take the opposite line, attributing the rise in strikes to the revolutionary spirit of syndicalism and, above all, to the influence of the militant leaders of the *C.G.T.* They accused the latter of planning strategy on a national scale, organising conflicts and inciting workers to revolt.[3]

The dispute was rather like the question whether the chicken or the egg came first. There was certainly evidence the revolutionary spirit was the result of strikes, rather than the other way round: this, indeed, was the syndicalists' own view. Once in existence, however, it had a life of its own and power to inspire further action. This was the case by 1902. All that Rist's correlation really showed was that the workers had acquired greater tactical freedom: they could choose the best moment for the next episode in the class war. That was how Yvetot saw it: "Formerly spontaneous, the strike has become calculated, organised, declared at the right moment, that which is most advantageous for the workers and most disastrous for the employers."[4]

[1] *The Times*, 16 April 1909.
[2] Rist, 'La progression des grèves en France et sa valeur symptomatique' in *Revue d'Economie Politique*, March 1907, p. 192.
[3] P. Gonnot, *La grève dans l'industrie privée*, 1912, p. 190.
[4] G. Yvetot, *A.B.C. syndicaliste*, 1906.

The tactics of the strike

Bernstein once wrote: "The strike is war and has, like every war, its rules for the preparation and conduct of battle, rules which have gradually developed into a whole science."[1] Given the importance syndicalists attached to the strike, they naturally showed much interest in its strategy and tactics. The question of strategy was closely linked to the *double besogne* of the C.G.T. and has already been discussed. Tactics grew out of the experience of the labour movement and were generally the same as in other countries. The French differed, perhaps, in their emphasis on *élan révolutionnaire* and in the advocacy of such refinements as sabotage and violence; other countries preferred to maintain a discreet silence when they indulged in similar practices. They also went further than most in trying to make a science of it. As Griffuelhes said, the strike was a natural form of struggle, inherent in capitalist society and imposed on the workers by economic necessity—it was up to the workers to learn how to employ it to best advantage.[2] The militant theorists were not slow in offering to guide the rank and file. On the whole, however, they remained true to their claim that they were only formulating current practice and drawing the obvious lessons from experience; only in more speculative moments, as in their discussion of the general strike, did they indulge in pure fantasy.[3]

ARDOUR NOT BENEFITS. Most *syndicats* were small and poor, membership dues low and receipts irregular; only few were able to pay adequate strike benefits when the need arose. On the whole, the older-established and richer *syndicats* (such as those of the *Fédération du Livre*) were reformist in tendency. The others, probably making a virtue of necessity, tended to oppose strike benefits in principle. They could argue that reliance on the meagre funds they had was to court obvious defeat: the workers' *sou* was no match for the capitalists' financial reserves. Temperament was another factor. The passive withdrawal of labour or 'waiting strike' (workers live on strike benefits and simply wait for loss of profits to force the employers to surrender) did not really appeal to the revolutionary activists at the head of the C.G.T. The syndicalists preferred more stirring forms of action and seem rather to have believed that starving men would fight better than well fed ones. Money only confused the issue: what really mattered was the spirit of the strikers. Griffuelhes, using rather dubious

---

[1] E. Bernstein, *Der Streik*, 1906, p. 49.
[2] V. Griffuelhes and L. Niel, *Les objectifs de nos luttes de classe*, 1908.
[3] Cf. E. Pataud and E. Pouget, *Comment nous ferons la révolution*, 1909.

Tactics of the strike

statistics, compared the relatively high proportion of successful strikes in France with the smaller proportion in Germany, where the unions had large financial resources. He attributed the French achievements to the fighting spirit of the French workers.[1] Indeed, the syndicalists never tired of criticising the respectable trade-union leaders of Britain and Germany who were so concerned with finance that they avoided strikes which might deplete their reserves. Pelloutier went so far as to oppose the suggestion that *syndicats* might be given the legal right to engage in acts of commerce. How many would strike, he asked, once they had capital invested and acquired a taste for property?[2]

To compensate, great emphasis was placed on the spirit of battle and revolutionary ardour. This was reflected in the hostility shown to the Waldeck-Rousseau–Millerand arbitration bill of 1908. Among other things, it would have made it illegal to declare a strike before all the workers concerned had been consulted in secret ballot. *The Times* commented that "the principle of a majority, which inspires all democratic government, would thus be introduced into the labour world".[3] This democratic principle, however, was a negation of the revolutionary spirit: it substituted discussion for action, the counting of heads for the leadership of the active class-conscious minority. One might have expected an attack on the 'superstitious belief in majorities' from the militant leaders; in fact most of the rank and file were equally opposed to this scheme of democratisation. They realised, perhaps, that the formal equality of the secret ballot was a poor substitute for the enthusiasm aroused by militant orators or for the feelings of solidarity generated at strike meetings.

In the most popular of all syndicalist pamphlets (over 100,000 copies sold), Yvetot described the role of militants in the following way. Normally their task was to give practical advice, to organise and to explain. In moments of tiredness or discouragement, and in order that sacrifices already made should not be wasted, their task was also to whip up new energies for the struggle and to set an example by their own action. If they incited the workers to violence, he was careful to add, they were also the first to participate in such action—and often it was they who had to pay the price. It was the leaders' task to arouse and maintain the battle ardour of their troops.[4] In 1909 *The Times* published Guérard's own account of how he had whipped up the enthusiasm of the postal workers, then on strike, by promising them the support of the railwaymen, a promise he knew could not be fulfilled. With remarkable honesty he told how he had arrived at a

[1] V. Griffuelhes, *L'action syndicaliste*, 1908.
[2] F. L. E. Pelloutier, *Histoire des Bourses du Travail*, 1902, p. 324.
[3] *The Times*, 25 August 1908.
[4] G. Yvetot, *A.B.C. syndicaliste*, 1906.

meeting of the strikers, only to find them disheartened and listless. "Anyone who knew anything about strikes could see that this was the end. I realised the effect I was expected to produce and that this effect had at all costs to be produced. I applied the whip vigorously and it gave the stimulus which was required."[1]

VIOLENCE. Syndicalists claimed that direct action distinguished the revolutionary strike from the passive—and legal—withdrawal of labour advocated by the reformists. Violence was another word for it—*la manière force*. Strictly speaking, the syndicalists had no theory of violence of their own; it would, indeed, have been difficult to complicate an idea so simple as that of the *coup de poing*. The theorists of the movement, however, did their best to complicate it. Taking their cue, perhaps, from Sorel's *Reflections on Violence*, they sometimes praised violence for reasons far more sophisticated than the simple fact that it might frighten their opponents into surrender. By the deep feelings it aroused and the shock it administered to both sides, violence helped to divide the classes; it was the most effective antidote to reformist and democratic efforts at glossing over the fundamental issues of the class war. Violence, moreover, was itself war and brought out the heroic qualities of the proletariat: it had an educative moral value.

For the labour movement as a whole, however, acts of violence were simply acts of violence, of no greater theoretical significance than the *coup de poing*. Sometimes stimulated by agitators, they were more often neither premeditated nor even deliberate: mounting bitterness as a result of continual disputes; personal hostility towards the employer; fraying tempers and growing tension; the final, spontaneous explosion of anger often set off by the introduction of blackleg labour or the intervention of the police. At such a time, in such a mood, the use of fists, stones, or even dynamite, could occur in any country; it was the more likely in a country where the call to the barricades was a stronger tradition than respect for law.

Violence could take the form of destroying property in the hope of terrorising employers into surrender. At Marseilles in 1902, for example, the dockers smashed cranes, fired warehouses and destroyed goods, until the commanding general was forced to declare a state of siege. At Brest in 1904 they threw overboard the cargo of one ship and emptied a number of warehouses in similar fashion, rolling fifty barrels of wine into the sea. At Mazamet in 1909 workers burnt down a wool mill and exploded dynamite cartridges in several others. At Meru the same year they sacked an employer's home as well as his factory. In so far as there was a motive in cases such as the last (apart from the obvious one of revenge), it was propaganda

[1] *The Times*, 21 May 1909.

Tactics of the strike

by the deed in the anarchist tradition. Monatte, reminiscing fifty years later, remembered that his first exploit on joining the syndicalist movement in 1902 had been to re-edit an anarchist pamphlet on the manufacture of bombs; whenever a strike appeared to be drawing out, one of his friends would leave for the scene of action in order to blow out a few of the employer's windows.[1]

More often, violence involved assault on persons and attacks on property outside the place of work altogether. Critics spoke of 'revolutionary vandalism masked as a strike' and 'movements which degenerated from a strike into insurrection'.[2] There was a tendency for strikes to turn into riots or, more often, into a brawl, for the workers to clash with organised society rather than with the employers concerned. A notorious example was the riot that took place at the Auteuil races in June 1909. The *Spectator* gave the following account. "A large part of the rioters had not any real motive for rioting. They joined in a riot that had already begun they knew not why. The lads and stablemen of the great training establishment at Maisons-Lafitte, who want to have their *syndicat* recognised by their employers, seem to have had nothing to do with the violence. It was begun by navvies armed with revolvers, who were mobilised by the C.G.T. and carried out their operations on the high-road. As for the rioters on the course itself, they broke into savagery only because the races were delayed two hours through the horses being held up on the road by the mercenaries of the C.G.T."[3] The *Times* gave details of the hold-up. "As the horses were being transported in vans from their stables to the race-course, some fourteen or fifteen stable lads, armed with revolvers, and a score of navvies sprang out of ambush into the roadside, stopped the vans and compelled them to return with the horses to the stables. The drivers were cowed into surrender by being told that if they did not obey they would find two thousand navvies waiting for them higher up the road."[4] While the activities of the crowd on the race-course had little to do with the C.G.T., those on the road were organised by Pataud, one of the best known and most powerful of the syndicalist leaders in Paris at the time. The summing-up of the *Spectator* was not unfair: "The characteristic of all labour troubles lately in France has been that there was no definite goal to be reached by a regular foreseen process; the policy, if such it can be called, was simply to produce chaos and see whether any advantage could be plucked out of it."

Most of the contemporary critics of syndicalism tended to assume that syndicalist action was wholly synonymous with violence or—the better to

[1] Monatte in *Révolution Prolétarienne*, March 1953.
[2] E. Levasseur, *Questions ouvrières et industrielles en France*, 1907, pp. 674/89.
[3] The *Spectator*, 26 June 1909.
[4] The *Times*, 22 June 1909.

8-2

castigate syndicalists—pretended to believe it so. 'Direct action means violence!' was the horrified phrase that ran through their accounts.[1] There was undoubtedly a great deal of violence in France during the first decade of this century, but it was by no means the major preoccupation of the *C.G.T.*, nor was it as extensive as one might suppose from reading such critics. The impressions of the time were coloured by a relatively small number of particularly notorious strikes which involved rioting and conflict with the troops (e.g. at Montceau-les-Mines, Villeneuve-Saint-Georges, Narbonne), and by an even smaller number of strikes in the public services which involved cases of sabotage and came near to paralyzing the country (e.g. the postal and railway strikes). The many isolated acts of violence which could be found in the minor strikes of the period did not really add up to a movement and it cannot be said that violence was a general characteristic of direct action. Nevertheless, they pointed to a sense of frustration and a spirit near revolt just below the surface of events.

THE STRIKE OF MACHINES. The immobilisation of factories during the strike was a form of sabotage. It could also be seen as the 'strike of machines', a protection against the employment of strike-breakers (blacklegs or soldiers) and thus a necessary adjunct to the withdrawal of labour. In an article published by the *Voix du Peuple* in 1905, Bousquet declared that the first duty of strikers, before leaving their place of work, was to immobilise their machines. He expanded his theme by detailed advice to workers in various sectors of industry: the smell of a few gallons of petrol, poured into the ovens, would make the baking of bread impossible for months to come; steel-workers could put sand in the oil cups, engineers remove vital parts that were difficult to trace.[2] The suggestion that railwaymen should immobilise their engines before going on strike caused uproar in the country when it was proposed at a *C.G.T.* congress (as a public service, of course, the railways were particularly liable to governmental strike-breaking). In practice, the *grève des outils* went little further than the cutting of telegraph and signal wires during the postal and railway strikes. This had some nuisance value, but failed to paralyze the services concerned. It was, however, another form of propaganda by the deed.

THE FOX HUNT. More effective than the immobilisation of machines was the exclusion of blackleg labour from strike-bound factories. Union members were of course forbidden to replace strikers; non-union workers (of whom there were many) were dissuaded, either by moral pressure or by

---

[1] Cf. M. Saint-Léon, *Histoire des corporations de métiers*, 1922, p. 774.
[2] *Voix du Peuple*, 21 May 1905.

force. Pickets have always been a source of violence in times of strike. Those who broke working-class solidarity could consider themselves lucky if they escaped with an insult or merely had their windows smashed at night. During the miners' strike of 1905 wholesale destruction of strike-breakers' houses occurred and many were seriously injured. The most notorious of such cases was that of a Havre worker who died in 1909 from his injuries. The trial of the secretary of the local *syndicat* on the charge of having premeditated and organised this assassination became a *cause célèbre*: a death sentence was pronounced, reduced to seven years imprisonment; when it was quashed altogether three years later the *C.G.T.* regarded it as a victory for its campaign in his defence. While the syndicalist *chasse aux renards* rarely ended in so disastrous a fashion, personal attacks on strike-breakers were not uncommon. Attacks on traitors—*sarrazins* and *renards*—were often more bitter and more vicious than attacks on the employers themselves.

SOLIDARITY. A historian of the labour movement, writing in 1906, claimed that the preceding years had seen a curious change in the form taken by strikes. The workers were more aware of the nature of their action and their planning was better; the number of isolated strikes was diminishing and a period of 'general strikes' beginning, either of a single industry or of different *syndicats* in a single town.[1] These were actually generalised rather than general strikes but they did reflect an important development in the labour movement. Action involving a whole federation, or at least of all the *syndicats* of the same trade or industry in a particular region, came with the growing strength of federations and Confederation *vis-à-vis* individual *syndicats*. There were obvious advantages in such unity. On the national level, however, only the miners, railwaymen and postal workers achieved anything like a generalised strike; and even these were never really universal. The strike of a number of different *syndicats* in one town was a more common occurrence, particularly in Paris; but there again it was generally restricted to the more revolutionary unions such as the builders, barbers and bakers.

There were also sympathy strikes where workers of another trade, with no immediate grievance, came out in support of their comrades. They reflected the growing class-consciousness of the workers as well as the local influence of the *Bourses du Travail*. An example was the Marseilles 'general strike' of 1904, when transport workers, road labourers and others, came out in support of the dockers. The dockers themselves had a record of sympathetic action that was probably better than any other trade, though

[1] H. Brisson, *Histoire du travail*, 1906, p. 498.

117

their efforts (such as the boycott of imported coal during the miners' strikes) were usually unsuccessful. Figures are suspect but it appears that the proportion of disinterested strikes increased every year. One commentator put them as high as 30% in 1905,[1] a figure, however, which must have included strikes by different trades united in a common interest, protest strikes (usually twenty-four-hour demonstrations) and *grèves de dignité* by the workers of a single enterprise in support of victimised comrades. Even so, figures for Britain in 1911 are given as: solidarity strikes (in support of other unions), 1%; sympathy strikes (in support of a member of one's own union), 9%.[2]

The weakness of the *C.G.T.* when it came to organising such strikes on a large scale was shown by the fiasco of the postal workers' strike in 1909. The confederal committee voted for an immediate general strike in sympathy. Only the electricians and builders declared themselves ready to strike; the railwaymen required at least a fortnight's notice, the gas workers and other trades a week. A manifesto was nevertheless issued over the signature of the secretary, Niel, who had declared only a few days before that the workers were nowhere near ready for a general strike: "The victory of the postal workers must be the victory of the whole proletariat, just as their defeat would be the defeat of the proletariat!" By that time only a hundred postal workers were still out, though they had been joined by over a thousand labourers, ready to drop pick and shovel at any time. The other union leaders failed to react. After three days, and after the issue of two more abortive manifestos, the *C.G.T.* had to call off its 'general strike'. The only result was widespread recrimination and the resignation of Niel. The solidarity of the workers, except in moments of excitement such as those of May 1906, never reached the level the *C.G.T.* like to claim.

THE STAGGERED STRIKE. The staggered strike, or *grève tampon*, was conceived as another expression of solidarity between workers of the same industry. The workers of each factory were to come out in turn, each group in turn receiving the financial support of those still at work. Strikes could thus be prolonged without undue hardship. The only publicised attempt to use this tactic was during a strike of the Paris jewelry workers in 1907; it was met with a general lock-out by the employers and failed. An even wider application of the idea was suggested at the Amiens congress of 1906 in connection with the eight-hour-day campaign. Clément, of the Paris locksmiths, proposed that each should strike separately at a favourable moment, supported during this period by the other federations of the

---

[1] Mlle Kritsky, *L'évolution du syndicalisme en France*, 1908, p. 402.
[2] K. G J. C. Knowles, *Strikes*, 1952, pp. 231/314.

118

C.G.T.—the result would be a cumulative series of victories. The *C.G.T.* was never strong enough, however, to consider the scheme practically.

STRIKE KITCHENS AND EVACUATION OF CHILDREN. Communal feeding arrangements—*soupes communistes*—sometimes replaced the strike benefits which the *syndicats* were unable to pay. They were an economical way of sustaining the strikers. At the same time, they were a symbol of unity; they strengthened the bonds of solidarity by bringing strikers and their families together. In a few cases, especially in the mining districts, strikers sent their children to the care of friendly workers in unaffected areas so that they could continue the struggle free from this responsibility. The main value of evacuating children, however, was the sympathy it aroused throughout the country: it was yet another symbol of proletarian solidarity. The organisation of such activities was made the province of the local *Bourses*. It was laid down in 1910 that all *syndicats* were to contribute to the central strike fund of their *Bourse* whenever a member *syndicat* was on strike; after five days the *Bourse* was to organise strike kitchens and, if necessary, the evacuation of children. The scheme was undermined by the fact that the level of its contribution was left to the decision of each *syndicat* rather than to the *Bourse* itself; in practice it was ineffective.

Subsidiary forms of direct action

There were several forms of direct action apart from the strike. Sabotage, boycott and the label were always quoted together as examples, and to this trio one could add intimidation and the 'self-granted' reform. None of them was essential to a theory of syndicalism. The subsidiary tactics were nevertheless important, theoretically at least, because the principle of direct action would have appeared rather empty without them. It was for this reason, perhaps, that the theorists of the C.G.T. tended to give them rather more space in their articles and pamphlets than they deserved. Judging by that alone, indeed, they often seemed to overshadow the strike. The same was true of the earlier congresses of the C.G.T. where such minor forms of direct action were debated at length and then adopted as principles—by contrast, again, to the strike. Boycott and label, however, were never of any importance in practice. Sabotage was. It was the principle which really aroused the bourgeois critics; often they identified syndicalism with violence and sabotage rather than with the more fundamental principles of the movement. At the same time, its practice did give an indication of the revolutionary temper of the syndicalists and the extent to which they were willing to defy the law.

SABOTAGE: THE PRINCIPLE. Sabotage was not a syndicalist invention. Already in 1881, apparently, telegraph operators so fixed the wires of the Paris exchange that, although engineers tried to locate the fault, the city was cut off for five days, after which the minister surrendered to their demands. The idea received its syndicalist baptism at the 1897 congress of the C.G.T. after the Prefect of the Seine had refused leave of absence to the delegates of the municipal workers. Pouget introduced a motion recognising the futility of a formal protest and calling on the city's employees to repay this veto with a hundred thousand francs' worth of damage. The motion never came to the vote but a few days later Delesalle presented the report of a special committee on boycott and sabotage. He pointed out that congresses had often enough affirmed revolutionary aims but had failed to adopt practical resolutions which would translate their words into action: it was time to think of other weapons to supplement the strike. He described a Scottish tactic known as Ca Canny—"if two Scotsmen walk together and one goes too fast, the other says 'ca canny' or slow down". The story behind this was as follows. In 1889 the Glasgow dockers had struck for higher wages. The employers replaced them with agricultural labourers, with whose work they declared themselves satisfied. When the dockers were forced to return, defeated, the secretary of their union was reputed to have told them: "The farm boys dropped their load now and then and two of them couldn't do as much as one of us; so do the same kind of work, ca canny, take it easy; only those fellows used to fall into the water, you needn't go as far as that." After a few weeks they got a rise. Delesalle suggested that French workers might follow this example. For a cheap price, the employers sold poor quality goods; the workers should do the same: the employers had no right to count on their charity; if they pay low wages, slow work or poor workmanship was the answer. If that was not enough, the employer could also be hit by careless damage to machines. Hamelin, of the printers, spoke in support. All means were legitimate, he declared; there were many easy strategems of which it was best not to speak openly. The main tactic that emerged, however, was bad work for bad wages rather than actual destruction. Perhaps for this reason, no voice was raised in opposition; a motion inviting the congress to adopt the conclusions of the report and to put them into practice at the earliest opportunity was voted unanimously. Pouget was the *rapporteur* in 1898. Practical details, he said, were a matter for the initiative and temperament of members. The committee was concerned only to advance the theory and ensure that sabotage entered the arsenal of weapons used by the proletariat in its struggle against capitalism. After the delegate of the kitchen-workers federation had won applause by telling how a famous Paris restaurant had been thrown into confusion when the cooks boiled bricks and baked the kitchen clock, the report was again adopted by acclamation.

At the following congress, in 1900, the first voices of dissent were heard. The chairman wished to remain neutral and remarked simply that sabotage was ineffective as a weapon and offended the dignity of labour. The latter was taken up by reformist delegates who feared that traditions of craftsmanship would be undermined and by others who thought that pride in work well done and a sense of responsibility for one's tools were the moral basis of the producers' society that syndicalism was supposed to promote. This time the special committee reported on the label, but the *rapporteur* found time to remark that while he admired the daring of the saboteurs, and had often laughed at the stories of their exploits, he had not their courage himself. He concluded that one should not ask others to perform what one dared not do oneself. This frank admission may have encouraged other delegates, previously reluctant to admit their lack of enthusiasm for such risky undertakings as the destruction of their machines. The principle of sabotage was put to the vote; this time there were 117 for but 76 against. Perhaps because the militants feared that voting might become even closer, sabotage was not discussed at subsequent congresses. It had, however, officially become part of the *C.G.T.*'s programme of action and various federations later voted for it at their own congresses. Pamphlets and articles counselled many forms of sabotage.[1] The invention they showed, however, was rarely reflected in practice.

SABOTAGE: THE TACTICS. The simplest, most frequently recommended and least dangerous form of sabotage was the slowing down of production —the strike on the job. As Pouget pointed out in 1898, many workers instinctively met unfair wages in this way, *en sabottant inconsciemment.* There was probably a great deal of this at all times and in all countries. On the other hand, it is impossible to determine how far 'ca canny' was consciously applied: no records exist.

Bad workmanship was another possibility, planned carelessness resulting in spoilt goods or damaged machines. A bulletin issued by the Montpellier *Bourse* in 1900 achieved some fame. It advised workers on how to organise accidents without undue suspicion falling on them: shop-assistants could allow fabrics to soil; garment workers could ignore faults in the material that passed through their hands; engineers could forget to oil their machines—the range of possibilities was almost inexhaustible. In 1911 the *Bataille Syndicaliste* published an anonymous circular that had been sent to building workers, pointing out that well-planned sabotage could involve the employer in greater damage than six months' strike and yet not involve the discreet saboteur in serious risk. It listed the technical tricks that could be played in workshop or timber-yard and added that it should, of course, be made plain to the employer that the standard of work would improve considerably if demands (in this case, the eight-hour day) were met. The press gave much hostile publicity to the spoiling of foodstuffs. In a few isolated cases nails and broken glass were found in loaves of bread; the syndicalists were accused of being murderers. It was a syndicalist principle from the start, however, that only the employer should suffer. Bakers, for example, were advised to burn bread so that it was obviously uneatable. Two campaigns were worth mentioning: in 1909 the postal workers organised a large-scale misdirection of letters as a protest against the dismissal of strikers; in 1910 the railwaymen similarly misdirected goods and side-tracked perishable consignments.

Sometimes, in moments of special ingenuity, the syndicalists reversed their motto to read 'For bad pay, extra-good work!', calculating that overscrupulous workmanship would also involve the employer in loss. A righteous note was often sounded. Builders on cheap houses should work with special care, regardless of time, and, where possible, use better

[1] Cf. E. Pouget, *Le sabotage*, 1910.

materials than the employer intended. Shop-assistants should no longer sell underweight or measure 95 centimetres of material instead of the full metre; in shops where the employer was honest, they could of course serve over-weight or cut 105 centimetres. A delightful variant was called the strike of the open mouth—the honest employee revealed the tricks of the trade to the customer. Tridon told the story of the waiters in a certain restaurant who gave diners an insight into the preparation of their meal.[1] Workers could also be overscrupulous in the performance of their duties, thus slowing down production, sometimes even creating chaos, by quite legitimate means. The work to rule strike suited the railwaymen especially well and was sometimes used by them: traffic could be thrown into confusion by the careful observation of all safety regulations and the rigorous inspection of tickets.

The principle of the strike of machines has already been mentioned. This form of sabotage was aimed less at the employers' profits than at their attempts to keep factories running during strikes. The syndicalists did not advocate the actual destruction of machinery; every worker, they suggested, knew one or two easily removed screws that could immobilise his own machine.[2] One of the few occasions on which this tactic was used with effect was during the 1908 strike of the Lyons tramway employees: they poured concrete into every switch in the town. The practice of sabotage became a major issue during railway and postal strikes. The strikers concentrated mainly on cutting telegraph or signal lines, perhaps because they believed this to be an effective interference with the service, but more probably because wires could be cut on a dark night with tempting ease. In any case, despite the near-panic fostered by the press, their efforts were quite unsuccessful.

INTIMIDATION. Intimidation was a form of direct action not listed as such by writers about syndicalism but it is a useful category. As Yvetot said, direct action consisted in forcing employers to make concessions either through fear or through self-interest.[3] Sabotage was generally aimed at the employers' interest (as was the simple withdrawal of labour); intimidation was the weapon of fear.

Sabotage itself could become a form of intimidation under certain circumstances. Wire-cutting activities actually reached their climax after the railway and postal strikes had collapsed. The hope was that fear of complete disorganisation in a public service would force the authorities to con-

[1] A. Tridon, *The New Unionism*, 1917.
[2] Cf. Bousquet in *Voix du Peuple*, 21 May 1905.
[3] G. Yvetot, *A.B.C. syndicaliste*, 1906.

cede the workers' demands (reinstatement of dismissed employees). Such tactics went beyond the principles of sabotage officially endorsed by the *C.G.T.* Pouget rightly called those involved 'guerillas'. Sometimes their activities were even more dangerous. In 1910 dynamite cartridges were discovered on railway lines at Marseilles and this was not an isolated example. The perpetrators were not typical of the *C.G.T.* nor were they really concerned with the interests of the labour movement as seen by revolutionary syndicalists. They were throwbacks, to the secret societies of *blanquiste* conspirators or to the progaganda by the deed of bomb-throwing anarchists. All these campaigns were, indeed, almost certainly organised by a few militant anarchists. That was the view of the authorities.[1] As late as 1910 the anarchist paper *Guerre Sociale* was still advising readers to form secret groups to engage in such activities.[2]

The use of violence to intimidate employers during strikes has already been described. Intimidation was used at other times as well. The most widespread case was probably the campaign for the closing of private employment bureaux. Intended primarily to influence the government, it was also directed against individual establishments, particularly against those which did not respect the law after it had been passed. Their offices were sacked. In the same way, employers who did not apply the law establishing the weekly day of rest found their windows smashed. The syndicalists' own favourite example was the tactic employed by the Paris barbers during their campaign for a reduction in working hours: they filled empty eggshells with caustic soda and threw them against shop-fronts at night, causing the paint to blister and peel away. They also put up notices informing clients of the regular closing time and adding that the consequences would be unfortunate for those who outstayed their welcome.

BOYCOTT. The principle of the boycott was adopted by the *C.G.T.* in 1897 at the same time as sabotage. What was suggested at the time was in fact a consumers' strike. The report told of the successful boycott of shops in Toulouse which remained open on Sundays and invited the *C.G.T.* to employ this tactic on a larger scale: higher wages or reduced hours of work might be extracted from employers by putting their stores on the index; patrons could be informed by posters, circulars, meetings, pickets and any other meetings the workers might think of. At best, a concerted refusal to buy at pilloried stores would only have been possible in the case of smaller shops and in areas where the population was overwhelmingly working-class; even then, it assumed an unlikely degree of solidarity among working-class housewives.

[1] Cf. *The Times*, 2 June 1909.   [2] *Guerre Sociale*, 8–14 June 1910.

Subsidiary forms of direct action

In practice the boycott was seldom employed. When employed, it was never a strike of customers; it was the employees who picketed the store in order to persuade them to stay away or, if persuasion failed, to drive them away. As appeals to solidarity rarely proved effective, the tactic usually degenerated into violence. This, indeed, Delesalle had foreseen. His report quoted the case of London shop-assistants who, to support their demand for a weekly half-holiday in 1893, reinforced their boycott by revolutionary means—such as storming a butcher's shop and throwing the hams into the street; they were victorious because they were audacious and energetic. This, however, was just another form of intimidation. The best known example of such direct action was the demonstration of boycotters outside the *Galleries Lafayette* in 1901; by smashing windows and frightening away customers, they forced the owners to accept 7 o'clock closing.

Another form of boycott was the black-listing of employers who refused to abide by the conditions of work or wage rates laid down by the *syndicat*, or who employed non-union (or rival-union) labour. This appeal to the solidarity of the workers was not very successful either, a fact hardly surprising as the *C.G.T.* only organised a minority of French workers and there were rival *syndicats* in the field. This form of boycott was often applied in conjunction with the strike in order to prevent the employment of blackleg labour. Here, too, the only effective form of action proved to be the picket; the workers no more boycotted the factories in question than the housewives boycotted the shops—they were kept away by force. The *chasse aux renards* has already been mentioned, as well as the violence it involved.

THE LABEL. While the boycott was directed against hostile employers, the label singled out the friend. It was awarded by the *syndicats* to employers who accepted their basic demands. It was evidence that the enterprise employed union labour, paid wages according to the union's tariff and respected the laws regarding conditions of work. Shopkeepers were issued a specially designed label to stick in their windows, while manufacturers were allowed to print a special mark on the articles they made. The idea was to mobilise the purchasing power of the working class and put it at the service of the labour movement, thus providing the unions with another bargaining counter. The possibility of increasing sales by the label might persuade employers to meet union demands; the threat of withholding it, on the other hand, would have the same effect as a boycott.

The label was first used by the printers. In 1895 the *Fédération du Livre* decided that all work composed and printed by its members should bear an inscription to that effect. It then brought up the subject at the congress of the *C.G.T.* in 1898 when the delegate of the Paris typographers reported that their label was being used by newspapers and magazines of all shades of opinion, while at the last election the posters of all parties had at the bottom the words "Travail exécuté des ouvriers syndiqués". The same delegate was *rapporteur* in 1900 when it was decided that each *syndicat* should prepare a stamp bearing the words "Syndicat de...Marque syndicale" and should organise an active campaign for its adoption. The congress also decided that it was the duty of every worker to support articles thus marked and to boycott any articles placed on the index by labour organisations. But there was still rivalry between organisations. Immediately after the decision of the *C.G.T.*, the congress of *Bourses du Travail* decided to create a label of its own. Labels of independent design were meanwhile being issued by several federations and even by some *syndicats*. After the fusion of *Bourses* and *C.G.T.* a special committee designed a new confederal label: a globe with clasped hands, surrounded by the words "Bien-être et Liberté, Confédération Générale du Travail". The *Fédération du Livre*, which had been made responsible for the practical side of the work, produced something quite different, omitting even the initials *C.G.T.* and there was an acrimonious dispute at the next congress. Eventually the confederal label was distributed by the *C.G.T.* to the federations and by them to the *syndicats* who were ultimately responsible for issuing it to deserving employers. This did not prevent some unions from using their own designs to emphasise their independence.

The idea was as simple as it could have been far-reaching. A syndicalist writer calculated that there were 800,000 organised workers; with families 2,500,000 consumers: the value of the label should be obvious to all, he concluded.[1] Nevertheless, it was quite ineffective. It gained no foothold in industry except for printing, where it was evidence of union strength rather than any mobilisation of consumers. In commerce, it had occasional success: it was used mainly by hairdressers and restaurant owners who perhaps found it necessary to reassure customers of their employees' good will. The importance of the label, however, did not lie in its application. The idea was interesting as an expression of the labour movement's determination to rely upon itself; it was conceived not merely as a form of pressure but also as a form of mutual aid.

A SELF-GRANTED REFORM. The campaign conducted by the *C.G.T.* for the eight-hour day deserves special mention. Of all the forms of action suggested by the syndicalists, the tactic chosen at Bourges in 1904 to obtain this long-demanded reform was in a way the simplest and most direct: the workers were to grant it to themselves without reference to employers or

---

[1] Sieurin in *Mouvement Socialiste*, May 1905, p. 106.

Subsidiary forms of direct action

state. They would take the law into their own hands and down tools every day after eight hours' work, thus presenting their employers with a *fait-accompli*. The congress resolved that the *C.G.T.* should organise widespread propaganda so that the principle could be implemented on 1 May 1906. Public meetings were held, the labour press was full of articles and, as the campaign drew to its climax, posters appeared in the streets. Shortly before the day itself, banners were posted on factory walls, in workingmen's cafes and over the doors of union headquarters: "Au 1er Mai nous ne travaillerons plus que 8 heures par jour".

A peaceful walk-out was not the only form of action considered. The report, which was embodied in the resolution, pointed out that suppression of the employment bureaux had been due to revolutionary action and said that the eight-hour day could only be achieved by similar methods. It was made clear that the campaign was to be directed against the employers and not the state (i.e. the aim was not legislation); but it was made equally clear that violence might be an integral part ("We must hit the employers with all the means at our disposal.") The strike was added as a third form of action at a special conference called in April of 1906. In line with its federal character, the *C.G.T.* left it to the federations to decide for themselves whether they advised members to walk out or whether they declared a strike in their sector. The walk-out was only tried in a few cases and was probably not successful in any. The campaign generally took the form of strikes and these became so widespread that they involved the government. Whatever the intention, therefore, it appeared in the end as pressure against the state.

Labour as a political pressure group

The original idea of direct action was that it should be directed against the employer; the purpose was to obtain concessions for the workers of a particular firm or, more broadly, a sector of industry, from the employers directly concerned. Such industrial action was sometimes supplemented by political action directed against the political institutions of society, government or parliament. The purpose, then, was to obtain concessions for the working class as a whole, indirectly, through legislation.[1] The activities involved were essentially coercive—*pression ouvrière* in syndicalist terms. This allowed the labour movement to remain *outside* the system; the principle of autonomy was maintained to the extent that action was autonomous. In its pure form, however, direct action was intended to by-pass the state entirely, thus challenging its continued existence in the long run. What was involved here, on the other hand, was an attempt to use the state. As a challenge to the constitutional order and, more immediately, as a threat to public authority, it tended to set the labour movement *against* the state. From that point of view, *pression ouvrière* was a more revolutionary form of action than the incidental forms of violence, riots and sabotage, discussed earlier. At first sight, nevertheless, it appeared to contradict a number of fundamental syndicalist principles. It is well, therefore, to discuss this particular tactic by analysing its relationship to such ideas as political neutrality, the autonomy of the labour movement and reliance on economic action.

THEORETICAL DIFFICULTIES. Campaigns directed against the state, and intended to force government or parliament to accede to the workers' demands, took the form of agitation more often than of strike. There was nothing particularly proletarian, however, much less syndicalist, about agitation as such: mass meetings, placards, demonstrations, marches, violence and rioting—these were forms of action employed by all sorts of political movements. Indeed, the very example of Griffuelhes gave of a successful campaign against the state was that organised by the bourgeois radicals in defence of Dreyfus.[2]

Pouget, on the other hand, described direct action as a normal function of unions and had added that it was 'meaningless elsewhere than in the economic field'.[3] The contradiction is apparent: it was not the normal function of

[1] Cf. C. Yvetot, *A.B.C. syndicaliste*, 1906.
[2] *Cit.* A. Pawlowski, *La C.G.T.*, 1910, p. 61.
[3] E. Pouget, *L'action directe*, 1910.

unions to agitate in the streets, nor could such action easily be described as economic. Reference to the Dreyfus affair clearly assimilated *pression ouvrière* to political action as practised by other pressure groups. And this was true not only of the form of action, but sometimes of the issues involved as well: the campaign against military service, for example, though logical in syndicalist terms, was not a purely economic question on the *C.G.T.*'s own definition (i.e. one that concerned all workers regardless of their politics). It could be argued, of course, that in so far as the campaigns in question were organised by the *C.G.T.* and its *syndicats*, the workers were fighting in their *cadres naturels* and as a class. This gave a blanket cover to all the activities of the *C.G.T.*—the fact of class distinction was enough to transfer the field of battle from the political to the economic. But this was a formal truth at best; in practice the mass in the streets did not behave differently when organised by the *C.G.T.*, either in procession or in riot, than when led by bourgeois agitators in a bourgeois cause.

Strikes were also sometimes a form of political pressure, designed to embarrass the community rather than the employer, thus forcing the state to intervene in order to restore vital public services and maintain public order. Some were part of a general campaign for legislative reform (e.g. May 1906); others, though originally directed against the employers, automatically took on a social character because of their wider repercussions. Such strikes remained within the *C.G.T.*'s defined sphere in at least half the sense of the definition: the weapon was economic, even if the aim was political and the opponent the state.

A further theoretical objection to *pression ouvrière* was that it seemed to breach the principle of the autonomy of the labour movement. The workers no longer relied wholly upon themselves but called on parliament to enact, and the government to enforce, their demands. Even granted the fact that the state was the executive committee of the capitalists, it meant a round-about attack on the exploiters and, in practice, an intermediary. According to Delesalle, however, direct action meant conflict between employers and employees without any person interposed.[1] A partial answer was that the *C.G.T.* did not act within the accepted framework of the political system; it did not play the parliamentary game. In its report to the Dublin congress, it defined its action as external pressure instead of penetration. This enabled it to retain its independence. The externality of the pressure was slightly modified, however, when union leaders came to confer with socialist deputies on reform programmes; it gave way then, in Leroy's phrase, to external collaboration.[2] Such exceptions apart, one could still say that pressure was direct in character, even if it was indirect in object.

---

[1] *Cit.* A. Pawlowski, *La C.G.T.*, 1910, p. 60.　　[2] M. Leroy, *La coutume ouvrière*, 1913.

Principles and practice of the C.G.T.

This brings one to the third objection to *pression ouvrière*. The demand for legislative reform contradicted the syndicalists' claim that such reforms were usually ineffective or, if effective, probably harmful (i.e. opium for the masses). At Montpellier in 1902, for example, Bousquet declared categorically that even the best-formulated laws were worthless; he cited the Millerand–Colliard law limiting hours of work for women and children: either it was not applied because of ineffective state supervision or its benefits were destroyed by the reduction of wages, the dismissal of children and the organisation of out-work for women. Delesalle went further, describing reformist action as conservative in character and likely to undermine the revolutionary spirit of the workers.[1] Of course the syndicalists did not entirely believe either of these things, or, if they did, it was on a level of theory unconnected with practice. If true, they would have made nonsense of such campaigns as those for the weekly day of rest. What the syndicalists *did* believe was that the only reforms of real value were those gained and upheld by the power of the working class. A logical question that followed was the one asked by Delesalle: if the workers had that power, why should they bother to use the state as an instrument to impose their will on the employers?[2] A partial answer, again, was that parliament could be considered as merely registering the will of the proletariat and the law as no more than a convenient means of ensuring its universal application. But this argument is not very convincing.

As late as 1910 Pawlowski could still write that the C.G.T. did not waste its time in trying to obtain legislation; "on the contrary, as all laws have the effect of reinforcing the state, the militants had only one thought, the destruction of existing laws".[3] *Pression ouvrière* should presumably have been negative: agitation to repeal laws, not to pass new ones.[4] Practice did not bear out their theory. Some labour legislation was accepted by the C.G.T. in principle and the concern was simply to modify the details by political pressure. In 1904 and in 1908 it resolved that the industrial injuries law of 1898 should be extended to all workers; in 1904 and 1910 that the decisions of labour tribunals (the *conseils de prud'hommes*) should be made binding. The pension law of 1910 was another example. The C.G.T. decided in 1910 that the labour movement should try by all means to prevent the application of 'a law which was useful in its principles, though contrary to labour interests in its provisions'. A successful policy of passive resistance was followed and few workers joined the scheme. In 1912 the C.G.T. could note that, 'thanks to long and vigorous agitation,

[1] P. Delesalle, *Les deux méthodes du syndicalisme*, 1903.
[2] P. Delesalle, *Les deux méthodes du syndicalisme*, 1903.
[3] A. Pawlowski, *La C.G.T.*, 1910, p. 59.
[4] Cf. the German anarcho-syndicalist, A. Roller, *Die direkte Aktion*, 1907, p. 50.

130

parliament and government were forced to make certain changes in the law'.

The syndicalists' rejection of reformist legislation was thus never as complete as their principles might have led one to suppose. This was not entirely a failure to relate theory and practice. The apparent contradiction reflected an ambiguity inherent in the syndicalist attitude to the state. On the one hand, doctrinal rejection of the state as such, springing from Proudhon and anarchism; on the other hand, concrete hostility to the bourgeois-democratic state, the result of disillusionment with the parliamentary system. While *pression ouvrière* contradicted the former, it was actually an expression of the latter. It reflected the syndicalists' refusal to abide by the rules of the democratic state or to play the parliamentary game. Le Bon quotes the phrase that sums up this attitude: "We shall not adapt ourselves to the system; the system must adapt itself to us."[1] Whatever their relationship with the state, this attitude underlay and coloured their approach. Seen in the framework of syndicalism as a whole, it had a distinctively revolutionary character.

THE CAMPAIGN AGAINST EMPLOYMENT BUREAUX. The private employment bureaux which had cornered certain trades, charging applicants exorbitant fees or offering cut-rate wages, had long been an object of attack. Parliament was first petitioned in 1881 to suppress them and the attempt to obtain legislative action continued for the next twenty years. In 1900 the Chamber at last voted a limited bill that would have allowed local authorities to close bureaux if they were willing to compensate the owners; it was rejected after much procrastination by the Senate in 1902. The workers' patience was exhausted and widespread agitation followed. Posters appeared bearing the slogan 'War on the Employment Bureaux'. Strikes were threatened by several federations. A clash between workers and police in the Paris *Bourse du Travail* ended with one dead and injured on both sides in 1903. The next day a question was asked in the Chamber: the committee which had been studying the issue for several months immediately presented another bill and it was voted three days later. When the Senate again delayed, the *C.G.T.* decided to organise a special campaign. This became quite violent: there were daily incidents inside and outside the bureaux, often involving the police. A hundred protest meetings were arranged simultaneously throughout the country on 5 December. The Senate thereupon invited labour leaders to give evidence but this they refused as a waste of time. The campaign continued: Christmas Day demonstrations led to over a hundred arrests in Paris; the workers of the food

[1] G. Le Bon, *Psychologie politique*, 1917, p. 206.

industry declared what was essentially a political strike. At the beginning of March 1904 the Senate passed the bill by a large majority.

It seemed as if direct action had won the day. That was certainly the syndicalists' own claim. In the report presented at Bourges that year, the Senate's capitulation was attributed to the fact that the campaign had become dangerous, to the acts of violence, intimidation, destruction and riot that it had entailed: "The suppression of the employment bureaux was conquered by revolutionary action." The conservative *Journal des Economistes* echoed this claim, albeit in different language: "The socialist unions have wrested the vote of Parliament by the pressure of rebellion."[1]

The law was only permissive. Many local authorities were slow to use it. Agitation continued, though now directed against the municipalities rather than the state. The workers also threatened to take the law into their own hands and close the bureaux by force if necessary. This they actually did in a number of cases: several bureaux were sacked; others were brought to a standstill by pickets. The point, however, is that it was a law that the labour movement had demanded; when passed, it took credit for it; and thereafter concerned itself with its application by the authorities.

THE CAMPAIGN FOR THE EIGHT-HOUR DAY. Equally unsuccessful petitions had been presented regularly since 1889 for the eight-hour working day. In 1904 the *C.G.T.* decided to concentrate on this reform and appointed a special committee to suggest ways and means. Its report, which was adopted by the congress, recommended a campaign of direct action similar to that which had led to the suppression of the employment bureaux. It also recommended, however, that the campaign should by-pass the authorities altogether: the workers should either implement the reform themselves (i.e. by leaving their factories on their own initiative after eight hours) or they should strike until the employers gave in. Organisation was entrusted to the committee and 1 May 1906 chosen as the day for action. Agitation soon spread through the country. Public meetings were held and posters of distinctively revolutionary tone distributed in large quantity.

Again, the syndicalists were not entirely consistent and the demand for government action tended to reappear. One poster read: "You will declare to the bourgeois government and to your exploiters that you will not cease the struggle until your demands are met; if the law made by the rich and the powerful shackles you, you will know how to force the rulers to change it." In an interview with the newspaper *l'Intransigeant*, Pouget refused to commit himself on what form the action of the *C.G.T.* would take on 1 May. Asked for a hypothesis, he replied: "None! A lucid sleepwalker

---

[1] *Cit.* L. Levine, *The Labour Movement in France*, 1912, p. 169.

could inform you better than I." He did say that it would necessarily be direct action—a discussion between labour and capital without intermediary. When pressed whether this 'discussion' would be peaceful or not, he replied that circumstances would decide but that government provocation might well lead to the resistance of the workers.[1]

As the day approached, strikes spread throughout the country and by May 1906 well over 200,000 workers were involved. Government intervention—'provocation' in syndicalist eyes—was inevitable. Clashes with the authorities increased, tension mounted and the situation appeared to be verging on revolution. Levine described the state of affairs in Paris: "The 1st May found Paris in a state of siege. Clemenceau had collected numerous troops in the capital. Since the day of the Commune, Paris had not seen so many. Among the bourgeoisie real panic reigned. Many left Paris and crossed the Channel. Those who remained spoke of the coming revolution which the *C.G.T.* was to let loose on society."[2] Government action, when it came, was spectacular. At the very last moment Clemenceau discovered the existence of a plot hatched by syndicalists, anarchists, monarchists and right-wing catholics to overthrow the Republic. Farce though this was, and it was treated as such even by the conservative *Débats Officiels*, it enabled the government to arrest Griffuelhes, Pouget, the treasurer of the *C.G.T.*, Lévy, and other strike leaders. Also arrested were the Comte de Beauregard, a leading bonapartist, and a man described as an anarchist millionaire. The list of those whose apartments or offices were searched read like a combined *Almanach de Gotha* and Catholic Directory.

The 'revolution' collapsed before it had started. The strikes were broken and the only gains recorded were by the printers who had negotiated separately for a nine-hour day. At the Amiens congress of 1906, however, it was unanimously decided to continue the campaign. Leadership was entrusted to a new permanent 'committee of propaganda for the eight-hour day and the general strike'. Pouget commented that the title showed that the movement was intended to be revolutionary in a wider sense.[3] Although the eight-hour day was treated as a special issue in all subsequent May Day demonstrations, however, little was achieved until 1919; and then it was established by law.

THE CAMPAIGN FOR THE WEEKLY DAY OF REST. The campaign for a weekly day of rest was of interest mainly to barbers, bakers, waiters, cooks and shop-assistants and was largely conducted by their federations. As far

---

[1] *L'Intransigeant*, 26 April 1906.
[2] L. Levine, *The Labour Movement in France*, 1912, p. 177.
[3] Pouget in *Mouvement Socialiste*, October 1906, p. 390.

as the *C.G.T.* was concerned, it was a subsidiary part of the campaign for the eight-hour day, with which it coincided. The demand, again, was for state intervention: the purpose of the campaign was primarily to speed through parliament a bill which had been introduced in 1902 by the socialist deputy Zévaès and held up in the Senate. The tactics were the same as those used against the employment bureaux, with violence and intimidation as the keynote and parliament again as target. In an open letter to the government in 1905, the Paris bakers declared that their patience was exhausted and that the streets would belong to them if the Senate did not deal with the matter immediately. The barbers put up posters calling for energetic pressure on the state as well as on the employers as 'parliament will only grant what it cannot refuse'. The windows of shops that refused to close were smashed, customers were frightened away by pickets and frequent brawls occurred. The movement was probably not extensive enough to force the Senators' hand, but the spectacle of continued disorder undoubtedly had its persuasive value. When the law was voted in 1906, it appeared to the syndicalists as another victory for direct action.

Antimilitarism and antipatriotism

The congress of Amiens, reaffirming an earlier resolution, adopted the principle of antimilitarist and antipatriotic propaganda as official policy of the C.G.T. and declared that it should become ever more intense and more audacious. This view was echoed at later congresses. Of all bourgeois ideals, patriotism was perhaps the most deeply cherished; it aroused the strongest and most irrational emotions. The antipatriotic tone of syndicalist propaganda, the open rejection of la patrie, aroused the fury of loyal bourgeois citizens. The scandal caused by these two doctrines was probably greater than that caused by any other revolutionary principle. As a result, contemporary critics gave them an importance out of all proportion to their real place in syndicalist theory; the significance they read into them, moreover, was largely foreign to the intentions of the movement itself.

THE ARMED FORCES OF THE BOURGEOIS STATE. As far as the rank and file of the movement were concerned, the resolutions they voted at the C.G.T. did not necessarily mean the lack of attachment of France that the critics saw in them. Antipatriotism was largely a corollary of antimilitarism. Antimilitarism, in turn, arose naturally from the workers' experience. Whenever an important strike movement occurred, the government seemed to call in troops to maintain public order. The result was a long history of bloody conflicts with the workers nearly always the victims, leading to a deep-seated belief that the main function of the army was to act as an auxiliary of the employers. Reference has already been made to the incidents at Fourmies, Raon-l'Etape, Narbonne, Villeneuve-Saint-Georges, Montceau-les-Mines and Draveil. It was the bitter experience of military intervention, not the abstract doctrine of Marx or the anarchists, which was the real cause of the C.G.T.'s antimilitarist propaganda. Its immediate purpose was not to promote the revolution but simply to dissuade soldiers, particularly conscripts of the working class, from playing the role of strikebreakers. From this point of view, it could be treated as an extension of the tactics of the strike.

In its report to the Dublin congress of 1903 the C.G.T. affirmed that the state never observed neutrality during industrial disputes. The need for syndicalist action followed from the recognition that the state was the executive committee of the bourgeoisie, which would use the armed forces at its command to protect its own interests whenever occasion arose. When the principle of antimilitarist propaganda was reaffirmed in 1908, two reasons were given: even when soldiers were not ordered to shoot down the

135

demonstrators outside factories, they were increasingly being employed as strike-breakers within. A similar resolution, passed in 1910, spoke of the intervention of soldiers during strikes, whether as 'assassins' or as *jaunes* (the name given to the anti-*C.G.T.* unions which tended to collaborate with the employers), as a monstrosity to be opposed at all costs.

Voivin of the leather-workers could therefore argue in 1912 that the anti-militarism of the *C.G.T.* was neither ideological in origin nor political in character; it was an economic question that could not be separated from the everyday action of the unions in support of their economic demands. He added that had the army been kept for the purpose for which it was raised, the defence of national frontiers, antimilitarist propaganda would have remained a strictly political issue and would have been pursued outside the *C.G.T.* in accordance with its principle of political neutrality.[1] While this may be doubted in view of the near-anarchist philosophy of so many of the Confederation's leaders, the use made of the army did enable the syndicalists to square the circle, adopting a policy that would otherwise have been labelled highly political while claiming to remain politically neutral.

ANTIMILITARIST PROPAGANDA. The first task of the militants was thus to dissuade soldiers from siding with the employers against their own comrades in periods of strike. They tried various means to make the conscripts aware of the class struggle and to strengthen working-class solidarity. The idea that close, personal contacts should be maintained with union members during their period of military service was first raised at the congress of 1897, when the task was entrusted to the newly-created local sub-committees for the general strike. In 1900 a four-point plan was adopted: public meetings should be organised at the time of the annual call-up; pocket money should be sent to the young soldier by his own union or *Bourse*; he should be invited to workers' homes in the garrison town; contact with him should be established by the secretary of the *Bourse* in that town. A special fund was created in 1910—known as the *Sou du Soldat*—mainly to finance propaganda in the barracks; the organisation to keep the conscript in touch with the local *Bourse* was strengthened at the same time.

There was a considerable output of antimilitarist literature. Yvetot's *Manuel du Soldat* went through many editions and enjoyed considerable popularity; the same was true of the special issues of the *Voix du Peuple* which appeared on the eve of the annual call-up and had a sale many times that normally reached by the paper. Both achieved corresponding notoriety in official circles and, together with the agitation of the militants within the barracks, led to a number of prosecutions. Of these Yvetot was certainly

[1] Voivin in *Mouvement Socialiste*, September/October 1912, p. 223.

Antimilitarism and antipatriotism

the chief victim. Despite the uproar, this propaganda could only claim one success, a revolt in the 17th Regiment at the time of the wine-growers' strike and the general unrest in the Midi during 1907. The regiment was locally conscripted, however, and local ties were probably the decisive influence.

THE BOURGEOIS STATE AND THE WORKERS' FATHERLAND. Anti-patriotic propaganda was a necessary aspect of antimilitarism. As the resolution of 1900 said, the bourgeoisie relied upon the patriotic sentiments of the workers to recruit them for the defence of bourgeois interests. A counter-attack was required to prevent the exploitation of this sentiment.

It is impossible to ignore the fact, however, that there were obvious political and ideological aspects to the antimilitarism and antipatriotism of the C.G.T. as well. The state was a capitalist institution. Its rejection, and the rejection of all it stood for, was only the logical conclusion of the extreme view of the class war taken by the syndicalists. Antipatriotism was simply the last and most spectacular expression of the syndicalists' principle of proletarian autonomy, the principle of the complete segregation of the working class. In this sense, of course, it was antimilitarism which was the corollary and not the other way round. The influence of Marx was clear. The reformist socialist Zévaès defined the syndicalist attitude as a drastically simplified, brutal and down-to-earth commentary on Marx's formula that the workers had no fatherland.[1] Thus Pouget could write in marxist vein that the idea of a fatherland was closely related to the idea of property and that patriotism without property was absurd.[2] In similar fashion, Griffuelhes declared that as he owned no property, the whole moral system of the nation was meaningless for him.[3] The syndicalists rejected the state as an instrument of the property-owning class and affirmed the common interest of workers throughout the world. This led them to the rejection of war, the extreme expression of state policy. War was a conflict of capitalist interests quite unrelated to the interests of the working class; a conflict, however, in which the working class was the major victim. Antimilitarist propaganda thus had a secondary purpose: the prevention of capitalist wars.

In practice this aspect of syndicalist propaganda did not mean any real lack of patriotism on the part of the great majority of the C.G.T. Despite the violent language of their resolutions, their purpose was essentially the same, to protect the immediate interests of the working class, whether against armed intervention during strikes or against the greater threat of war. The attempt to dissuade the government from warlike actions took

[1] A. Zévaès, Le syndicalisme contemporain, 1912, p. 144.
[2] E. Pouget, Les bases du syndicalisme, 1906.
[3] Griffuelhes in Mouvement Socialiste, August 1905.

137

Principles and practice of the C.G.T.

several forms: demonstrations of solidarity with foreign workers; the incitement of troops to disaffection; the threat of a strike of reservists or of a general strike of all workers in case of mobilisation. From a doctrinnaire point of view, syndicalism implied the absolute rejection of state and *patrie*; in practice the rank and file supported a limited antimilitarism which reflected the workers' distrust of French foreign policy during the international crises of the time (Morocco, Balkans). Antipatriotism was used as an argument of propaganda for peace.

WAR AND THE GENERAL STRIKE. A distinctively revolutionary note nevertheless entered some of the antimilitarist resolutions of the *C.G.T.* and this cannot be ignored either. The *C.G.T.* openly threatened a workers' revolution should war be declared. The resolution of 1908 introduced the idea that any such declaration should be met with a revolutionary general strike, though it was careful to commit the *C.G.T.* to no more than propaganda and to specify that the strike should be international. In October 1912, at the time of the Balkan crisis, the *C.G.T.* called a special anti-war conference in Paris. The delegates, speaking—so they claimed—on behalf of the united French labour movement, affirmed in a long resolution their determination to oppose a bourgeois war by all means but to profit from a declaration of war, should it come, by a counter-declaration of the revolutionary general strike which would achieve the emancipation of the proletariat.

This resolution proved a hollow threat in the light of subsequent events. Perhaps it was never meant to be more than a threat. More likely, it represented the ideas of a small but vociferous minority—notably Yvetot and Hervé—who secured by their eloquence the vote of the rank and file, ever ready to support revolutionary slogans, if not revolutionary action. On the other hand, even though the antipatriotic and antimilitarist principles of the *C.G.T.* were swept away overnight in 1914, one must not underrate its genuine efforts to avert the coming war. Their failure was at least partly due to lack of co-operation by the labour organisations in other countries. In 1903 at Dublin, and in 1905 at Amsterdam, the international labour congress refused to place the question of antimilitarism on the agenda at all. Griffuelhes met with a sharp rebuff when he visited Berlin in 1906 to arrange simultaneous anti-war demonstrations in France and Germany. In July 1914 Jouhaux failed in the same attempt; Legien, leader of the German trade unions, did not even answer the telegram calling for united action to protest against the warlike policies of the two governments. The *C.G.T.* had cause to be disillusioned.

It has been claimed, even from the calmer distance of 1948, that the

138

Antimilitarism and antipatriotism

entire syndicalist movement was not simply hostile to the army and its use at home but opposed that most certain principle of patriotism, the defence of national territory.[1] While the one was true, the other was more apparent than real. In 1914 the workers went enthusiastically to the front. Patriotism (or, to use a less pleasant word, nationalism) proved a stronger and deeper force than class conscience; the syndicalists were as loyal as the bourgeoisie in the defence of national territory. The war showed them, moreover, that *patrie* and state were inseparable; in the face of national danger, the leaders of the *C.G.T.* collaborated bravely with the bourgeois government of the time.

[1] R. Goetz-Girey, *La pensée française syndicaliste: militants et théoriciens*, 1948, p. 47.

Genealogy of the general strike

The idea of the general strike occupied a central place in the development of syndicalism. It had a threefold importance for the movement. From a historical point of view, the doctrine of the general strike marked the breach between socialists and syndicalists. Its adoption in the face of socialist opposition was the French labour movement's declaration of independence. Thereafter, belief that the emancipation of the proletariat could be achieved by no other means was the test separating the two. From a theoretical point of view, it was the apex of syndicalist ideas. If syndicalism was to be regarded as a closed system, leading to the emancipation of the proletariat, then its logic depended entirely upon the general strike. If that was not possible, syndicalism was an overture to which the curtain could never rise; if it was possible, then so was the whole of syndicalism. If syndicalism was seen as a movement, rather than a theory, then the importance of the general strike depended less on its feasibility than on the power it had to inspire the workers in their everyday struggle. The concept of the general strike as a 'means of acting on the present' was largely due to Georges Sorel but some syndicalist leaders came close to expressing the same view. From a psychological point of view, finally, there was a deep-rooted, fairly widespread belief in its possibility, at times in its imminence, among labour militants at the turn of the century. "Men who participate in a great social movement always picture their coming triumph as a battle in which their cause is certain to win", observed Sorel with some reason. The general strike was a picture, however blurred, of such a triumph. Looking back at the history of the movement, it becomes irrelevant whether it was a 'myth' or a practical weapon. The belief existed and its existence was sufficient to affect the policies and actions of the *C.G.T.* for a time. Ideas about the general strike, its form and significance, changed almost from year to year and any discussion must take account of these stages of development. The present chapter traces the history; subsequent chapters will consider the general strike in its changing theoretical and psychological aspects.

In Pouget's words, "the idea of the general strike had no ideological coat of arms; it came from the people".[1] The nearest to a *blason idéologique* the idea can show was Mirabeau's warning to the Third Estate just before the Revolution that the people, to be formidable, need only become immobile. Another precursor was Girardin who urged, after Louis Napoleon's *coup d'état* of 1851: "Let the merchants cease to sell, the customers to buy, the labourers to work, the butchers to slaughter, the

---

[1] Pouget in *Mouvement Socialiste*, June/July 1904, p. 165.

Genealogy of the general strike

bakers to bake, let everyone cease to work, even the national press; let Louis Napoleon find neither compositor to set up *Le Moniteur*, nor a printer to run it off, nor a bill-poster to put it up! Isolated, solitude, emptiness all round this man! With nothing but folded arms around him, he must fall. Let us organise the universal strike."[1]

Both were thinking of a citizens' strike. As a weapon of the proletariat it was first advocated by the anarchists in the First International. Indeed, it was one of those bitterly contested points which led to the split between marxists and others. The rump congress held at Geneva in 1873 ended by deciding that the time was not ripe for an answer to all the questions raised by the idea of the general strike; it urged the workers to concentrate meanwhile on socialist propaganda and the organisation of trade unions. After the Commune the anarchists were scattered and suppressed. The marxist party imposed the principles of parliamentary and political action on the French labour movement. The idea of the general strike disappeared for a while. As Pouget said, new ideas were often elaborated by one generation, only to be forgotten; the next generation, unaware of the work already accomplished, was forced to start again at the beginning.[2]

A new stimulus came from America in 1886. News of the eight-hour-day campaign, with its agitation for a general strike and its climax in the Chicago Haymarket riots, reached Europe. Belgian, Dutch and German socialists began to write about the political mass strike. Interest was strong in Belgium and France but the reaction in the two countries was quite different. In Belgium the socialist party voted for the mass strike as a means of obtaining universal suffrage. Strikes were declared in 1893 and in 1902, involving 200,000 and 300,000 workers respectively, both lasting about a week; the former was a partial success, the latter a complete failure. The French socialists, on the other hand, considered such action unscientific even for political and reformist ends. It was not the intellectuals (with the exception of Briand) but the militant workers who took up the idea and they gave it a sense entirely different from that it acquired in the countries of northern Europe; they advocated the industrial general strike as a means of achieving social revolution.

The idea found fertile soil in France and immediately struck root in the labour movement. Broadly speaking, there were three reasons for this. It followed logically from the militants' exclusion of the conquest of state power by party-political means and their recognition of the impossibility of a workers' insurrection. The general strike was the only means left to achieve the emancipation of the proletariat. Looked at from another point

---

[1] *Cit.* W. H. Crook, *The General Strike*, 1931, p. 28.
[2] Pouget in *Mouvement Socialiste*, June/July 1904, p. 169.

of view, it also followed logically from the growing strength of the trade unions. As Pouget said: the strike was the obvious weapon of the *syndicat*; generalisation of the strike followed naturally as the movement grew stronger; from the generalised strike of a federation to the general strike of the entire Confederation was but a step in thought.[1] Finally, there was the anarchist tradition. By 1890 the anarchist and revolutionary movements had recovered from the aftermath of the Commune. As the old spirit of insurrection surged up once more, it found in the general strike the obvious, indeed the only plausible, outlet for its energies. It was the anarchists who spread the idea during the next few years. Much was due to Tortelier, a Paris carpenter, a fiery speaker and a dedicated anarchist. He had little success as a delegate to the international congress of 1888 but in the Faubourg Saint-Antoine and among the Paris labourers he had considerable support.

The decision of the *Fédération nationale des syndicats* at its 1888 congress in Le Bouscet nevertheless came as a surprise. Led by the *blanquiste* Boulé, a Paris stone-cutter by trade, the sixty-nine delegates decided with much enthusiasm but little debate that the complete cessation of work could alone lead to the emancipation of the proletariat. They declared that the general strike was the equivalent of the revolution. This was rejected two days later by the congress of Guesde's *Parti ouvrier*. By contrast, Allemane's *Parti ouvrier socialiste révolutionnaire*, probably the most proletarian of the French socialist parties of the time, came out in support of the principle in 1891. The *allemanistes* joined the anarchists as active propagators of the general strike in the labour movement. The *blanquistes* accepted it as a possible revolutionary weapon at the same time, thus leaving marxists and right-wing socialists isolated together.

The adoption of the general strike as a fundamental principle of the labour movement, however, dated from the Marseilles congress of 1892. There Aristide Briand, delegate of the *Bourse* of Saint-Nazaire, made himself its chief advocate and his eloquence triumphed in the face of Jules Guesde himself. Briand later claimed 'paternity' and his claim was strong in the sense that he, more than any other single person, swung the congress over. Tortelier, however, had laid the groundwork and so had Fernand Pelloutier who, also a delegate of Saint-Nazaire, had successfully introduced an almost identical resolution at a regional socialist congress in Tours a few days earlier. A long resolution declared that the workers could never obtain their just rights through parliamentary action. Among the weapons legally at their disposal was the universal withdrawal of labour. This would immediately, certainly and peacefully lead to

[1] Pouget in *Mouvement Socialiste*, June/July 1904, p. 166.

victory. The emphasis on legality reflected Pelloutier's belief in peaceful revolution.

In 1893 the Paris *Bourse du Travail* was closed by the authorities and it was in the shadow of this event that a joint congress of *Bourses* and *syndicats* was held. Ramelin of the printers, an *allemaniste*, was *rapporteur* for the general strike: "It is time to leave the path of theory and enter that of practice", he exclaimed. Nevertheless, a resolution calling for an immediate general strike as a protest against the government's action was rejected. As far as the principle was concerned, on the other hand, there was only one vote of dissent. A permanent committee for the organisation of the general strike was appointed. The title, changed shortly afterwards, was a little misleading: its task seems to have been conceived as the organisation of propaganda (meetings, leaflets and posters were mentioned), rather than the organisation of the strike itself. No clear pattern emerged from the debate and it is difficult to tell exactly what the delegates had in mind. Was the congress thinking of the possibility of a national strike in the near future with limited ends (it was resolved that the new committee should prepare actively for the declaration of a strike in case of further governmental aggression); or was it thinking of a revolutionary general strike, and, if so, in the near or distant future (the committee itself declared that the strike, when it came, would be the social revolution)? Perhaps the distinctions were not clear to the delegates themselves. They did close their proceedings, however, with the cry "Vive la grève générale! Vive la Révolution sociale!"

Next year the *Fédération des syndicats* held its congress at Nantes. Girard, secretary of the new committee, reported on a 'vast referendum' that had been organised among the constituent groups. To the first question, "Are you a partisan of the immediate general strike?" forty affirmative replies had been received; all eighty answered affirmatively to the question "Are you a partisan of the general strike if the organisations of the working class are threatened?"; only two said that they were actually opposed to the general strike as a principle. The issue was again debated and Briand was again the protagonist. His attitude was equivocal. To the guesdistes he declared: "The general strike is a weapon; you say you already have one, but if it fails here is another." He accepted that there were other weapons, not only the ballot box, but guns and swords also, and he would march with others if they chose them. He spoke of the strike as a means of obtaining reformist legislation by embarrassing the government during the forth-coming international exhibition. His closing challenge was that of a defence counsel and open to various interpretations: "I ask you to vote the general strike as a formula; I do not ask you for its immediate application; what can it harm you to vote for it under these conditions?" The majority voted for the principle and the guesdistes withdrew. The split led to the foundation of the *C.G.T.* in 1895.

Questions of organisation dominated in 1895 and the principle was voted without discussion. At Tours in 1896 Guérard of the railwaymen was *rapporteur* and the question was examined more practically than before. He made it clear that the labour movement was not yet sufficiently prepared for a general strike; a good deal of propaganda was still necessary. He added that such a strike could in any case not be organised in advance; it would break out suddenly, when the time was ripe, perhaps as the result of a railway strike which would act as a signal for wider revolt. He therefore suggested a change in title from 'committee for organisation' to 'committee for propaganda for the general strike'. This was accepted almost unanimously. A new realism could be seen in the debate. The picture of the general strike changed (discussed in the next chapter), as did its importance, the place it occupied in the whole body of syndicalist ideas. It had originally been voted, as Hamelin said, "to leave the path of theory for that of practice". It was now realised that the movement must after all restrict itself to theory (i.e. propaganda) for some time. The result was naturally to shift attention to other possible fields of action such as enlarging the scope of ordinary strikes, boycott and sabotage.

In 1897 at Tours the general strike and the generalised strike of an industry or trade were both on the agenda. The delegates first voted for the former in principle, then declared themselves in favour of the generalisation of strikes. The result was a certain amount of confusion. The term 'general strike' was used indiscriminately thereafter to describe the revolution proper and national strikes within a single industry (including one, for example, of the two thousand members of the match-makers federation). It was probably not only in the formulation, but in the mind also, that the distinction tended to vanish. The principle was voted in 1898 at Rennes and two years later in Paris. The wording in the latter case made the strike appear as one of the only means for the emancipation of the proletariat, without excluding others in other fields of action. Léon Blum read into this a profound change of spirit.[1] The compromise was probably superficial, however; the *C.G.T.* was being careful not to offend the foreign trade-union movements with which it was trying to co-operate at the time.

In 1898 there was some hope that a general strike might emerge from the proposed national strike of railwaymen. But the latter was a failure: the government intercepted strike orders in the post and prevented any widespread movement from the start. In 1901 there was talk of a generalised strike by the miners' federation and hopes were again expressed that other

[1] L. Blum, *Les congrès ouvriers et socialistes français*, 1901, p. 190.

workers might profit from the opportunity. At the Lyons congress that year the committee reported that the principle of the general strike was by then sufficiently understood; repeated postponements meant the dissipation of revolutionary spirits and gradual discredit of the whole idea. What better opportunity than the present? it asked: let the miners give the signal and the *C.G.T.* would follow their lead. The congress thereupon voted yet again that any general strike would be the equivalent of revolution, though it reassured itself by declaring that the failure of a movement in support of the miners would not impair this principle; it would in any case be a valuable expression of working-class solidarity. The delegates were sufficiently optimistic, however, to call on all *syndicats* to express their views about the organisation of society after a successful revolution. The miners' federation voted for a generalised strike if the government did not meet their demands by 1 November. When the day came, their demands had not been met but the miners' committee, rent by political and personal conflicts, was unable to organise a national strike. By 1902 the failure of the movement was complete and the *C.G.T.* disassociated itself completely.

When the *C.G.T.* was reconstituted at Montpellier in 1902, questions of organisation again dominated. A revolutionary motion, drawn up in general terms without actually mentioning the strike, was adopted without debate by 355 votes to 1, with 37 abstentions ("The congress calls on the executive committee to continue energetically its revolutionary and trade union work which alone will permit the overthrow of bourgeois society.") In the years that followed, the labour movement grew in strength and, finding it possible to obtain material concessions after all, also grew in realism. The general strike lost much of its importance and was only mentioned incidentally in debates (e.g. in relation to antimilitarist resolutions). The principle was nevertheless reaffirmed at regular intervals and remained part of the official doctrine of the labour movement. It was embodied in the Amiens Charter, the fundamental declaration of principles of the *C.G.T.* to which all members subscribed. This stated quite clearly: "The Confederation works for the complete emancipation of the proletariat which can only be achieved by the expropriation of the capitalists; as the means of action it recommends the general strike."

A new twelve-member committee for strikes and the general strike was set up by the *C.G.T.* statutes of 1902. Though responsible for general strike propaganda, it was also responsible for the organisation of a central strike fund and was primarily interested in the support and co-ordination of generalised strikes throughout the country. Sub-committees had already been set up earlier in some *Bourses du Travail* and these were extended. In accordance with the federal structure of the *C.G.T.*, their composition and function were left to the *Bourses* concerned. The main task was seen as propaganda, indeed a confederal circular of 1910 suggested that their sole task was "to profit from important events in order to create a solid agitation which would prepare their forces for a possible general strike". In practice, they showed more interest in the organisation of generalised strikes in their area.

As May Day 1906 approached and the campaign for the eight-hour day reached its climax, interest in the general strike quickened once more. Once more, as in 1898 and 1901, it seemed as if a strike movement might really grow into revolution. The result was no different than before. It was nevertheless decided at Amiens that year that agitation should continue and Delesalle, the *rapporteur*, recommended the setting up of a new committee to continue the agitation, a committee of propaganda for the eight-hour day and the general strike. Despite past failures, revolution still seemed possible. The report even sketched the campaign plan for which propaganda could be made: (1) generalised strikes of federations as troop manoeuvres; (2) withdrawal of labour throughout the country on a given date as army manoeuvres; (3) complete and general standstill, placing the proletariat in a state of open war with capitalist society; (4) general strike—revolution.

The changing picture of the general strike

The *Encyclopaedia of the Social Sciences* distinguishes three types of general strike in its article on the subject. The element common to all was the complete paralysis of economic life; the difference lay in the ends this paralysis was intended to serve. First: "The general strike may be economic, aimed at the redress of specific injustices in industrial relations, sympathetic in nature and directed at the outset at least against the employers." The syndicalists often used the term in this sense, meaning no more than a generalised strike in support of limited demands. Second: "It may be invoked as a weapon to wrest some new constitutional right for the working population; in this instance it is directed against the government and is political in character." This was the mass strike advocated by socialists in certain other countries. Syndicalist threats of a general strike in case of war also came into the category of political strikes as, perhaps, did the eight-hour day campaign (the object of attack was the government even if the issue was not constitutional). The *C.G.T.* in fact issued a pamphlet advocating the reformist, as well as the revolutionary, general strike; the former could be used to obtain quite minor benefits from the state.[1] Third: "It may be considered the opening wedge in a revolution against the entire established order, in which case it is revolutionary in character." It was the general strike, not merely revolutionary in character but the revolution itself, which was the peculiar contribution of syndicalism to the history of socialism.

The syndicalist general strike was not a clearly defined concept. It is difficult enough to disengage the meaning at any one moment, for there were at all times differences of opinion amongst its advocates; there were ambiguities in the resolution which they voted; and one is left to guess the unformulated pictures in the mind of the rank and file. It is impossible to discover any doctrine valid over a longer period of time: the idea of the general strike changed with changing circumstances. It is only by simplification that one can impose a broad pattern of evolution.

At first it was visualised in negative terms: the workers merely down tools and wait with folded arms for society to surrender its riches to them. Gradually a more positive attitude developed. It was realised that the strikers would have to seize food supplies to avoid starvation; then that they would themselves have to take over the means of production rather than

---

[1] C.G.T., *Grève générale réformiste et grève générale révolutionnaire*, 1903.

await their voluntary surrender by the capitalists. This would involve violence. At first, again, it seemed as if this might be incidental and the task brief. Finally, however, it dawned on the workers that the overthrow of the state would involve a lengthy struggle in which the use of force would be at least as important as the cessation of work. The concept of the general strike merged gradually with the older concept of insurrection.

Parallel to this development was a change in the expectations of how the general strike would occur. First it was supposed that a nationwide cease work order would be issued for a specified day. From this, support veered to the idea of spontaneity: the strike would break out at an unpredictable moment and almost of its own accord. There would be a sudden explosion of forces when the time was ripe. Finally this picture gave way to the idea that the general strike would emerge gradually from the widening of some ordinary strike movement. Still unpredictable in time and form, it could nevertheless be brought nearer by ordinary strike action.

In the early days it was widely supposed that the general strike was imminent and all hopes were therefore pinned on it. As the unions became more concerned with everyday reformist matters, it receded into the background of syndicalist thought and its coming was postponed to an unspecified future date. At the same time, from the theorists' point of view, the earlier sharp distinction between the reformist strike and the revolutionary general strike gradually dissolved and the one was assimilated to the other.

FROM FOLDED ARMS TO INSURRECTION. The picture presented by its earliest advocates was notable for its simplicity, its highly dramatic nature and its extreme convenience. The revolution would involve nothing more difficult than a national agreement to cease work on a particular day. The workers would declare a Grand National Holiday as suggested half a century earlier by William Benbow in England. With one accord they would leave factories, shops and fields, donning their Sunday best for a stroll along the boulevards or for a picnic *en famille* in the Bois de Boulogne. As the furnaces died out and the machines ground to a halt, the capitalists would at last realise that only labour was truly productive; faced with the manifest determination of their former employees not to serve them any longer, they would have no choice but to submit with the best grace possible. As the paralysis spread, as press, transport and other services failed, the government would be faced with the isolation, solitude and emptiness that Girardin had wished Louis Napoleon; they too would be forced to capitulate. A single gesture and the revolution would be accomplished. *Une idée simpliste*, as an anarchist, probably Delesalle, wrote in 1901, not that many years later.[1] Something of this attitude remained until the end, however, perhaps because it appealed to the workers' belief that labour was the only vital element in the social order. This view was expressed by Griffuelhes and Niel in a pamphlet published as late as 1908: labour was the beginning and end of all things; its withdrawal would leave the capitalist system powerless; the general strike was the curtain that would go down on the old society and rise for the new. They were aware by then, however, that several acts would have to be played before the drama was over.[2]

The emancipation of the proletariat was not merely conceived as a peaceful event but as an entirely legal one. The Marseilles resolution of 1892 spoke of the universal strike as 'among the legal means unconsciously put at the disposal of the workers'. The strike in one industry was legal, the sympathetic strike of all industries must therefore be within the law also. Theirs was to be a revolution by permission of the *Code Napoléon*. Pelloutier, leading advocate of the general strike at the time, in any case opposed violence. In an open letter to Jules Guesde he declared categorically that it was a peaceful and legal weapon and repudiated any form of insurrection.[3]

Guesde and his marxist supporters countered that even if the workers were not starved into surrender, the state would intervene and settle the strike by force. These two points were soon taken up. It was clear that the first victims of a strike might easily be the workers themselves; they and their families would feel the pinch of hunger long before the employers would feel any need to capitulate. In 1893, therefore, the committee on the general strike felt bound to ask whether the suspension of work alone might not after all prove a boomerang and suggested that the workers should at least seize adequate food supplies. This was the narrow wedge of revolutionary action. From the argument that the pennies of the workers could not compete with the employers' millions, it was but a short step to the argument that the strikers must take the offensive all along the line: if they did not have the advantage of wealth, they at least had that of numbers. This point was made in 1894 by a delegate who denied the possibility of a peaceful general strike. At the same time, the workers realised that they could not expect the factories, mines, railways and fields to fall into their lap as the gift of the owners. The proletariat would have to take over the wealth of society on its own initiative. Thus both Pouget and Griffuelhes came to define the general strike as a two-sided activity: negatively, the suspension of work; positively, the seizure of the means of production.[4]

[1] Groupe des étudiants socialistes révolutionnaires internationalistes, *La grève générale*, n.d
[2] V. Griffuelhes and L. Niel, *Les objectifs de nos luttes de classe*, 1908.
[3] *Cit.* A. Zévaès, *Le syndicalisme contemporain*, 1912, p. 112.
[4] E. Pouget, *La C.G.T.*, 1908; Griffuelhes in *Mouvement Socialiste*, June/July 1904, p. 159.

Principles and practice of the C.G.T.

Even so, it seemed as if it would be a relatively simple task for the workers to enter into their inheritance. Some violence might be required to dispossess the capitalist but not much. The troops would certainly be called out but they would be scattered throughout the country, guarding vital points against sabotage and leaving the employers isolated and helpless. A simple calculation was reported by Guérard to the Tours congress of 1896: there were 300,000 soldiers available to guard 39,000,000 metres of railway track, one man for every 130 metres and none left for the stations, arsenals and public buildings, not to mention the factory gates themselves. The strike would thus be short and decisive, its repression physically impossible.

This belief could not last for long either. Bitter experience taught the labour movement what a major strike implied in terms of state intervention and clashes with armed force. How then could a general strike avoid an open battle between the proletariat and the army, chief defenders of the bourgeois state? The capitalists would not passively surrender the factories; the strikers would be met with a declaration of war. They might as well, therefore, take the initiative themselves. Violence, in that case, would then not simply be dictated by outside forces, it would express a reborn spirit of revolution on the part of the proletariat itself. A delegate at the 1900 congress, in a speech sounding more like a call to the barricades than anything else, declared openly that the workers must fight in the streets. This sentiment was shared by others. While anarchists still professed that a victory in the streets was almost impossible,[1] memories of Bakunin and Blanqui stirred. The picture of the general strike merged imperceptibly into civil war and in civil war all weapons were legitimate if opportune. This was illustrated by Pataud and Pouget in their utopian short story *Comment nous ferons la Révolution*. At the start, strikers would use force to bring out recalcitrant workers and close the factories. They would raid food stores and arms depots. Sabotage of public services would be carefully planned. As the conflict sharpened, barracks were burned and the troops disarmed. The climax was a march on parliament at the Palais Bourbon.

One may sum up this development by reference to the 1902 report of the C.G.T.'s general strike committee which expressed views that seem fairly typical of the time. It accepted both folded arms and insurrection. The former was said to be infallible but the latter was threatened as an afterthought. The peaceful strike was the proletariat's only effective weapon; the immobilisation of national life, bringing terrible consequences, would force the government to capitulate within a very short time. If it did not, the workers would rise in revolt from one end of France to the other.

[1] Groupe des étudiants socialistes révolutionnaires internationalistes, *La grève générale*, n.d.

Changing picture of the general strike

FROM ORGANISATION TO SPONTANEITY. The earliest advocates tended to assume that the general strike could be proclaimed by some central committee at a suitable moment, not far distant. All that was required was a little more propaganda, a few more resolutions, a slightly better organisation. This belief gradually gave way to the notion that it would be spontaneous and break out without any warning. This, of course, is something of a simplification; to a certain extent the two views existed side by side. In 1888, at the first congress at which the principle was adopted, a delegate affirmed that although the workers were not yet sufficiently organised, the general strike existed in a latent state and might be compared to the explosion which could occur in a gunpowder store. The more enthusiastic rejected the argument that the labour movement was insufficiently prepared for an immediate declaration of the strike. But in the following years the view spread that it would not take place on some date carefully fixed in advance but would be sudden, spontaneous and unforeseeable. In 1893 a delegate went so far as to reject any organisation as a waste of time, preferring rather to surprise the government—and presumably the labour movement also. In 1894 another delegate affirmed that it was materially impossible to organise the general strike, which must be a spontaneous act.

Spontaneity and organisation did not necessarily contradict each other. Griffuelhes, writing later, said that at the time the general strike appeared to the militants as an imminent explosion for which it was necessary to prepare. While the workers could not predict, much less decide, when the fatal day would dawn, they could make ready for it.[1] In other words, it was impossible to organise the strike but it was necessary to organise for it. Indeed, some form of co-ordination would obviously be required to ensure the universal and simultaneous suspension of work when the moment came. This, presumably, was thought to be the function of the committee of organisation for the general strike.

The situation changed as soon as it was realised that there was no absolute need for all workers to strike immediately and in unison. By 1893 the report pointed out that the same effect could be obtained by strikes in a number of key federations, above all the railwaymen and miners. These would bring all other branches of industry to a standstill within a very short time. The same point was made by Guérard in 1896 when he pointed out that the general strike would not be the result of a co-ordinated suspension of work at all, but would be enforced by shutting down such vital industries as fuel, power and transport.

From this it was but a short step to the idea that the strike of a key federation might become the impetus for a wider strike movement. This

---

[1] V. Griffuelhes and L. Niel, *Les objectifs de nos luttes de classe*, 1908.

151

Principles and practice of the C.G.T.

was a rather different notion, however. The general strike was no longer seen as a single, decisive event but as a movement, a wave of strikes spreading gradually through the country from one industry to another until the majority of workers were involved. The question of organisation thus became irrelevant. Some major strike, declared for quite unrevolutionary reasons, would be the spark which set the revolution aflame. Once the labour movement was imbued with the right spirit, almost any crisis would be sufficient—though which crisis it would be no one could tell in advance. The task of the *C.G.T.* was limited to preparing the ground in order to hasten the day.[1]

This idea had also been suggested by Guérard in 1896. The strike of a key industry would automatically force some other industries to close; at the same time, it would be the signal for the *C.G.T.* to persuade workers to leave unaffected industries in sympathy. If one is to believe Griffuelhes, looking back in 1908, the militants expected such an event almost daily. The general strike committee was convinced that the revolution was at hand; they met regularly to watch developments.[2] Their hopes were raised by the railway strike of 1898 and its failure was a blow to their optimism. It was not fatal, however, and similar hopes were expressed on later occasions. During the miners' strike of 1901, for example, Pouget wrote in the *Voix du Peuple* of the great actuality of the subject: the unions should be even more vigilant so as not to miss an opportunity; the workers should accustom themselves to thinking of the revolution as a task to be accomplished in the near future.[3] Reference has already been made to the events of May 1906. Despite the failure of the eight-hour-day campaign, it was decided at Amiens that the new committee should fix another day for a national strike. The militants still believed that if only the campaign was well organised, a revolutionary situation could be created which they could utilise.

A VISION OF THE GENERAL STRIKE. The picture of the general strike as the culmination of a series of strikes and as a period resembling civil war emerged from Pataud and Pouget's pamphlet-novel of 1909, which was published in English as *Syndicalism: How shall we bring about the Revolution?* by the anarchist paper *Freedom*. It was probably quite typical of the ideas that passed through the minds of the militants when, in an idle moment, they speculated about the coming revolution. The authors foresaw a period of depression and growing industrial unrest. "When the crisis was lessened in one union, it became envenomed in another. Strikes

[1] C.G.T., *Grève générale réformiste et grève générale révolutionnnaire*, 1903.
[2] Griffuelhes in *Action Directe*, 23 April 1908.
[3] *Voix du Peuple*, March 1901.

152

followed strikes; lock-outs were replied to by boycotts; sabotage was employed with ruinous intensity." Tension mounted rapidly. "Everywhere, on the least occasion, trouble and collision between labour and capital grew into violent conflicts, into strikes showing an always growing bitterness." An incident occurred, a clash between demonstrators and the troops; as had happened before, blood was shed; but the revolutionary ferment had been at work—this was the unpredictable spark, the signal for revolt. "This massacre—no more murderous than many preceding ones— precipitated and created a revolutionary situation." A sudden anger swept the labour movement. "News of the fray spread with the spontaneity of an electric spark. There was at first stupefaction, consternation. Then fists were clenched, anger blazed forth. The mass of the people, distressed, indignant, were intensely agitated, and the excitement reached a climax. The storm burst." The *C.G.T.*, after a hurried meeting of its council, called upon the workers to show solidarity with their murdered comrades and to suspend work until the government had punished those responsible. "On the threshold of this strike, the consequences of which were going to be so incalculable, the issue narrowed down to an ultimatum to the government. But there is nothing surprising in this. It is the same with social upheavals as with living organisms, they are born from a cell, from a germ, which develops gradually; at the beginning the new being is feeble, the Revolution is shapeless. The latter, indeed, is so unformed that even its most ardent supporters, those who in their inmost minds call for its coming, and would carry it through to all its ultimate developments, desire it rather than feel a presentiment of its coming." From the suspension of work, the proletariat passed to the offensive. By means of sabotage, the boycotting of the quarters of the rich and the incessant harrying of the troops, they reduced their enemies to impotence. Meanwhile they organised the distribution of food; seized and operated the factories; issued labour notes to replace money; as the revolt spread to the countryside, the peasants took over the land. Society was gradually transformed, even while the last battles were still being fought. As a climax the workers marched on the Palais Bourbon and invaded the Chamber of Deputies. "A demonstrator, climbing into the chair, pushing out the bewildered Speaker, took his place and, frantically ringing his bell, quieted the crowd and obtained relative silence. He profited by this to proclaim in abrupt, vigorous phrases, that fell like stunning blows, the downfall of Parliament and the dissolution of the bourgeois state." The socialist deputies, anxious to capture the revolution, cried 'To the *Hôtel de Ville!*' They were ignored; no new government was set up; the final, proletarian and anarchist revolution was accomplished.

Principles and practice of the C.G.T.

FROM ROMANTICISM TO REALISM. The importance of the general strike to the syndicalists diminished, roughly speaking, almost from the day it was first officially adopted. From a theoretical point of view, it changed from being the unique weapon of the proletariat to the mere culmination of a series of strikes; at the same time it tended to lose its industrial or strike character and take on that of a general insurrection. From a practical point of view, attention was focussed more and more on obtaining immediate concessions and as a result it was pushed further and further into the future. This development can be divided into three phases: the early period of revolutionary romanticism, the period of the twofold task of the C.G.T. and finally, the period of new realism.

The early tendency was not only to see the general strike as the sole means of emancipation but as the only form of action worth while at all. Griffuelhes later described the militants as believers because they believed in the revolution and nothing else.[1] The ordinary strike was at best a minor skirmish, perhaps training the worker for the real thing. As late as 1900, however, a report was approved by two hundred votes to seven which declared, among other things, that partial strikes should not be encouraged because the results were never worth the sacrifice involved and could not in any case be of real importance. Given the belief that revolution was imminent, 'all or nothing' was a natural attitude to take. It faded towards the end of the century and only revived at moments of high tension.

In 1903 the general strike committee of the C.G.T. issued a pamphlet in which it declared that while the general strike was still the sole practical means of emancipation, happy results might nevertheless be obtained by reformist, generalised strikes.[2] Such strikes were also seen as a vital training ground for the coming revolution. In other words, to prepare oneself for the general strike now meant to devote oneself to everyday strike movements. As Griffuelhes wrote in a pamphlet of 1908, the strike was necessary because it hardened and educated the worker; from it emerged a sense of confidence, an *élan*, a sharpness of vision, a feeling of solidarity.[3] Thus two birds—reform and revolution—could be killed with one stone. There was a difference, however, between the two statements. In 1903 the general strike was considered in terms of 'possibilities that can be realised under existing circumstances'; in 1908 the need for a lengthy period of training was stressed. The general strike had moved further into the future.

At the same time interest shifted from the revolutionary to the reformist goals, from total emancipation to the possibility of immediate practical

[1] Griffuelhes in *Action Directe*, 23 April 1908.
[2] C.G.T., *Grève générale réformiste et grève générale révolutionnaire*, 1903.
[3] V. Griffuelhes and L. Niel, *Les objectifs de nos luttes de classe*, 1908.

154

Changing picture of the general strike

gains. In the first issue of the *Voix du Peuple* one could read that the action of unions, although homogeneous, had a twofold aspect; practical in the present, theoretical as regards the future.[1] As time went on the general strike became more and more theoretical. Finally, as all attention was concentrated on immediate issues and reformist strikes, the doctrine was evolved that the general strike itself would grow out of the reformist movement, almost as a by-product, when the time was ripe. The syndicalists could thus devote themselves to the present in confidence that the future would look after itself. This was reflected in the history of the general strike committee of the *C.G.T.* In 1904 its work was temporarily suspended; the explanation given was that the eight-hour day had become the absorbing preoccupation of the movement. When it was reconstituted, its main function was officially declared to be the continuation of that campaign.

By the end of 1906 interest in the general strike as a practical weapon had probably evaporated. The slogan remained, so, probably, did the belief in an ultimate emancipation of the proletariat, perhaps even in an ultimate revolution. But the picture of this tended to recede to the furthest corners of the mind, becoming quite divorced from action at the same time. This was accompanied by the gradual redefinition of the concept of revolution. By 1912 Lagardelle could write of syndicalism as a form of permanent revolution.[2] The general strike was no longer a central element in syndicalist theory but merely the last strike in a long series, the last of a long line of partial expropriations. The revolution had become an evolutionary one.

[1] *Voix du Peuple*, December 1900.
[2] Lagardelle in *Mouvement Socialiste*, February 1912, p. 134.

The general strike as myth

So far, the general strike has been discussed from an analytical point of view, as a rationally constructed theory of conduct, consciously held by members of the C.G.T. and seriously intended as part of the strategy of the labour movement. It cannot, however, be treated entirely on its face value in this fashion. The interpretation of the general strike in terms of social psychology, as an intuitive mind-picture rather than as part of a rational theory, as a verbal symbol of faith rather than as a practical guide to action, was the contribution of Georges Sorel and Henri De Man to the understanding of syndicalism. As it is now impossible to conduct an empirical survey, all one can do is to touch on some ideas, necessarily speculative and incapable of substantiation.

PSYCHOLOGICAL COMPENSATION. In his *Psychology of Socialism*, De Man claimed that "socialism cannot be understood except by those who realise that the essential function of socialist doctrine is to supply this creed with its guiding symbols". He spoke of the eschatological sentiments or dispositions which inevitably arise when there is a great discrepancy between the aspiration of the masses and the possibilities of immediate success. This discrepancy was particularly marked in France where the revolution of 1789 had awakened high demands but where the labour movement was not a force capable of their realisation. His argument could be summarised as follows. Who suffers, hopes; and who hopes, believes. Every unpleasant emotional state arouses the compensatory idea of a happier state, a happier future. Man always believes in what he yearns for and the belief grows more vivid if he cannot do anything to alleviate his condition. Such faith is a psychological need. The faith of the masses in a socialist state of the future was not the outcome of scientific cognition but the expression of an eschatological hope. Such notions as the social revolution which ushered in the future society were, from the outlook of social psychology, nothing more than myths, that is to say verbal symbols of faith.[1]

The word 'myths' brings one to Sorel and the *Reflections on Violence*. He, however, provided a somewhat different reason for the faith of the masses in the coming revolution which the general strike symbolised. For him it was not a compensatory dream of the underprivileged and powerless, of De Man's inferiority complex. On the contrary, he described it as the expression of a determination to act and said: "One thing always seemed to me quite evident—that men who participate in a great social movement

---

[1] H. de Man, *The Pyschology of Socialism*, 1928, pp. 133/9.

156

always picture their coming action as the battle in which their cause is certain to triumph."[1]

Possibly De Man's explanation came nearer to the truth. Belief in the general strike was strongest when the labour movement was weakest and the struggle consequently almost non-existent; it tended to fade as soon as the workers engaged in effective action and the conflict with employers— formerly verbal—became concrete, for then the discrepancy between hopes and possibilities diminished. As De Man wrote, admittedly with a perspective lacking to Sorel at the time of his *Reflections*: "If we study the history of the labour movements down to our days, we note that the eschatological element is most marked in the early phases. It gradually passes into the background when the movement becomes crystallised into organisations and when the purely propagandist activities of the start are replaced by concrete and immediate tasks."[2]

PIOUS SLOGAN. Another point may be made at the same time. The French character, for reasons of history, was particularly suited to the perpetuation of such ideas as the general strike. All French socialists were vulnerable to dramatic phrases and the witchery of formulae. As Gustave Le Bon remarked in his *Psychology of Socialism*: "At times they have been great speakers, lovers of logic and words; very little concerned with facts, they greatly love an idea, so long as it is simple, general and presented in elegant language."[3] Thus, once established in the labour movement, the words 'general strike'—just as the word 'revolution'—had a life of their own. They remained in use in speeches, pamphlets, resolutions and arguments long after the intensity of the belief which had launched them had evaporated and any real belief in their coming had vanished almost entirely. There was of course truth in Le Bon's observation that certain words have the power to evoke images. Slogans could intoxicate, revolutionary slogans more than most. But when the original emotional drive behind these images had gone, the intoxication tended to last no longer than the convivial atmosphere of the congress debate or mass meeting. At this stage, the general strike lost its 'mythical' content and became mere 'doctrine', moving from an emotional to a verbal level at which it was a much less potent force. Griffuelhes said that the early advocates of the general strike were convinced of seeing the revolution. The *C.G.T.*, in its early years, lived in the shadow of this romantic faith. A comparison with religion is tempting. The words of faith are repeated, partly from habit, partly from piety, and in

[1] G. Sorel, *Reflections on Violence*, 1916, p. 22.
[2] H. de Man, *The Pyschology of Socialism*, 1928, p. 138.
[3] G. Le Bon, *Psychology of Socialism*, 1899, p. 130.

that repetition they may momentarily convince, but the inner conviction of their truth may have died.

INTUITION. This raises the question of the meaning of the term 'myth' in the context of syndicalism. Sorel was full of allusions but deliberately avoided clear definitions. The myth was said to be a group of images and these in turn, were the convictions of a group expressed in the language of the movement. The images arose out of the movement and could only be grasped intuitively by involvement. To clarify his meaning, Sorel contrasts the myth with the utopia, an intellectual construction which can thus be described and conveyed to others by description. It is hard to see that the idea of the general strike presented itself to the labour movement originally in this spontaneous and intuitive fashion. Indeed, the early idea of the folded-arms strike was an excessively rationalistic construction and it was in its elementary logic that its appeal lay. The 1888 resolution was based with apparent logic on one simple notion, the indispensability of labour; the strategy of a universal withdrawal of labour on a given day was equally simple. It is also hard to see why a utopia should not have provided an image as vivid as that of a myth. In this case, reason rather than intuition provided the highly dramatic picture of the coming revolution and there is no reason to believe that it was less firmly held because of its intellectual origins.

It has been seen that this simple concept did not last long; it changed as the workers became more active and the class struggle sharpened. Sorel's definition became more relevant. The basic conviction of almost any group involved in a war is that of its own inevitable victory. The language of the movement in this case was obviously that of industrial conflict and industrial action. Workers, accustomed to thinking of the class struggle in terms of the strike, automatically drawing on their own experience to visualise the last battle, saw ultimate victory as a bigger and better strike. A reservation must again be made. Political action, insurrection and the barricades, were as deeply ingrained a part of the language of the labour movement as economic action. This was the legacy of a long history of revolution in France, nourished later by strike riots involving clashes with army or police. The final battle was thus understandably visualised in other terms as well. Pataud and Pouget drew a picture composed in equal parts of strike and civil war.

However, the whole point of Sorel's myth was that it must not be described. He was sometimes ambiguous on this score and it was not always clear whether he meant that the observer could not understand the workers' myth by analysing it or whether he meant that the workers should not

The general strike as myth

attempt to analyse their own myth. Probably both. For the militants, its capacity to inspire would evaporate. It would no longer be an effective myth, and an ineffective myth was no myth at all. It followed that "the general strike must be taken as a whole and undivided, and the passage from capitalism to socialism conceived as a catastrophe, the development of which baffles description".[1] The same applied to the student of syndicalism: the myth had to be swallowed whole. It has already been noted that, for Sorel, to understand meant to participate; it also apparently meant to believe. This doctrine would make rational exposition impossible. It would also make it useless to speculate about the exact nature of the images associated with the words 'general strike' in the minds of the revolutionary syndicalists.

The militants did, however, formulate many of their ideas about the general strike. Sorel notwithstanding, therefore, one may treat their explanations as an indication of the unformulated pictures held by their followers. Here it is only necessary to repeat the three elements that appear to stand out in these pictures. First, that inherited from the period of the folded-arms strike: the picture of a sudden standstill of production and the immediate, peaceful collapse of the capitalist system. Second, and of course largely contradictory: the picture, drawn from first or second-hand memories of the barricades, of a great battle with the forces of the state, culminating in the victory of the proletariat. Third: the picture of revolution as the culmination of a long strike movement, possibly following a gradual transformation of society through an even longer series of unrelated strikes.

These descriptions refer to what Sorel called utopias rather than myths, for the latter are unexpressed and inexpressible. His demand that the general strike must be conceived as a catastrophe which baffled description ignored a fundamental characteristic of the French people. Le Bon called them lovers of logic and words. This made it unlikely that they would be content to hold ideas without describing or analysing them. The syndicalist militants were often caught in the trap. They often disclaimed any ability to predict comparable to that of the scientific socialists; they often stressed the importance of spontaneous activity and natural creativity. Yet they tended as often to construct utopian pictures of the coming revolution and the future society. This did not really matter. Sorel rightly warned of the dangers of overestimating the rational factors in the general strike, only to swing to the opposite extreme by proclaiming the irrational as the sole force behind it. Whether the pictures of the general strike were intuitive or speculative was of less significance than Sorel would have one believe. A

[1] G. Sorel, *Reflections on Violence*, 1916, p. 164.

159

valid point is made in an essay on Sorel: "An intelligent and intelligible plan of social change, however blurred it may be, must and will exist; a myth is therefore a utopia that has caught on, that has fired the passionate imagination of the mass into action."[1]

APOCALYPTIC VISION. A more important aspect of the general-strike myth—using the word in its widest sense—was its apocalyptic character as a revelation of ultimate victory. However blurred the image, it included a double faith: that the revolution was possible and that victory was inevitable. One need not argue whether the origins of this faith lay in its being a psychological compensation for lack of effective power, as De Man maintained, or whether it can be traced to the door of Karl Marx, who gave it scientific credentials (a vulgar marxism was in the air and must have affected many workers even when they rejected marxist socialism). Confidence in the collaboration of natural and supernatural forces was shown to an extraordinary degree by Pataud and Pouget in their story of the general strike. Not only was the revolutionary situation the result of economic forces outside the control of the workers (a depression) but the spark which set the revolution itself alight was equally fortuitous as far as they were concerned (a clash with the troops). Though a sensible assessment of the sort of conditions under which a general strike was likely to occur, it accorded ill with the syndicalist insistence on free will and the oft repeated slogan *vouloir, c'est pouvoir*. The final chapter had a psychological significance of far greater importance. It was a dramatic account of an attempted foreign invasion to suppress the revolutionaries. The invaders were not met by the fighting ranks of the working class but were annihilated by a secret weapon providentially invented at that very moment. This reliance on a *deus ex machina* was more than a literary trick; it reflected the extent to which the workers trusted providence.

STIMULUS TO ACTION. The value of a myth lay above all in the certainty of victory it gave. As De Man said: "There is no science of the future, there is only faith in the future, and among the forces which combine to bring the future into existence, the faith in its coming is one of the most effective."[2] It did this because it provided an incentive to the everyday struggle: the general strike, as token of ultimate victory, reassured the contestants when the battle seemed long and progress slow; it stimulated them to further efforts just as a mirage might stimulate the wanderer in the desert. On this interpretation, the general strike became a battle hymn, in

---

[1] J. H. Meisel, *The Genesis of Georges Sorel*, 1951, p. 265.
[2] H. de Man, *The Pyschology of Socialism*, 1928, p. 133.

The general strike as myth

Leroy's phrase 'a sort of *Marseillaise*'.[1] It was in thinking of, and preparing for, the general strike that the proletariat found the hope and courage necessary for a victorious struggle.

The general strike was not only the most effective myth in the class war because it was easily understood and expressed in the language natural to the labour movement, but above all because it brought out in a flash the essence of that war, dividing the revolutionary labour movement sharply from the parliamentary socialists and making all democratic compromise a waste of time. Thus for Sorel the general strike was "a body of images capable of invoking instinctively all the sentiments which correspond to the different manifestations of the war undertaken by socialism against modern society", for in its light "the slightest incidents of daily life become the symptoms of the state of war between the classes, every conflict is an incident in the social war, every strike begets the perspective of a total catastrophe". He added: "Strikes have engendered in the proletariat the noblest, deepest and most moving sentiments they possess. The general strike groups them all in a co-ordinated picture and, by bringing them together, gives to each one of them its maximum intensity; appealing to their painful memories of particular conflicts, it colours with an intense life all the details of the composition presented to the consciousness."[2]

This was why Sorel called the myth a means of acting on the present. It was to be judged in that sense alone. Any attempt to discuss how far it could be taken literally as future history was devoid of sense. Belief in the general strike was enough, its truth as irrelevant as the analysis of its meaning. This, of course, was a Sorelian and not a syndicalist point of view. For Sorel, what was important was the present rather than the future. There might, probably would, never be a general strike; what mattered was that the workers should fight nobly on the assumption that there would. Sorel was something of a Nietzschean, basically concerned to restore a heroic quality to modern life. The syndicalists, had they read him, would hardly have appreciated this view of their movement.

Vilfredo Pareto also took up the question of the myth in his *Mind and Society*. In his own pseudo-scientific terminology he wrote: "The capacity of influencing human conduct in the form of derivations that overstep experience and reality throws light upon a phenomenon that has been well observed and analysed by Georges Sorel, the fact namely that if a social doctrine (it would be more exact to say the sentiments manifested by a social doctrine) is to have any influence, it has to take the form of a myth. The social value of a doctrine, or the sentiments which it expresses, is not

---

[1] M. Leroy, *La coutume ouvrière*, 1913, p. 547.
[2] G. Sorel, *Reflections on Violence*, 1928, pp. 137/145.

to be judged extrinsically by the mythical form it assumes, which is only its means of action, but intrinsically by the results it achieves."[1] This was essentially De Man's point that socialist doctrines could only be understood as providing a socialist movement with guiding symbols. The concept of the general strike guided the proletariat in the most beneficial direction. Pareto reduced this to a utilitarian calculus far removed from Sorel's hope that the myth would inspire heroism in the working class. According to him, the purpose of the symbol was to induce individuals to advance to a point where they would enjoy a greater utility than at present. To rouse them, it was wiser to place before their eyes a point where they would enjoy an enormous, altogether fantastic, amount of utility. In making for this point they would be hampered by all sorts of practical checks. Thus, while never attaining their imagined goal, they would reach a level of utility they would not otherwise have achieved.[2]

DOUBLETHINK. Sorel's moral-utilitarian and Pareto's material-utilitarian interpretations were both clearly limited to the observer. They could not be shared by those participating in the myth for they, by definition, must be believers. If the militants had digested either writer, they would have lost their faith and the myth its effectiveness. There was a problem, however. Sorel claimed that every effective social movement known to history had been the result of the widespread acceptance of a myth. If no myths were accepted by the masses, talk about revolution would remain talk indefinitely. It was therefore necessary to inspire the proletariat. The correct myth had to be discovered and propagated: "We must know what forces exist in the world and then take measures whereby we may utilise them."[3] This was quite different from the suggestion of hostile critics that Sorel advocated the invention of myths after the fashion of Plato's noble lies.[4] It was only of Mussolini and the fascists (influenced by Sorel, it is true) that Ernst Cassirer could write that "henceforth myths can be manufactured in the same sense and according to the same methods as other weapons—like guns and aeroplanes".[5] What the syndicalist leaders of the labour movement had to do, presumably, was to discover the myths already latent in the movement, capable of arousing the workers because they appealed intuitively to them.

It was far from clear how this could be done, given the nature of myth as belief. At one point Sorel said that the general strike could be accepted

---

[1] V. Pareto, *Mind and Society*, 1935, section 1868.
[2] V. Pareto, *Mind and Society*, 1935, section 1869.
[3] G. Sorel, *Reflections on Violence*, 1916, p. 166.
[4] Cf. W. M. McGovern, *From Luther to Hitler*, 1941, p. 429.
[5] E. Cassirer, *The Myth of the State*, 1946, p. 282.

although one knew it to be a myth. In so far as this applied to the militants of the *C.G.T.* (for they alone could in practice inspire the rank and file), it is hard to see whether this would have made them machiavellians or Orwellian doublethinkers. As they were not cynical, it was presumably the latter: preaching the general strike as a useful means of stimulating the class struggle and at the same time believing in it themselves. Such acrobatic feats would have suited the French character well and are not unknown elsewhere. Pouget, for example, at one point declared that the popularity of the general strike among the militants was due to its propaganda value.[1] Griffuelhes, at a time when he appeared genuinely to believe in the general strike, was also well aware of this aspect. He wrote later, in 1911, that the worker, in his everyday struggle, needed to feel himself a link in the chain of history; he needed to be supported by memories and hopes—by a sometimes legendary tradition on the one hand, by ideals, perhaps inaccessible, on the other.[2]

Finally, one must ask what influence the idea had. Sorel thought that "the idea of the general strike has such power behind it that it drags into the revolutionary track everything that it touches. In virtue of this idea, socialism remains ever young; all attempts to bring social peace seem childish."[3] At first sight, this seems like putting the cart before the horse, the concept of the general strike being the result, rather than the cause, of social conflict and revolutionary temper. In so far as ideas, once formulated, have a life of their own, it must nevertheless have helped to perpetuate that situation.

Pareto pointed out that while the myth could be a dynamic force in society, in so far as it was rationalisation it had little power to change the course of human action. Man was essentially a logical creature in that he wanted to know why he should move in a particular direction. And so a person who was moved by instinct, interest or other pressures, exercised his imagination and hitched his waggon to the star of an imaginary goal. The latter acquired a force of its own; it became a 'sentiment' which helped to drive him along the original course. It also exerted an influence on other people who found the sentiment ready-made in the society to which they belonged. On the other hand, in so far as the imaginary goal was a mere explanation, it satisfied the human desire for logical, or pseudo-logical, justification but could do little or nothing in the way of determining conduct.[4] In other words, the direction of the labour movement was determined by social and economic pressures. The general strike was a

[1] Pouget in *Mouvement Socialiste*, June/July 1904, p. 174.
[2] Griffuelhes in *Bataille Syndicaliste*, 28 May 1911.
[3] G. Sorel, *Reflections on Violence*, 1916, p. 145.
[4] V. Pareto, *Mind and Society*, 1935, section 1871.

Principles and practice of the C.G.T.

'pseudo-logical rationalisation', determined by the course the workers were already following, assuring them that they were moving in the right direction, probably encouraging them to move further than they would otherwise have done.

Basically, then, the general strike assured the syndicalists that they were in fact heading towards the final emancipation of the proletariat, this being vital to their peace of mind from a theoretical point of view, even if it was often irrelevant in practice. Whether one thinks of it as an intuitive myth, a rational utopia or a bewitching slogan, this is at least a plausible explanation of the central doctrine of revolutionary syndicalism. French politics were often less pragmatic than British, but not overwhelmingly so. While the English admitted with pride to muddling through, however, and often chose to do without system or principles, the French preferred to fit their actions into a coherent body of doctrine and to explain them by reference to theory. At the turn of the century a socialist theory, to be complete, required the final emancipation of the proletariat. The general strike justified the tactics of the *C.G.T.* by explaining how they fitted into a wider strategy. Those tactics enabled the movement to fight the battles that had to be fought. As the final battle never came, the strategy was never tested.

The epitaph on the general strike, remarkably enough, could also be found in Sorel: "We know that these social myths in no way prevent a man profiting from the observations which he makes in the course of his life and form no obstacle to the pursuit of his normal occupations."[1]

[1] G. Sorel, *Reflections on Violence*, 1916, p. 134.

Organised labour and the syndicalist utopia

The discussion so far has centred round the strategy of syndicalism. The aim, the emancipation of the proletariat, was seen in terms of the destruction of the capitalist system. This, however, was only the negative aspect of the social revolution; the positive side, the final goal, was the new society that would take its place. It is with this syndicalist 'utopia' that the present chapter is concerned. Not surprisingly, perhaps, this vision played only a small part in the practice of the *C.G.T.* More surprisingly, it played an equally small part in syndicalist theory.

DESTRUCTION AND RECONSTRUCTION. The future was a subject in which the militants showed relatively little interest. When they treated it, it was with great discretion. In earlier days, when the possibilities of action were limited and there was not much alternative to speculation, this self-imposed restraint reflected an optimistic faith that verged on naïvety. They simply assumed that capitalism and the state were the twin sources of all evil: once these distortions of human life were destroyed, a natural harmony would assert itself; peace and freedom would reign of their own accord. To plan for the future was thus unnecessary. 'Only destroy and the future will look after itself!' This nihilist doctrine was common to Bakunin and Blanqui, even, in a sense, to Marx, and part of the revolutionary tradition of the country. For the anarchists and syndicalists, however—and in that sense they differed from Blanqui and from Marx—there was to be no dictatorship of the proletariat, no period of central control, preceding the withering away of the state. A free society could only develop freely and that meant spontaneously. Blueprint utopias, imposed on the workers by some future revolutionary government, would merely involve the reintroduction of the state in another form. In any case, there were more important things to do than talk about the future; there was the revolution to be prepared. Planning would only dissipate energy better spent on the task in hand.

In later years, as the reformist element overshadowed the revolutionary, the cause of this discretion changed somewhat. After 1902 the syndicalists were immersed in the everyday struggle, their real hopes were pinned more on immediate gains than on final emancipation. The latter probably became something of a slogan, symbolising the ultimate victory of the proletariat but empty of positive content. Indeed, it is reasonable to assume that the negative aspect of emancipation was at all times more important than

165

the positive. What mattered to the workers emotionally was to escape from capitalist oppression; the life thereafter stood in no direct relationship to their own lives and left them relatively indifferent. From a slightly different point of view, it can be argued that the syndicalist movement was the expression of a revolutionary spirit that was itself primarily destructive: it was a revolt against something (i.e. capitalist economy, bourgeois society, parliamentary democracy) rather than a revolt for something (i.e. a better society).

There was, however, another strand to the revolutionary tradition of France, that of utopian socialism. When all qualifications have been made, the syndicalist movement undoubtedly produced its own utopian vision of a socialist society, however blurred and unanalysed it may have been in the minds of the majority. In 1902 the *C.G.T.* published the answers received from member unions to the question: "In your opinion, what form will the organisation of society take immediately after the Revolution?" This report, edited by Bourchet, was perhaps the only clearly syndicalist statement of ideas about the future. In its optimism, the picture was very close to that of the earlier anarchist tradition. It was, one could say, an anarchist society seen through working-class eyes and reorganised to suit workers' interests. The workers projected their own experience into the future; the economic order they visualised was that already familiar to them in the trade-union movement. The syndicalist utopia was, in fact, the *C.G.T.* writ large. One may argue whether Proudhon was a utopian socialist or not. He had a clear picture of how society was to be reorganised, but this reorganisation was to take place in the present as much as in the future. The syndicalists, marked by Proudhon as well as the anarchists, had the same idea.

THE CHARACTER OF LABOUR ORGANISATIONS. At this point, therefore, it is necessary to look again at the nature of the French trade unions and the structure of the movement. The *syndicat* was the unit on which all else was built. It was small enough for all its members to meet regularly, to get to know one another, to discuss questions of mutual concern and thus to reach decisions which either reflected the 'sense' of the union or to which all felt bound by ties of personal loyalty. It was also a homogeneous group, bringing together men of common background, common skills and common interest. They spoke the same language, that of their locality as well as of their trade. Their interests were sufficiently similar, the area small enough, for them to have a genuine overview of all matters with which the *syndicat* was directly concerned. In all these senses it was a cell; it had, ideally at least, the makings of a genuinely integrated organ of self-government.

Syndicalists often claimed that their unions represented a more demo-

The syndicalist utopia

cratic (i.e. direct) form of government than the parliamentary system (whether applied to central or local government). Real power lay with the members, not with elected representatives or permanent officials. Direct democracy, decisions taken by a general meeting, was possible in many cases. Officials and representatives could be controlled quite easily through everyday personal contact and because their functions were limited to matters understood by the rank and file. The fact that they were only part-time leaders was equally important. The syndicalist official, unlike the politician, did not belong to a distinct caste, not even to a separate profession; he enjoyed no special privileges and acquired no higher status. Reviewing Michel's *Political Parties*, Lagardelle claimed, therefore, that the iron law of oligarchy could not be transferred from the field of politics to the syndicalist movement.[1] This belief was the basis of a sharp syndicalist distinction between trade-union and parliamentary-political forms of organisation. On the one hand, the *administrateur*; on the other, the *gouvernant*. Pouget amplified this distinction in the *Voix du Peuple*: while the politician had a blank-cheque mandate to legislate on whatever subject and in whatever fashion he fancied, the union secretary was a temporary delegate, charged with the execution of specified and limited tasks in a field with which he was directly acquainted and in which there could be no conflict of interests.[2]

The *syndicat*, basis of the labour movement, was seen also as the basis of the new society. This idea was constantly repeated, from Tolain's pamphlet of 1863[3] down to the 1906 Charter of Amiens. It accorded well with the doctrine that the administration of things would replace the government of men after the revolution. It arose, more practically, from the hostility of the workers to the bourgeois-dominated parliamentary system and their desire to establish their own comprehensive institutions. Above all, perhaps, it was a simple projection of the familiar present into the unknown future: if the workers had to plan, they planned on the basis of what they knew.

The federations united the *syndicats* of the same trade or industry on a national basis. The *syndicats* remained autonomous, however, and the main task of the federations was to co-ordinate. Federal decisions had often to be taken by mandated delegates or *ad referendum*; the danger of remote control or a shift of power to career leaders was thus lessened. The *Bourses* were equally democratic. Their local character was important and, in a sense, they too were natural 'cells'. In them, the worker recognised himself as not only a builder, baker or railwayman, but as a member of the working class. It was true that the immediate advantage—and the immediate cause

---

[1] Lagardelle in *Mouvement Socialiste*, July/August 1912, p. 136.
[2] *Voix du Peuple*, No. 21, 1903.
[3] H. Tolain, *Quelques vérités sur les élections de Paris*, 1893.

—of this unity lay in the organisation of sympathy strikes and strike funds. Projected into the future, however, it was not difficult to see that the *Bourse* might replace the *Hôtel de Ville* as the centre of communal life. Just as the *syndicats* and federations were the natural organs for the administration of industry, so the *Bourses*, bringing together all the producers of the area, were the natural organs for the administration of communal affairs. The importance they attached to education has already been mentioned. Their wider, long-term citizenship function was an important part of the syndicalist programme for the new society.

Finally, the Confederation. It has been described as a committee for the discussion and co-ordination of common problems. Its powers, in theory at least, were strictly limited: the autonomy of its constituent parts was guaranteed; the *syndicat* was confirmed as the basic unit of the movement by the equality of voting rights. The whole was founded on a pluralist, organic theory of workers' organisations. The *syndicat*, based on direct government, was the cell of the labour movement; co-ordination at the level of an industry or trade was achieved by the federation, local co-ordination by the *Bourse*, the whole linked by the Confederation. One need merely replace the words 'labour movement' by the word 'society' to have the framework of the syndicalist utopia.

THE BLUEPRINT FOR THE FUTURE. The syndicalist revolution would bring the overthrow of the state and all its institutions: government, civil service, police, army, law—all would be swept away. The expropriators would be expropriated—an end to the capitalist economy, private enterprise and private property. But society would hardly notice their absence. The administration of things would replace the government of men and the limited tasks of administration would be performed competently by the already existing organs of the labour movement. The *syndicat* would replace the employer and the workers would organise production in their workshops. The federations would be responsible for technical co-ordination within their industries and would run such national undertakings as the railways or the postal service. The *Bourses* would replace the town hall in communal affairs and would at the same time become centres for the distribution and exchange of goods. The Confederation, finally, largely in the shape of a statistical bureau, would be the nearest approach to a central administration. The new order merely required the extension of existing institutions to cover the whole society. The basic slogan was simple: 'The workshop will replace the government'.

The character of this new society was expressed in another such slogan: 'The free worker in the free workshop'. Bourchet presented a picture of

The syndicalist utopia

paradise regained in his report to the 1902 congress on the organisation of society the morning after the general strike. Drudgery and discipline vanish overnight. The worker chooses the occupation that suits him and a workplace where he finds sympathetic colleagues. There are no rules to bind him. He is free to come and go as he pleases. Working time is agreeably lightened by conversation. The workshop, rebuilt, is attractive. Work itself becomes a joyful act of creation and as a result the worker gives freely of his strength and ideas, seeking to produce fast and well. But he does not have to do this in the sweat of his brows. Technical progress and fairer distribution enable him to fulfil the needs of society in three hours of work a day. If production presents no difficulties, nor does organisation. The worker is quite capable of running his own factory. A few statistical centres will solve all questions of planning and exchange: a bulletin of materials required and surplus products available will be prepared at the *Bourse* and circulated throughout the country. This distribution need cause no headaches either. The twin limitations, wages and prices, are replaced by the last of the slogans: 'The theory of value is abolished'.

The free worker will replace the employer.
The free workshop will replace the government.
The administration of things will replace the governing of men.
Mutual aid will replace the market economy.
From each according to his ability, to each according to his need.
In place of the state, free associations freely federated.

A theory of syndicalism

Syndicalism was a movement rather than a theory. It was a general trend within the French labour movement, a range of ideas rather than an agreed body of doctrine. Primarily, indeed, it was a way of looking at politics, a temper which was expressed in action, rather than in clearly formulated ideas. The *C.G.T.* adopted a number of principles, never a philosophy. Nor did its theorists produce a really unified body of thought. They wrote for the worker rather than the social philosopher. They dealt with issues of the moment. Their ideas were scattered in newspapers, pamphlets and speeches. Nowhere did they attempt to bring these ideas together within the covers of a single book. It would have been difficult for them to do so. Their views changed; they did not always agree. Even at the level of the printed word, therefore, no integrated system of ideas, certainly no definitive philosophy, was produced by the syndicalists themselves.

It is nevertheless possible to deduce a theory of syndicalism from the ideas and practices of the labour movement and from the statements of its leaders. Was such a theory implicit, merely waiting to be disengaged by the student, or is it an independent construction? Probably the truth lies between the two. The syndicalists, certainly the militants, clearly had an overall picture of ends and means; however scattered and fragmentary their pronouncements, these appeared to them as different aspects of their own 'philosophy' and fitted in their minds into some sort of picture. It has been said, however, that to analyse is to destroy. If that is so, to force syndicalist ideas into a system means not only describing something that never existed in that form but distorting what actually did exist. Systematisation is necessary for coherent discussion even at the risk of some artificiality.

THE CLASS WAR. At the root of syndicalist theory lies the idea of the class war. Society is divided into two naturally antagonistic groups, capital and labour, bourgeoisie and proletariat, between whom a constant struggle is necessarily waged. The terminology is marxist but the concept shorn of its theoretical foundations and reduced to a simple slogan: exploiters and exploited, oppressors and oppressed. The class war is taken as an obvious fact, a fact experienced every day by the workers and not a theory in need of proof.

No legislative reforms, however well meaning, no agreements with he most benevolent of employers, can free the workers from the dual yoke of exploitation and oppression. Only the complete overthrow of the existing social, economic and political order, the abolition of property and the destruction of the state, can bring the final emancipation of the proletariat.

The syndicalists ignored dialectical materialism with its prophecy of the automatic intensification of conflict, the inevitable revolution and the predestined victory of the proletariat, all due to the forces of history itself. They saw the conflict between capital and labour as a war like any other. Though they, too, were sure of victory, when it came it would not be the gift of impersonal forces but the result of their own efforts.

The spread of democratic ideas, while not appreciably lessening the exploitation of the workers, may weaken the class struggle. If the war is to be won, it must be fought; and if it is to be fought, its existence must be constantly reaffirmed. It was Ramsay MacDonald who said that while others had played with the idea of class war like a child plays with a tin sword, only the syndicalists had constructed from it the appropriate and logical theory of action. To be effective, it required a complete breach between the two classes, a breach carried into all fields of life. The proletariat must not only oppose the bourgeoisie at all points, it must isolate itself from bourgeois society and the bourgeois state.

In order that the division of society into two great hostile camps may be clearly seen by all, any overlapping between the classes must be prevented. Syndicalism must remain an exclusively proletarian movement: bourgeois supporters only blur and confuse the issue. Moreover, as the basis of the class war is the conflict between employers and workers, only workers have a natural interest in the overthrow of the existing order. Parlour socialists and socialist intellectuals have at best an abstract, therefore superficial, interest; in practice they show a strong tendency to fraternise with the class enemy, to compromise and thus betray the workers. To maintain its revolutionary spirit, the movement must restrict itself to those bound by ties of common exploitation; it must organise itself entirely within its own class.

The proletariat must carefully guard its identity for another reason. If it is to create a new society based on producers' interests, it must not allow its own values and institutions to be influenced by socialists whose bourgeois background necessarily gives them a different ideal.

THE REJECTION OF POLITICS. Political parties, even when they claim to represent the interests of the working class, by their very nature deny the class struggle. Party membership cuts across class barriers; parties draw on persons of different social background, even different economic interest. Socialist parties tend to be dominated by intellectuals and professional politicans. The basis of party is ideological. It depends on transient and superficial agreement on matters of philosophy. Unlike the class, it is an artificial form of organisation; without the bond of direct economic interest, it lacks true solidarity. Its first aim, moreover, is to attract voters; programmes are inevitably watered down to widen its appeal. It tends, therefore, to lose whatever revolutionary character it may originally have possessed.

Political action leads to the same sort of confusion. The party appeals to the worker for support at times of election, that is to say in his role as citizen which he shares with other classes. Its activities take place on the terrain common to all parties and all classes, in parliament. It tends to associate, rather than differentiate, the proletariat and the bourgeoisie.

Democracy itself contradicts the idea of the class war. Its essential characteristic is agreement, if only agreement to differ. To participate in a democratic system, even under the banner of a revolutionary programme, means to collaborate with the bourgeoisie and is an implied recognition of the existing political order.

In any case, the proletariat did not form a majority of the electorate in France at the turn of the century. The socialist party must therefore make electoral agreements: the class enemy becomes the friend of the polls. The same thing necessarily occurs in parliament. The socialists' only hope of ministerial office lay in collaboration with bourgeois parties. Policy degenerates into bargaining, concessions and ultimately a betrayal of the working class. The parliamentary *milieu* is itself bourgeois and thus a further corrupting influence.

Whatever benefits may be gained for the working class as a result of compromise, they cannot compensate for its dangers. Democracy is a system designed by the bourgeoisie for bourgeois domination. It is a façade to hide the real nature of social conflict; its ideology—universal franchise, equality before the law—distracts from the real economic inequality that it protects. The parliamentary game is, in the last analysis, but a means of diverting the energy of the proletariat into harmless channels.

Social legislation is part of this attempt to stifle the class war. Reforms do not alter the fundamental property relations and concede nothing of real importance. They do, however, undermine the class struggle by creating an impression of benevolence and social harmony. They are the crumbs the rich man throws from his table to satisfy the hunger of a proletariat that would otherwise be driven to revolt. Genuine concessions are never achieved through parliamentary action but only through the direct action of the workers themselves.

Syndicalists did not merely oppose the parliamentary system, they opposed the state as such. They followed Marx in calling it the instrument of capitalist domination, the executive committee of the ruling class. They denied, however, that it could be used by the revolutionaries for its own destruction.

Here they took up the anarchist line of argument. A change in government is merely a change of rulers, the substitution of one executive committee for another. The dictatorship of the proletariat is not likely to differ in practice from any other form of dictatorship. Power corrupts and the state will not wither away of its own accord. Freedom, in any case, cannot be established by decree from above. The state exists for the government of men, the new society will be based on the administration of things and there is no connection between the two. A *coup d'état* is therefore no better than the parliamentary conquest of power. The state must be overthrown in its entirety and replaced by a quite different system.

THE ROLE OF THE UNIONS. In place of the party, syndicalists put the trade union. This is the autonomous organisation of the working class. It is wholly proletarian in character and excludes mere sympathisers. At the same time, it unites the workers not on the base of some ideology or sentiment but in their very quality as workers.

The union clearly differentiates the working class from the bourgeoisie, emphasising simultaneously its proletarian and its non-political character. Disregarding questions of philosophy in this fashion, it unites the workers on the basis of inescapable common economic interest. Members joining a union are not asked to subscribe to any specific political programme; they simply enter a relationship with their fellows that is forced on them by the class struggle itself. While the party is an association of choice, the union is an association of necessity. Therein lies its strength.

The *raison d'être* of the union is the organisation of workers against employers. It thus stands at the very point where the class struggle arises, organising the worker at the moment he separates himself from all other classes and takes up the struggle directly against the class enemy.

In place of the state, the syndicalist also puts the union. Just as parliament is the natural expression of bourgeois society, so the union (with horizontal and vertical federations) is the natural form of organisation in a proletarian society.

The union therefore links the present with the future. It organises the worker in his everyday struggle against the employer, obtaining thereby material concessions of immediate value, and it prepares him for the coming revolution. It is at once destructive and constructive, battle formation and cell of the new order. For this reason syndicalists declared that their movement was self-sufficient and that their organisations fulfilled all needs. The capitalist society carries within itself the means by which it will be over-thrown as well as the skeleton of the new order that will replace it: the seeds of its own destruction are at the same time the seeds of the new society. Every action that strengthens the union is a step in this direction.

DIRECT INDUSTRIAL ACTION. The emancipation of the proletariat can-not be achieved by political means but only by the workers themselves, through their own efforts. This is the doctrine of direct action. The syn-dicalists interpreted the marxist formula that the emancipation of the workers must be the act of the workers themselves to mean that it must be achieved by the workers acting as workers and without intermediaries. Just as the union is the proper form of organisation for the proletariat, so the industrial sphere is its proper field of action.

The syndicalists advocated various forms of industrial action, such as boycott and sabotage. Agitation, and even pressure on parliament were also employed, though not entirely industrial in character and only direct in half the sense of the word. The strike, however, is direct economic action *par excellence* and as such dominated the strategy of the movement. It is the clearest possible expression of the class war, placing the workers in an im-mediate conflict with the employers and illuminating sharply the deep antagonism between capital and labour.

The worker can no longer hope to achieve anything by direct political action (i.e. insurrection) because the bourgeoisie controls the armed forces of the state. The strike is the most effective weapon available to him. It has the advantage of involving the immediate and inescapable interests of the working class. It mobilises energies that political issues fail to arouse. It draws even the apathetic into a movement that can be turned to revolu-tionary ends by the militant leadership.

The strike fulfils a double function. Like the union, it has a reformist and a revolutionary aspect. Even if intended only to obtain some immediate concession from the employers, such as a wage increase, it furthers the cause of revolution at the same time. If it is successful, the concession gained is more than an immediate benefit: it is a partial expropriation of the expropriators, a blow directed at the capitalist system, a weakening of the power of the bourgeoisie. At the same time, every strike—whether suc-cessful or not—increases the hostility between the classes and thereby further stimulates the conflict. It encourages a feeling of solidarity; it strengthens revolutionary *élan*; it is a training ground for greater battles yet to come. It is in the use of the possibilities of the ordinary strike that the strength of the syndicalist programme lay.

The climax of a long series of such strikes, growing ever larger and more widespread, becoming better organised and at the same time more bitter, will be the general strike. The general strike will finally overthrow the capitalist system, emancipate the proletariat and usher in the new society. The concept of the general strike completed the syndicalist theory. Capitalism will never voluntarily surrender its power and privilege. It is therefore the corner-stone on which all else must ultimately rest, for it alone can bring the class war to a victorious conclusion.

The general strike is closely linked to the ordinary everyday strike. The revolution will not come out of the clouds but will be the outcome of the continuous intensification of the struggle of the workers against the bourgeoisie. It is the last link in a long chain: it follows a process of partial expropriation on the one hand and, what is more important, a process of military training on the other. Although it may involve more workers, lead to more violence and last longer than previous strikes, it will not differ essentially from them.

THE NEW SOCIETY. Emancipation was essentially a synonym for the destruction of the capitalist system and the bourgeois state. Syndicalism was above all a strategy of action to achieve this end. Capitalism and the state are the twin sources of all evil; once abolished, a natural harmony will assert itself. Syndicalism tended to maintain a voluntary discretion about the society that would emerge after the revolution. It could not be organised from above but would grow spontaneously out of the labour movement. Utopias therefore played only a small part in syndicalist thought. In so far as they considered the future, it was an anarchist society seen through working class eyes and reorganised to suit working class interests. The workers would run the factories, the trade unions organise production and exchange.

The syndicalist programme of action was thus remarkably homogeneous. The strike, natural form of everyday conflict, is also the form of revolution. The revolution itself would not be a once-for-all affair in the distant future. Every strike is a partial revolution and a step towards the final conflict. The unity achieved between ends and means was equally remarkable. While the class war is being fought, the future is being created. Final emancipation will not create something entirely new but merely allow an order already in existence to take over. The union, natural formation of battle, is also the natural cell of the new society. There is no major problem of transition to be faced. Syndicalism meant that the labour movement was sufficient unto itself.

Conflicting voices in the C.G.T.

The tendency has been to speak of the French labour movement during the first decade of this century as syndicalist. Syndicalist attitudes appeared to dominate, giving the period its special character. How far did this appearance reflect reality? How syndicalist was the movement in fact? Syndicalism was a revolutionary doctrine and as such bound to attract attention. Its militant theorists were heard louder than other trade-union leaders. It was easy at the time, and is still easier at a distance, to identify syndicalism with the entire labour movement. If one looks more closely, however, placing the syndicalists in perspective, the picture is rather different.

If syndicalism is defined as the principles and practice of the *C.G.T.*, the first point to note is that the *C.G.T.* itself represented only a small proportion of the working class. In 1906 France had a population of over 40,000,000; there were over 12,000,000 wage and salary earners; 836,000 were organised in some form of union; the *C.G.T.* had a nominal membership of 300,000 and a paid-up membership of 200,000. Even in its heroic age, therefore, it represented little more than a tenth of the proletariat, and that included a fair number of transient members and other passengers. It is true that its influence was much wider than such numbers indicate, that in a real sense it spoke for the labour movement as a whole. It was nevertheless a minority. On the whole, it probably organised the militants, the more active workers or those with the strongest opinions; its membership was not a typical cross-section of the working class.

If syndicalism is expressed in the principles adopted by the *C.G.T.*, another question arises. How representative were its congresses? The system of representation (one *syndicat*, one delegate, regardless of size) and the failure of many *syndicats* to send delegates at all, must be taken into account. One cannot be certain how far individual delegates, who might represent as many as ten *syndicats*, really expressed the ideas of rank and file. Congress resolutions may thus have represented a minority even of *C.G.T.* members. The *C.G.T.* was certainly not united on questions of doctrine, even on immediate policy. There were other trends beside the revolutionary syndicalist and even if they were in the minority, which is by no means clear, they expressed strong currents of opinion. The movement did not speak with one voice; its principles and practice were not uniformly syndicalist.

THE SYNDICALIST MAJORITY. Less than half the *syndicats* adhering to the *C.G.T.* were represented at its congresses. Some were 'limpers', excluded because they were affiliated to only one of the Confederation's two sections; many more simply abstained:

1902	1,043 syndicats	458 represented
1906	2,399 syndicats	1,040 represented
1912	2,837 syndicats	1,292 represented.

Did the absent unions share the outlook of those present? Some were probably too poor or too small to send delegates, though this problem could be overcome by giving a mandate to the delegate of another union or to a resident in the town where the congress was held. They may also have been more apathetic, less interested in the wider aims of the movement. The congresses tended to bring together the militant sections of the *C.G.T.*, staunch anti-syndicalists as well as syndicalists. If the views of the passive unions had been taken into account, the general direction, though remaining antipolitical, might well have been less revolutionary.

Some delegates were given definite, though not constitutionally binding, instructions on important matters such as relations with the socialist party. On the other hand, they were probably more militant, in whatever direction, than the rank and file. Something of a permanent nucleus of delegates emerged, many representing several *syndicats*: the number of participants never rose much above 400. The same names appeared year after year and they were the names of union leaders, speakers, writers and organisers. A delegate may well have been chosen because he was active in union affairs rather than for his opinions. He was likely to be a union official, enjoying some independence despite syndicalist theory, or a persuasive orator to whom the more apathetic willingly resigned this task. The delegates were the militants of the movement; their views did not necessarily reflect those of the members they represented.

The system of representation employed by the *C.G.T.* undoubtedly introduced major distortions. Obviously the vote of a single delegate tells nothing about the division of opinion within his *syndicat*; it tells even less when, in some cases, he cast his vote on behalf of ten *syndicats*. The real issue, however, arose from the fact that each *syndicat* had an equal vote at the congress, each federation an equal seat on the council. It was thus possible for the smaller *syndicats* and federations to outvote the larger on any issue. The opponents of syndicalism claimed that this was happening all the time. For that reason, indeed, the question of proportional representation became inextricably linked with the conflict of tendencies within the Confederation.

The disparity between size and voting power is clear enough when one considers the *C.G.T.*'s confederal council. The number of federations and national *syndicats* entitled to representation was 30 in 1902, 61 in 1906 and 53 in 1912. These numbers included a few large federations (e.g. railway-men, printers, builders, metal-workers, miners and clerical workers) and a host of very small ones, often with a total membership below 1,000. While the railwaymen had over 50,000 members, the laundrymen had only 80 and the apprentice pharmacists under 50. Less than ten federations probably accounted for three-quarters of the total membership. These large federations appear to have been evenly divided between supporters and opponents of syndicalism. The builders and metal-workers were revolutionary; the railwaymen, printers and clerical workers were reformist; the miners supported the socialist party. The small federations, on the other hand, were generally on the side of revolution. Their disproportionate influence, however, was not only due to their voting power; they were often the most active elements in *C.G.T.* campaigns (e.g. barbers and foodstuff-workers).

The effect of the equality rule at congresses is much harder to judge. However large or small a federation might be, the size of the *syndicats* which composed it tended to be round the 100/200 mark. There were exceptions, some relatively large *syndicats* which were clearly under-represented. The opponents of syndicalism always maintained that syndicalist principles were adopted by the *C.G.T.* only because of its voting procedure, which was rigged so that decisions represented only a minority opinion. There was some truth in this argument. This can be seen by analysing the vote for antimilitarism at the 1908 congress:[1]

> For: 670 *syndicats* with 114,000 members
> Against: 406 *syndicats* with 127,000 members.

It is reasonable to assume that the smaller *syndicats* were mainly revolutionary in outlook: smallness probably meant that only the more militant workers had bothered to join or that it was established by a small group of militants in an area of trade-union apathy. This seemed particularly true of the rural *syndicats*. In 1904, for example, the thirty delegates of the agricultural workers of the Midi and the forty wood-cutters all belonged to the revolutionary wing. But it is impossible even to estimate the number of revolutionary syndicalists in the *C.G.T.*

RIVAL DIRECTIONS. The syndicalists always faced strong opposition within the *C.G.T.* It was unity of organisation that was achieved in 1902 at Montpellier, not unity of outlook. Many of the large federations adopted policies radically opposed to those of the *C.G.T.* 'majority' and there was no way of making them toe the party line. All shades of opinion were

[1] Cf. C. Franck, *Les Bourses du Travail et la C.G.T.*, 1910, p. 345.

represented on the confederal council. An even more confusing picture emerges from the study of congress debates: the opinions expressed ranged widely. In 1902 the *C.G.T.* was under the control of the syndicalists. They were led by Griffuelhes (general secretary), Pouget (assistant secretary responsible for the section of federations and editor of the *C.G.T.* paper), Yvetot (secretary responsible for the section of *Bourses*) and Delesalle (assistant secretary for that section and secretary of the committee for the general strike). Their opponents were united only in their opposition to the doctrines of direct action and the general strike and to the anarchist tendencies of the leaders. They ranged from moderate reformists to politically-minded revolutionaries. At the Amiens congress, in order to simplify the debate and to give all parties an equal opportunity to present their case, it was agreed that time should be divided between three main currents of thought: the revolutionary (i.e. syndicalist), the political (on the whole marxist, but including supporters of other parties) and the reformist.

The reformists were led by the veteran Keufer, secretary of the printers' federation from 1884 to 1920. They were as staunch supporters of labour autonomy *vis-à-vis* the socialist parties as were the syndicalists themselves; Keufer, indeed, was one of the first to oppose the parliamentarisation of the movement as far back as 1880. Instead of direct action, however, they advocated negotiations with the employers, seeking where necessary, though without political alliances, the intervention of the state. By 1902 this line was a little old-fashioned, though it did not disappear. More important were the advocates of close alliance between the *C.G.T.* and the socialist parties, led by Renard, secretary of the textile federation. This wing was particularly strong among the miners and textile-workers of the north, where local party organisations had managed to retain their association with the unions.

The congress of 1902 had been dominated by questions of organisation. At Bourges, in 1904, however, the differences of outlook made themselves felt. The attack was led by Keufer, supported by 128 printers' *syndicats* (the figure itself was a measure of their feeling: two years earlier only thirty *syndicats* had been represented). His first complaint was that the council had failed to observe the principle of political neutrality: the antipolitical propaganda it organised was as one-sided and political as that of the party. He also denounced its policy of violence: reprisals would leave the workers the real victims. The answer was given by a delegate of the rival compositors' union who accused the printers of themselves failing to observe the statutes of the *C.G.T.* by preaching social peace. The council's report was then approved by 812 votes to 361. A motion to introduce proportional representation was defeated by the same majority. This, in the words of its own official history, was decisive for the future orientation of the *C.G.T.*[1] At Amiens in 1906 the council's report was adopted by an even larger majority: 781 to 115. The subsequent debate hinged on the question of the *C.G.T.*'s relationship with the newly unified socialist party. The centre of opposition had shifted and the attack was led by Renard. His motion, calling for close collaboration, obtained no more than 34 votes against 774. In view of this, a motion tabled by Keufer, calling for strict political neutrality within the *C.G.T.* and parallel parliamentary action outside, was not even put to the vote. The official resolution, afterwards called the Charter of Amiens, was then adopted. It appeared to settle the dispute between the politicals and the antipoliticals: it affirmed the neutrality of the *C.G.T.* and its affiliated organisations; it allowed members to take part in whatever political activities they wished as individuals; it recognised the right of the parties to pursue their task outside and parallel to the *C.G.T.* Often described as the charter of revolutionary syndicalism, the wording was actually a compromise. The reformist could accept it as a guarantee against militant anarchism, not unfavourable to Keufer's support of parallel action. The socialist could read into it a recognition that his party had a contribution to make to the joint cause and the right of informal co-operation. The syndicalist, finally, could regard it as a statement of his own principles: the autonomy of labour, direct action and the general strike. The near unanimity of the vote—830 to 8, with 1 abstention—indicates that it was all things to all men. This was shown by the relatively small majority (488 to 310) obtained for a motion on antimilitarist and anti-patriotic propaganda. What the Charter did, however, was to place leadership firmly in syndicalist hands.

At Marseilles in 1908 Renard strongly attacked the revolutionary policy of the leaders, blaming them for the bloodshed and defeats of the preceding years; the workers, he declared, were at the mercy of a few lunatics. The report of the council was nevertheless again approved by a large majority though some of the vote may have been cast in sympathy with the leaders, then in prison, rather than in agreement with their policy. Yvetot's motion on antimilitarist and antipatriotic propaganda, which had hardly been discussed at the previous congress because of pressure of time, aroused the most heated debate and produced violent recriminations. His demand that the workers should answer any declarations of war by a general strike was accepted by only 681 votes against 423, with 43 abstentions.

The conflicts grew more bitter as time went on. The hold of the syndicalist leaders was weakened, first by their arrest, then by personal accusations.

[1] C.G.T., *La C.G.T. et le mouvement syndical*, 1925, p. 92.

Conflicting voices

Some irregularities in the administration of the new *C.G.T.* headquarters were made the excuse for vicious attacks in which personal rivalries mingled inextricably with political differences. In 1909 Griffuelhes, Pouget and the treasurer, Lévy, all resigned. The reformists succeeded in electing Niel, a conciliator, as general secretary by a majority of one in the confederal council. A syndicalist and a reformist were elected as assistant secretaries for the federations and the *Bourses* (Yvetot remained at the head of the latter section); another syndicalist became treasurer. Niel's failure to cope with the postal strike of the following year gave his opponents an opportunity to force him out again, manoeuvres about which he complained. He was replaced by Jouhaux, a close collaborator of Griffuelhes, at the time a supporter of the revolutionary wing. The domination of the syndicalists was largely reestablished.

As the bitterness of the conflict grew, so it became more personal. The papers of the time were full of acrimonious, often personally insulting polemics. The *C.G.T.*'s official *Voix du Peuple* devoted almost as much space to attacks on Renard and those who wished to co-operate with the socialists than to attacks on capitalists or government. The syndicalists also quarrelled amongst themselves. There were frequent disputes between the *Voix du Peuple* (edited by Pouget), the anarchist *Temps Nouveaux* (on which Delesalle was an important collaborator) and Hervé's revolutionary antimilitarist *Guerre Sociale* (with contributions by Yvetot). The reformists founded their own fortnightly *Action Ouvrière*.

In 1909 a committee was formed to oppose anarchist (i.e. syndicalist) tendencies within the *C.G.T.* Its first manifesto included the signatures of the reformist Keufer (printers), the socialist Renard (textiles), the marxist Guérard (railwaymen) and the conciliator Niel. The preoccupation with internal differences slowed the *C.G.T.*'s growth, a situation reminiscent of earlier conflicts. There was talk of a crisis of stagnation in the labour movement. In a series of articles contributed to the *Mouvement Socialiste*, the leaders of the different trends blamed one another.[1] Keufer attributed the trouble to the revolutionaries' attack on the reformist federations, Yvetot to the reformists' attack on the leaders of the *C.G.T.* after their arrest in 1908. Merrheim, secretary of the metal workers, also blamed the reformists, though on different grounds: it was not a domestic crisis, he wrote, but a crisis of domestication. Nowhere was there unity of outlook. Every shade of opinion was represented. Some differed on matters of fundamental principle, some only on immediate tactics; some were undecided, some willing to conciliate, some intransigent. The closer one looks at the French labour movement, the less clear is the voice with which it spoke.

[1] *Mouvement Socialiste*, various articles, 1909 to 1911.

Leaders and followers, theory and practice

The previous chapter asked how many syndicalists there were in the French labour movement as a whole and, more specifically, in the *C.G.T.* To complete this perspective, two other points must be considered. Key positions in the *C.G.T.* were occupied by a small number of militant syndicalists who were able to exert considerable influence on the formulation of policy. To a certain extent they may have imposed their own ideas upon a relatively passive, itself by no means so revolutionary-minded, rank and file. How far was syndicalism really the creation of these few leaders? There is also the problem of the relationship between theory and practice. It was not unusual, perhaps, for Frenchmen to separate the two. It is sometimes hard to assess, therefore, how far syndicalist principles were intended as serious guides to action and how far they were mere doctrine, ideas for their own sake, propaganda slogans divorced from real life.

THE ROLE OF THE MILITANTS. A few militant syndicalists occupied the key post in the *C.G.T.* during the heroic period of syndicalism: Griffuelhes, Pouget, Yvetot and Delesalle. They were also the theorists of the movement. Between them, they were responsible for most of the pamphlets, and a large share of the articles, in which syndicalist ideas were expressed. Syndicalism has been defined as the principles adopted by the *C.G.T.*—'adopted', not 'formulated'. Most of the important resolutions were drawn up by them. According to Dolléans, they drafted the Amiens Charter in a restaurant.[1] The *C.G.T.* declarations published in the *Voix du Peuple* were, in the nature of things, written by the members of the bureau. Some critics saw them wielding almost dictatorial powers behind the scenes, with Griffuelhes as the organiser and Pouget as the theorist.[2] This did not mean that they had power to direct the labour movement as such (the autonomy of its organisations has been sufficiently stressed), but it was probably their voice that spoke when the *C.G.T.* spoke. It was of course inevitable, in this as in any other movement, that resolutions should be formulated by a small group of leaders. The real question is, whose ideas did they express: their own, those of the majority of delegates or those of the rank and file? Looked at another way, how many of those who apparently accepted syndicalist principles were consciously committed to

---

[1] E. Dolléans, *Histoire du mouvement ouvrier*, 1936–9, vol. 2, p. 136.
[2] Cf. M. Leclercq and E. Girod de Fléaux, *Ces messieurs de la C.G.T.*, 1908, p. 81.

syndicalist ideas, how many followed the militants without really making those ideas their own?

Congress delegates were chosen from the more active sections of the membership and thus not truly representative. They were usually union officials. The same names occurred again and again. There was a relatively small, fairly permanent core of militants. How small the number of those actively interested in syndicalism may have been is shown by the circulation figures of the *Voix du Peuple*. Despite the fact that it was the official organ of the *C.G.T.*, it never managed to sell much more than 6,000 copies (and a third of these must have gone to the *syndicats* who were bound to subscribe according to the statutes). The other syndicalist papers, *Action Directe* and *Bataille Syndicaliste*, had an even smaller circulation. The workers clearly found the bourgeois press more entertaining. Pouget himself described his readers as the most active militants, members of union bureaux and councils, adding that it was through them that syndicalist ideas were diffused. A hierarchy can be seen: at the top, the official theorists who wrote for the paper; below, the militant subscribers, mainly officials, capable of understanding and spreading the doctrine; at the bottom, the passive mass of workers.

There were complaints about the apathy of ordinary members, many of whom considered their duty done in normal times if they paid their dues regularly and once in a while elected a secretary or delegate. It was the militants who had to prepare the labour movement for its struggle, who stirred up temporary enthusiasm for revolutionary doctrines and violent action.[1] Dolléans was not far wrong in describing Pouget as the animator of direct action campaigns mounted by the *C.G.T.*[2] Certainly, the work of propaganda and organisation was in the hands of relatively few men, travelling from town to town, making key speeches at local conferences and public meetings, standing behind the more significant strikes. The syndicalists were aware of this state of affairs. They considered themselves an elite whose task it was to lead the masses (the active, class-conscious vanguard of the proletariat, in fact). Pouget was particularly outspoken: the inactive or indifferent, having missed their opportunity, must accept the decisions taken by others.[3] That, indeed, he saw the fundamental between 'democratism' and syndicalism. Democratism, universal suffrage for example, meant rule by the slow and uninspired masses; the syndicalist method was to allow the conscious minority, who carried the future, to act regardless.[4] The contradiction between this view and the claim that syndica-

---

[1] Cf. Petit in *Temps Nouveaux*, 18 August 1906.
[2] E. Dolléans, *Histoire du mouvement ouvrier*, 1936–9, vol. 2, p. 119.
[3] E. Pouget, *La C.G.T.*, 1908.
[4] Pouget in *Mouvement Socialiste*, April 1910, p. 267.

Principles and practice of the C.G.T.

lism was a popular movement, based on truly democratic labour organisations, is only too apparent.

Can one say then that there were only a few revolutionary syndicalists in the labour movement and that the majority which accepted syndicalist principles were either the passive recipients of other men's ideas or the passive followers of other men's leadership? Pouget, who wrote that all action would have been paralyzed if the labour organisations had been democratic,[1] claimed elsewhere that all the members of those very organisations were militants, acting on their own initiative and thinking their own thoughts.[2] Both views can be argued. The leaders played a considerable role in the formulation of policy. But the *C.G.T.* cannot therefore be dismissed as the tool of a few revolutionary leaders, nor can syndicalism be explained as their private creation. Syndicalism lay in the development of the French labour movement. History brought the syndicalist leaders to the fore when the time was ripe for their ideas. History explained the following they obtained. A third statement of Pouget's is relevant: "I can tell the workers to arm themselves, but that is a long way from announcing the revolution; one can no more make a revolution than a cyclone or an earthquake; one can only prepare the play; I have studied social philosophy long enough to avoid the imbecility of thinking one can do more."[3] It was history that explained their ultimate failure.

THE LEVEL OF COMMITMENT. There was a tendency in France to adopt revolutionary slogans as normal figures of speech, often divorced from the realities of action. Syndicalists sometimes accused the socialists of *verbalisme révolutionnaire*. Can this accusation be turned against them also? How deeply were they attached to the principles they advocated: firmly convinced or temporarily enthusiastic? To what extent were even firm principles held on the level of theory but never intended for practice? One must obviously distinguish between the more extreme and the more down-to-earth doctrines. It was in the former that a dichotomy between thought and action was often to be found.

Antimilitarist and antipatriotic resolutions had been voted year after year, almost as a matter of course. The *C.G.T.* was officially committed to the view that, whoever the aggressor, a war between capitalist powers could only harm the proletariat and that any mobilisation should therefore be met by a general strike. In 1914 war was declared and the call-up ordered. No one thought of calling a general strike, of sabotage, or any

[1] Pouget, *Mouvement Socialiste*, November 1904, p. 44.
[2] Pouget, *Mouvement Socialiste*, July 1906, p. 275.
[3] Pouget, *Mouvement Socialiste*, March 1905, p. 373, quoting the American labour agitator August Spies.

184

other opposition to the war effort. The most ardent revolutionaries became overnight as ardent patriots and hastened to arms like any loyal bourgeois. A delegate, discussing this phenomenon at the first post-war congress of the *C.G.T.*, remarked that on the first day of mobilisation one saw so-called revolutionary workers shouting 'To Berlin!'; many syndicalists ran to the front *comme des fous*. At best 1914 showed that the principle of the class war was less deeply ingrained than that of patriotism. Jouhaux, writing later, saw it rather differently: the workers responded to the call to arms with the same *élan* that they had devoted until the last moment to their agitation against war.[1] In other words, they did their best. His use of the word *élan* is significant, however, for it suggests that so long as the militants had a rousing idea to inspire them, they were satisfied; what was needed was a battle cry and whether the enemy was the *boche* or the bourgeoisie was a matter of secondary interest.

Were the revolutionary principles ever seriously intended for practice, or were they *la doctrine*, belonging only to the meeting hall and the editorial office? Syndicalists at times appeared to suffer from the same vice they condemned in socialist intellectuals. They spent much time fighting the battles of doctrine. Merrheim, a member of the *C.G.T.*'s council, was struck by his colleagues' love of theory and complained that this had become the exclusive preoccupation of many militants.[2] The general strike was a seductive idea. Neat, simple and conclusive: Cease work and the bourgeoisie will surrender...a little violence perhaps, but overwhelming numbers are on our side! Who could resist the bewitching formulae? It made plausible the emancipation of the proletariat without the help of despised parliamentarians and without waiting on the slow, inevitable march of history. The orators and editorialists were no doubt convinced, so were their listeners and readers, but when it came to practical affairs the syndicalists were neither so bewitched nor so logical. There was no general strike. The time was never ripe perhaps, but perhaps, in part of their mind, they recognised it as a myth.

At the level of the possible, to pursue the limited aims set at various times, direct action was consistently employed. Even if it never developed further than widespread strikes, manifestations and occasional clashes with the troops, the implications were revolutionary: it was violent action, outside and against the law. Revolutionary in that limited sense, but how much more? Whatever the Paris bourgeoisie may have thought in 1906, there was no serious possibility of overthrowing the government. How many had the serious intention? In any case, despite the reiteration of

---

[1] L. Jouhaux, *La C.G.T.*, 1937, p. 192.
[2] Merrheim in *Mouvement Socialiste*, November/December 1909, p. 292.

Principles and practice of the C.G.T.

revolutionary principles, the *C.G.T.* became more and more reformist in practice. An attempt was made to adapt syndicalist theory to changing practice but a gap remained between the two. In the quiet of their offices and in their everyday work, the syndicalists increasingly saw advantages in co-operation with the state, the politicians and the employers; many compromised, theory notwithstanding.

The strike was another, perhaps the most important aspect of syndicalism. Griffuelhes claimed that one could measure the intensity of the labour movement by its strikes; by their spirit, they indicated the degree of labour activity.[1] The actual figures, however, did not show an upward trend and, to that extent, failed to show an increase in syndicalist strength despite the propaganda efforts that went into the major campaigns of the period:[2]

1902	512 strikes	212,000 strikers	4,675,000 strike days
1904	1,026 strikes	271,000 strikers	3,934,000 strike days
1906	1,309 strikes	438,000 strikers	9,438,000 strike days
1908	1,073 strikes	99,000 strikers	1,752,000 strike days
1910	1,502 strikes	281,000 strikers	4,830,000 strike days.

It should be noted, on the other hand, that Griffuelhes specifically referred to spirit rather than to numbers.

It may be interesting to look at Britain. The following statistics take all the years 1902 to 1910 together:

| France | 9,110 strikes | 1,965,000 strikers | 36,937,000 strike days |
| Britain | 3,703 strikes | 4,018,000 strikers | 38,110,000 strike days. |

Any real comparison would be misleading because of the very different economic and political conditions in the two countries. Some points nevertheless suggest themselves. France had more than twice as many strikes as Britain. The much smaller size of the French *syndicats* is a partial explanation: thus the average number of strikers involved was only 215 in France, compared to 1,080 in Britain. Another explanation, however, is that it was easier for strikes to break out in France: the French workers were relatively strike-prone. This may reflect a higher level of militancy and revolutionary *élan*. It is not surprising that the total number of workers involved should be higher in Britain, considering the higher level of industrialisation there. Surprising, on the other hand, is that the total number of strike days should be so similar for it means that the average duration of strikes was much longer in France than in Britain: nineteen and nine days respectively. In view of the relative poverty of French *syndicats*,

[1] Griffuelhes in *Mouvement Socialiste*, March 1906, p. 249.
[2] Cf. *Internationales Handwörterbuch des Gewerkschaftswesens, 1930–1932*.

Leaders and followers

this may also indicate a relatively high level of militancy on the part of French workers.

It is in the character, rather than the number of strikes, that one is likely to find evidence of revolutionary spirit. Three points may be made. Strikes frequently involved violence, conflict not only with the employer but with the state, leading on occasion to pitched battles with army or police. There was a tendency to generalise strikes, so that they became more than a simple issue between a group of employers and their workmen, shifting towards a wider conflict between capitalists and proletariat. Often it was only a case of concerted strikes within a single industry, or local sympathy strikes, but even this was described by some commentators as a *généralisation révolutionnaire*.[1] In the absence of large strike funds, successes could be attributed to the revolutionary *élan* of the workers. The workers' victories, according to Griffuelhes, could only be explained by the fact that they did not separate their desire for immediate gains from their revolutionary ideals.[2] It is impossible to prove this now. But French strikes of the time were played on a stage with a revolutionary back-drop.

[1] Cf. M. Leroy, *La coutume ouvrière*, 1913, p. 671.
[2] Griffuelhes in *Action Directe*, 23 April 1908, pp. 254–5.

IDEOLOGICAL CONTEXT

The revolt against reason

Julien Benda, in an essay on existentialism, speaks of a permanent philosophical position which exalts life, experience, action, existence, at the
cost of thought and ideas.[1] France is often described as the country of
Reason, but rationalism is only one strand of French thought and the
existentialism of which Benda speaks is a recurrent phenomenon in French
philosophy. Thus Pascal is the companion of Descartes, Rousseau of
Voltaire, Bergson of Comte, Sartre of Maritain. And if France produced
its rational socialists, from Saint-Simon to Jules Guesde, then by Benda's
definition syndicalism belonged to the existentialist camp, to the revolt of
life against reason. It was often no less theoretical for that, but then
Reason, in France, is the delight even of its opponents; anti-intellectuals
are often intellectuals themselves.

This current of thought, loosely described as the revolt against Reason,
became particularly prominent in the first decade of the twentieth century,
when it spilled over from the realm of philosophy to religion, art and
politics. The irrationalist political doctrines of this period can be explained
in terms of the history of ideas; they can also be explained in terms of the
social, political and economic circumstances which, by creating a particular
mood, made popular those philosophies which catered for it. The following
chapters are concerned with both these explanations. They attempt to
place syndicalism first in an ideological context, then in the context of its
own time.

The existentialist position has no real genealogy; it represents no clear
line of thinkers, no unbroken development of thought. It is, rather, a recurrent phenomenon, a tradition based on similarities rather than on
continuity. If the link between one philosopher and another is often weak,
that between philosophers and historical events is even weaker. The evidence for the influence of philosophy on politics is small at the best of
times. One author, tracing the origins of fascist ideas from Luther to Hitler,
maintains that the fascist regime was the result of a political philosophy
which had crystallised slowly throughout the nineteenth and early twentieth century.[2] A better explanation is that the objective situation in
Germany and Italy made the fascist leaders sympathetic to certain ideas
invented at an earlier date. The link with philosophy is especially tenuous
in the case of syndicalism. Syndicalism, a working-class movement, was
almost entirely divorced from that world; the militant workers had neither

[1] J. Benda, *Tradition de l'existentialisme*, 1947, p. 61.
[2] W. M. McGovern, *From Luther to Hitler*, 1941, p. 7.

191

the opportunity nor the inclination to study the writings of philosophers, nor did they wish to contribute in that field themselves. At first sight, therefore, one would expect syndicalism to stand outside whatever line of irrationalist thought that historians of ideas may trace. It was not true of the syndicalists, as it was of the fascists, that their situation made them sympathetic to the ideas of earlier thinkers, but rather that a similar situation and a similar temperament gave rise to similar ideas; the causes of the syndicalist revolt were in part at least those of the wider revolt against Reason. All revolutionary movements and ideologies that coexist at any time always have a lot in common.

This view needs some qualifications, however. Syndicalism was elaborated, if not created, by a few theoretically-minded leaders. It is largely with their ideas and those of Sorel that the following chapters are really concerned. The relationship between Sorel and the irrationalist philosophers is clear enough. Except for some rather weak links that Sorel provides, it is impossible to show a direct link between the militants of the French labour movement and the philosophers of the revolt against Reason. Schumpeter makes the point, referring to this problem, that while they are the product of the same social processes and in many ways react in a similar way to similar necessities, they cannot at the same time avoid borrowing from each other and splashing each other with their colour.[1]

The Age of Reason began with Descartes who proclaimed it the only key to knowledge and sole test of what was true or false. Once it had established a foothold, Reason gradually invaded all fields of human concern. French thought in the eighteenth century was largely an endeavour to apply this principle not only to philosophy and science but also, beyond Descartes' intention, to religion, morality and politics. The cartesian spirit, however, was characterised by its scepticism: having sometimes found my senses deceitful, I will distrust all they teach me. This brought with it its own reaction. The advance of reason in philosophy tended to undermine man's faith in Reason itself as an instrument for the discovery of truth. At the same time, having destroyed old faiths, Reason alone proved an insufficient faith to live by, offering but little scope for sentiment, still less for imagination and the hidden activities of the mind, The vacuum was soon filled by more inspiring, if less rational, philosophers. Two movements, therefore, contributed jointly to the revolt against Reason: the anti-intellectual and the romantic. Anti-intellectualism is the attempt to arrive rationally at a just appreciation of the limits of rationality in human affairs; it does not reject thought but regards it as only a limited guide to human affairs. Romanticism, by contrast, rejects thought in favour of

---

[1] J. A. Schumpeter, *Capitalism, Socialism, Democracy*, 1943, p. 340.

intuition and exalts non-rationality as a desirable mode of conduct. The two are related in so far as the former provides argument for the latter.

INTUITION AGAINST REASON. Romanticism was foreshadowed by Pascal, whose famous dictum 'The heart has its reason which Reason knows not of' was made in defence of the autonomy of religious truth. It was Rousseau, however, who provided the real impulse to the romantic movement. Hostile to the philosophy of his own time, he did not try to demolish it on its own ground: the heart rejects, conscience condemns, and from this verdict there is no appeal. He first made vocal a newly awakened fear that rational criticism might go too far. His revolt was essentially that of the common man who abruptly declares that he knows what he likes because he does not understand the philosophers and, in his heart, both fears and despises their apparently superior arguments. All his moral judgements turned on the worth of common feelings; philosophy was mere intellectual frippery. The syndicalists' reaction was much the same. Rousseau rejected the artificiality of existing society in favour of a society based on natural virtues and natural instincts. This led him to a direct attack on philosophers and intellectuals, an attack which was to become an important theme of the revolt against Reason. "These vain and futile declaimers," he wrote, "go forth on all sides, armed with their fatal paradoxes, to sap the foundations of faith and nullify virtue." "A thinking man is a depraved animal", he added, swinging to the opposite pole. He appealed against Reason to the inward light of conscience; against the 'principles of a high philosophy' to those 'written by nature in ineffaceable characters in the depths of his heart'. Rousseau's appeal to intuition, emotion, sentiment, so familiar afterwards, was popularised in *Emile* and *La Nouvelle Héloise*. It came as a relief to many people, then and later, that they could do without philosophy and without philosophers.

Hans Kohn sums up the Romantic movement: "The irrational forces in men and society seemed not only the true directives, but they seemed also the only creative forces able to lift men to enthusiasm and great deeds, to liberate them from the dryness and mediocrity of intellectual life."[1] Wordsworth called upon man to 'close up those barren leaves'. The cultivation of sentiment, the dismissal of learning, the worship of nature—that was the Romantic's position. If one substitutes 'experience' for 'nature', one may see in it the direct precursor of the later, political, revolt against Reason: of the conservatives who said with Burke that one sure symbol of an ill-conditioned state is the propensity of people to resort to theories

[1] H. Kohn, *The Twentieth Century*, 1950, p. 49.

and who appealed instead to tradition, the accumulated experience of the past; and of the syndicalists who, equally hostile to the terrifying apparatus of the philosophers, claimed to draw their ideas from the practice of every-day life.

PHILOSOPHY AGAINST REASON. Hume, rational and sceptical, pro-vided in his *Treatise on Human Nature* the mine which, according to Bertrand Russell, eventually blew the edifice of Reason sky high.[1] He showed that the rigorous application of rationalist empiricism led to results which few persons could bring themselves to accept. The reaction to this unbearable agnosticism took a more subtle form in Germany than that which Rousseau had given it in France. Kant, whom Russell described as a pedantic version of Rousseau's savoyard vicar,[2] brought back into philo-sophy the appeal to a non-rational faculty, the moral intuition, by his distinction between 'pure' and 'practical' reason. He opened the gates to the Romantics, though he was hardly the villian McGovern paints him in *From Luther to Hitler*: "As time went on his definition of true reason led to the growth of philosophical and political systems which were openly irrational in character."[3]

If Hume undermined the place of Reason in philosophy, it may be argued that Schopenhauer, writing at the very time when the philosophy of Reason appeared triumphant in the works of Hegel, was the man who dethroned it. Hegel proclaimed that history was the self-unfolding of Intelligence; Schopenhauer countered that it was the creation of a blind life-force, of aimless Will. Far from rational, the Real was irrational. Of the mind, as of the earth, we knew but the crust; in the depths under the con-scious intellect lay the unconscious Will, a persistently striving vital force, the cause of spontaneous activity. The Will of life dominated man who could use intellect to bring order to this blind whirl of forces but, in the last resort, remained its servant. It is only by intuition that this reality can be grasped, a doctrine which has been interpreted thus: "In real life the scholar is far surpassed by the man of action, for the strength of the latter consists in perfect intuitive knowledge. Philosophy must be brought back to the recognition of the richness of an immediate and direct knowledge of reality. It must learn that the meaning of things is to be realised more by living than by thinking."[4] The doctrine that Will was paramount was later held, in one form or another, by many philosophers. Russell sees Nietzsche,

[1] B. Russell, *Let the People Think*, 1941, p. 63.
[2] B. Russell, *History of Western Philosophy*, 1948, p. 731.
[3] W. M. McGovern, *From Luther to Hitler*, 1941, p. 139.
[4] M. Beer, *Schopenhauer*, 1914, p. 80.

The revolt against reason

Bergson and James in this tradition.[1] It acquired a popular vogue outside the circle of professional thinkers. The syndicalist leaders often spoke in a similar vein.

SCIENCE AGAINST REASON. Science joined philosophy to undermine man's faith in Reason. The trusting rationalism of the eighteenth century met its first challenge as an expanding knowledge of foreign cultures showed the relativity of all beliefs and institutions. Montesquieu and Burke had already pointed out that social and political arrangements were less the creation of Reason than of tradition and environment. The new anthropology—Frazer in *The Golden Bough*—showed that many beliefs were primitive myths in disguise. The economic materialism of Marx showed that others were mere superstructure, reflecting the modes of production of the time. The behaviouralist psychology of Pavlov showed that many actions were the result of automatic reflexes, either natural or conditioned. Freudian psycho-analysis showed the extent to which man was dominated by deep, pre-rational instincts and unconscious motives, inborn or formed in early childhood. More important, perhaps, was the study of social psychology, which attracted widespread attention towards the end of the nineteenth century. Tarde, Durkheim and Le Bon enjoyed considerable popularity in France. In different ways such writers provided evidence that mental processes and resulting activity were influenced by non-rational forces within society and within the individual.

A distinction has been made between the anti-intellectual and the Romantic movements. The social psychologists, for example, were not themselves necessarily hostile to Reason. Graham Wallas, while stressing the place of instinct, emotion and habit in political life, remained a rationalist and a democrat, seeking to bring the forces of unreason under control. Some took the opposite view: while Le Bon considered the group mind the lowest form of psychic life, Durkheim tended to see the collective consciousness as the highest. The newly discovered irrational forces of society could be interpreted either in terms of the romantic realism of Burke, as the accumulated wisdom of past generations, or in terms of the romantic idealism of the Nazis, as an expression of the *Volksgeist*. The same was true of the discoveries of psychology. Freud hoped to submit the irrational to the control of Reason. Herbert Read, in his *Politics of the Unpolitical*, took the opposite view. It could be argued that the full expression of man's personality meant opening the barriers of intellect which tended to repress natural instincts and the unconscious mind. This claim was advanced most successfully in the fields of art and literature. In France at this time, for

[1] B. Russell, *History of Western Philosophy*, 1948, p. 787.

13-2

example, André Breton was trying to register the richer truths of the irrational by means of automatic writing.

Kohn summed up the consequences: "Man seemed subject to biological forces (in the widest sense) against which his reason was powerless, of which his reason, perhaps, was only an instrument. Organic and vitalistic theories gained ground in all the social sciences."[1] The triumph of *bios* over *logos* had considerable repercussions. Paul Tillich describes the new atmosphere: "Against the imperious reign of technical reason, yielding the detached impersonal knowledge of mechanistic naturalism, there arose a demand for knowledge concerned with life, in which the very nature of the knower is involved. Existential truth was the new goal. A truth which concerns us as living, deciding men has a character quite different from the truth which reason was supposed to provide."[2] Socialist theory did not escape this influence. Marxism had earlier transferred the rationalist categories of Hegel to the economic processes of a material world; it now seemed that the internal forces of the mind, neither rational nor predictable, were more important than the external objective forces on which the scientific socialists had based their philosophy. The path was open for a reinterpretation. Sorel and De Man were among those who offered it for syndicalism.

[1] H. Kohn, *The Twentieth Century*, 1950, p. 49.
[2] P. Tillich, *The Christian Answer*, p. 55.

Nietzsche and the transvaluation of all values

Friedrich Nietzsche, Schopenhauer's immediate heir, carried his argument to its logical conclusion while turning it upside down. The former saw salvation in the denial of Will, in the Will-less life of pure contemplation, in Nirvana. The latter, touched by a more heroic temper, scorned this escape. Nietzsche preached a joyful acceptance of the irrational, a Yea to life and to the struggle it entails. "Wherever I have found life, I have found the Will to Power." The force Nietzsche discovered at the centre of all things was the urge, experienced by every man, to dominate his fellows and control his environment. For him eternal strife was the father of all things, an echo, transformed, of Darwin and Marx. From this understanding of life, and its acceptance, all else follows.

Knowledge is both subjective and instrumental. Man's understanding evolves in accordance with his need to master the external world; to say that an idea is true is only to say that it has proved useful to his preservation—therein lies its cause and its justification. The same is true of values: they express the needs of a community and differ with different needs. If nothing is true independently, then nothing is really true and Nietzsche concludes, naturally enough, that all must be permitted, man must penetrate beyond good and evil, a notion that had already occurred to the Marquis de Sade. Nietzsche's own view of life, however, led him not to the destruction of ethics but only to their reinterpretation. His transvaluation of all values followed from his affirmation of life. What he saw around him, and in history, was the denial of the Will to Power: his wrath was great and he attacked with a hammer.

Nietzsche hated the rationalist tradition of Europe. Socrates, its first martyr, was for him (as for Sorel) the villain of subsequent evils. The old Greeks were creatures of instinct and habit, fighters and revellers, athletes and singers; in so far as they thought at all, it was simply to find ways of satisfying their natural desires. But then a change took place in the Greek way of life: philosophy replaced poetry, science art, talk games. Socrates, the first intellectual, taught Athenian youth to think about what they wanted of life rather than to rely upon instinct, to think, indeed, rather than to live. This subordination of Will to Reason was the deformation of man. Nietzsche's attack on the civilization of his own time was no less bitter. The bourgeoisie was rotten to the core, its ideals were the final travesty of life: sordid materialism, vulgar pleasure-seeking, complacent mediocrity.

Ideological context

Democracy, the slaves' attempt to remake the world in their own image, the rationalists' talking-shop, the rule of nonentities—that was the final decadence. Heroism had been killed by reason, nobility driven out by the mob, adventure banished by the self-satisfied, joy expelled by the virtuous: "Today the little people are masters, preaching submission and modesty and policy and the long boring toll of little virtues", he wrote, and: "With their virtue they have made a wolf a dog and man Man's best domestic pet."

The verdict: "The world hitherto has been a dispiriting place; it is impossible to believe in anything that has existed." The conclusion: "The meaning that must be inherent in this vast creation is in the future, not in man but in Superman." Thus spake Zarathustra! The concept became notorious, though Nietzsche was as discreet as Marx about the future. He tended to ask How shall Superman be brought into being? rather than What will he be like? Some have suggested that Superman should be understood as a poetical substitute for God, an ideal towards which one may strive but which must necessarily remain mysterious. He showed the path and inspired men to follow it. Nietzsche probably intended to spur men on to greater affirmation of life here and now rather than to speculate about some future utopia. The Sorelian myth springs to mind as a parallel. Like Sorel and other activist philosophers, he was more concerned with the movement than with the end.

Nietzsche in fact preached the full life, an old doctrine but with a difference: the complete man of earlier tradition was replete with all the virtues; Nietzsche wanted him to have all the vices as well. Such men had existed in pre-Socratic Greece: "The value judgements of warlike aristocracy were founded on a powerful bodily constitution, on flourishing health, not forgetting what was necessary to the support of this overflowing vigour: war, adventure, the hunt, the dance, games and physical exercises." He praised the ancient heroes' terrible gaiety and profound joy. In Renaissance Italy, in the person of Cesare Borgia, he found these virtues linked with a taste for beauty and the spirit of creation. War and courage, discipline and pride, had done more great things than charity but, a philosopher himself, he saw the same virtues accessible to philosophers: in Schopenhauer he admired the adventurer's impulse to discovery, the enjoyment of dialectical chase, the love of battle and of victory. The range of aphorisms which constitute his distinctive style was almost endless and by their selection one can establish almost any picture of his hero: the blonde beast and the stoic, the warrior and the poet. It is well to remember that he wrote in *Ecce Homo* "I know both sides because I am both sides."

Relevant here is Nietzsche's romantic attack on the cult of Reason. It was the pulsations of the Will to Power that determine man's thoughts; instinct was the direct operation of this Will, unfalsified by consciousness. Thus "instinct is the most intelligent of all kinds of intelligence" or, as Zarathustra proclaimed "there is more wisdom in your body than in your subtlest learning". Warriors and poets did not require such learning. Nietzsche was generally interpreted as preferring the man of action who, by the simple argument 'I will', scorned to conceal his desires under the cover of Reason. The intellectual, preferring Reason to the promptings of life-force, rejected life itself. It was the man of action who expressed the life struggle and embodied the Will to Power that was its true essence.

Reliance on instinct and glorification of struggle—both themes were echoed by Sorel. "Proletarian violence, practised as a pure and simple manifestation of the feeling of class struggle, appears as a very beautiful and very heroic thing; it is at the service of the primordial interests of civilization; it is perhaps not the most appropriate method for obtaining material advantages but it may save the world from barbarism."[1] This scorn of the utilitarian in favour of the heroic was pure Nietzsche. E. H. Carr has made the point: "While the goal is the goal of Marx, the voice is the voice of Nietzsche."[2] If one looks at Sorel's own philosophy, rather than at his interpretation of syndicalism, one might be as inclined to write: The goal is the goal of Nietzsche, the voice is the voice of Marx. Either way, the synthesis can be found.

The transvaluation of all values has on occasion been interpreted in socialist terms. Charles Andler in France, for example, claimed that, having shown the decadence of the bourgeoisie, he hoped to see it replaced by a working class that would be a class of masters; "One may legitimately call the system of Nietzsche a socialism."[3] It was true that Nietzsche disliked the socialism he knew, but that was because he saw in it not heroism but only envy. If, however, the older socialism represented the worst expression of slave morality, the rise of syndicalism, according to Sorel, meant a fundamental change in the character of the socialist movement. The syndicalists were fighters. Opposed to the sentimental humanitarianism of the bourgeoisie, with its doctrine of social peace, he saw a syndicalist morality founded on war and its virtues, on class struggle, violence, courage and discipline. As producers, the syndicalists were creative; as workers, not deformed by intellect. Sorel reinterpreted Nietzsche's transvaluation, blending his distinction between master and slave moralities with Marx's proletarian and bourgeois moralities. The proletarian revolution was to be the coming of Superman.

[1] G. Sorel, *Reflections on Violence*, 1916, p. 130.
[2] E. H. Carr, *Studies in Revolution*, 1950, p. 156.
[3] C. Andler, *Nietzsche, sa vie et sa pensée*, 1920–31, vol. 5, p. 321.

Bergson and creative evolution

For Bergson the world was divided into two conflicting forces, life and matter. Life was a force, an impulse (*élan vital*), making a path for itself through the material world which Bertrand Russell summarised quite neatly: "Meeting the resistance of matter, struggling to break through matter, learning gradually to use the matter by means of organisation; divided by obstacles it encounters into diverging currents; partly subdued by matter through the very adaptation which matter forces upon it; yet retaining always its capacity for free activity, struggling always to find new outlets, seeking always greater liberty of movement amid the opposing walls of matter."[1] This continuous adaptation of the life was evolution, a concept which lay at the beginning of Bergson's philosophy. Bergson argued that the orthodox doctrine of adaptation to environment by survival of the fittest could explain the way in which the process took place but not its cause; that could only be explained by the existence of a life-force, perpetually striving to transform matter in accordance with its own need to achieve a greater freedom of action. In that sense evolution was itself both free and creative. The upward surge of life created its own path at every movement, a path that could not be mapped in advance towards a goal that could not be predicted.

One bifurcation of the life force was the separate development of plants and animals; another was the development of some animals in the direction of instinct and others in the direction of intellect, at the end of which process stood man himself. Intellect was an organ to control man's environment, evolved to deal with matter and adapted to matter. Like the eye, a similar organ, it was far from perfect. There were thus many aspects of reality which the intellect was unable to grasp. Bergson made a distinction between time and space. The material world existed in space; it was divisible and measurable. Life, on the other hand, flowed like a river through time. The natural sciences, servants of intellect, measured, counted and weighed; they were determined by the utilitarian purpose they served, control of the material world. It was a mistake to apply this quantitative-intellectual method to life. If one attempted to measure time after the fashion of science, by dividing it into moments, one was forced to do so in spatial terms, symbolised by the swing of the pendulum. The intellect, trying to grasp true psychological time, merely created an artificial material time. In its struggle with the material world, thought became deformed by its object; it got in the habit of understanding—or misunderstanding—everything in spatial terms.

[1] B. Russell, *History of Western Philosophy*, 1948, p. 820.

Bergson and creative evolution

The split in the life force which led to the specialisation of man in the direction of intellect instead of instinct was, for Bergson, the moment of original sin. Reflection, abstraction, division, analysis, these were his vices. Life—'real time'—was a process, an indivisible whole, a constant flow, a continual Becoming. To divide this process into separate parts, and then to classify the parts, was to arrest the flow, destroy the whole and falsify what remained. Bergson accepted that it was necessary for science to analyse reality in terms of the abstract categories of the intellect, with its mechanical representations, but argued that one could never reconstitute reality from such elements. The analogy he used was that of the cinema film. The intellect can only see the isolated frames. To see the film in motion, to grasp life as a whole, required another faculty, one capable of seizing life in its immediacy. While intellect observed life from the outside, instinct sprang directly from life and was a continuation of life. Instinct, however, was not self-conscious: it determined action but itself provided no knowledge. It was to a synthesis of instinct and intellect, therefore, that man needed to turn in order to understand reality—to an instinct which had become aware of itself and was capable of reflection.

Intuition means to penetrate into life, *Einfühlung*. Of its working little can be said, though the difference between intuition and intellect can be suggested by thinking of the visual faculty of the artist, and the faculty for abstract thought of the logician. The exponents of the philosophy of life tended to the former way of thinking. It was significant that Bergson relied heavily on metaphors to convey his ideas. The same approach can be found in the existentialist writers: Sartre found it simplest to convey the essence of his philosophy in novels and plays. If the philosopher is to translate intuitive pictures into words, these must of course be submitted to the intellect; only the painter and the musician can convey direct experience directly. Nevertheless, the writer must also rely on the suggestibility of his work, rather than on its logic, to convey his ideas to the reader as immediate experience, as *données immédiates*; these cannot be recreated by the reader himself through intellectual analysis. It was Goethe who said that truth, in the last resort, can only be created and can only be seen. The case arises, however, where intuition remains inarticulate. Sorel described the general strike as an image which presented itself directly to the mind. While such a myth-picture might inspire men to action, it was not necessarily translated into words, the more so as workers were not creative writers. To the extent that the workers had intuitive knowledge which defied intellectual analysis, it becomes difficult to explain syndicalist ideas. To understand the syndicalist movement requires some empathy—that is a lesson to be learnt from Bergson.

Ideological context

Henri Bergson lived from 1859 to 1940. In his time, particularly the early years of this century, he was a major, perhaps the dominant, figure in French thought. While his own contributions to philosophy are now generally discredited, his earlier influence was considerable. It was an influence that spilled out well beyond the field of professional philosophers. In 1913 A. O. Lovejoy could write that his philosophy had ceased to be merely a body of arguments and conclusions contained in certain books; it had become an influence to be reckoned with in the life of that time.[1] Some twenty years later another student concluded more cautiously that in the preceding years some attempt had been made to utilise the Bergsonian point of view in the sphere of political thought.[2] In practice, this meant that Bergson's terminology was borrowed by writers of the most diverse allegiance, from the syndicalist Sorel to the neo-catholic Le Roy, all of whom found his language useful for their own purpose. In the case of Sorel this adaptation was especially clear, indeed self-avowed. Bergson himself, on the other hand, never dealt with social questions and, as he himself pointed out, it was false to the spirit of his philosophy to pass from his conclusions in one field of study to another field. He was consulted about his relationship with the syndicalists and his reply was published in 1910. He admitted that Sorel and his close collaborator Edouard Berth quoted certain of his ideas correctly, but added that this could as legitimately be done by sociologists of quite different schools. That, from his point of view, was the extent of the link.[3]

It has nevertheless been claimed that syndicalism could be interpreted from some points of view as an application of Bergson's philosophy to the field of political economy and that Sorel and his circle might be called the left-Bergsonians, just as earlier in Germany Marx and Engels had been left-Hegelians.[4] According to Bergson evolution was creative and Sorel proceeded to apply this doctrine to the phenomena of social change. For the life force he substituted action or violence. Bergson's *élan vital* pushed life on to ever new forms; Sorel saw the evolution of society (a matter not considered by Bergson) as the creation of a similar *élan*, the urge of a class, unhampered by intellect, expressing itself directly in action, in conflict with environment. This conflict was the class war and out of it new forms of society arose. *Elan vital* was spontaneous; its direction could not be

[1] Lovejoy, 'Practical Tendencies of Bergsonism' in *Journal of Ethics*, April/July 1913, p. 253.
[2] Jacques, 'Significance of Bergson for Recent Political Thought in France' in *Transactions of the Royal Society of Canada*, series 3, section 2, 1932, p. 5.
[3] *Cit.* Goldstein, 'Bergson und die Sozialwissenschaften' in *Archiv für Sozialwissenschaft*, vol. 31, 1910, p. 15.
[4] G. Serbos, *Une philosophie de la production*, 1913, p. 49.

predicted in detail. Sorel thus excluded any logical analysis of the socialist movement and any real discussion of the future socialist society: the syndicalists should not ask where they were going or even what exactly they wished. Sorel translated Bergson from the individual to the social sphere, interpreting intuition in terms of class conscience. And just as the one urged an awakening of intuition, so, in his fashion, did the other. The purpose of course, was different: intensification of the class war. In this Sorel was a reasonable interpreter of the militant syndicalists who themselves rejected scientific socialism in favour of a more intuitive approach, believing that too much thought not only distorted the truth but fatefully weakened the springs of creative action.

James and the pragmatic approach

William James, in his pragmatic philosophy, evolved a theory of perception very similar to that of Bergson. While earlier writers usually took the view that experience is composed of distinct sensations between which the mind interposes connections, James, like Bergson, reversed this argument to show that experience in fact came as a continuous whole in which the mind then interposed distinctions. "Consciousness does not appear to itself chopped up in bits" was the way he put it. A world of immediate experience which was a vast indeterminate flow would, however, prove impossible to live in from a practical point of view; therefore it was the first task of mental activity to break up this flow, separate it into parts, analyse it into objects and their relations, reduce it to manageable proportions. This analysis was dictated by the interests and temperament of the perceiver: the mind discriminated; it is only selected but added in relation to his purpose. This purpose reflected the demands of life, but within that limit perception was conditioned by will and thus an expression of choice. In other words, man made his own reality and that reality was the one which best served his purpose. Action was of prime importance in this process, for it was in action that man's purpose lay: all knowing was relative to doing. Goethe again is often quoted at this point: "In the beginning was the deed!".

James approached the question of truth in similar fashion. He pointed to the barrenness of the internal consistency doctrine, favoured by the rationalists, which allowed a hundred and one theories to exist side by side, all apparently logical, without any one of them bearing a direct relationship to the problems of everyday life. Science, on the other hand, directly concerned with the control of environment, proceeded by hypotheses, purely utilitarian truths only accepted because (and so long as) they produce useful results. James maintained that a similar process actually (and justifiably) took place in the ordinary affairs of men. He came to this conclusion by studying the psychology of thinking. What the mind held to be a truth, he found, was really a hypothesis or convenient formulation of experience, a truth-claim to be tested and validated in action. The truth of a belief was established if it proved useful in furthering the purpose in hand; truth was the cash value of an idea. In James' sense there could never be an absolute truth. All one could say was that certain hypotheses appeared consistently more successful in coping with the demands facing man and thus, over time, became established as truths. In this way man made his own truth, just as he made his own reality, and both were linked to a utilitarian purpose. The essence of pragmatism was that a belief was true if it worked and not for some abstract logical reason; it was good if it was effective and not because it accorded with some abstract ethical system. A belief formulated to meet the needs of action, in other words, was really a policy for action, just as a scientific hypothesis was really a policy for research. It led to action and if the action it stimulated had the desired effect it became true. More likely, almost certainly, given the difficulties of prediction in the social sciences, the effect would not be entirely what was expected. A continuous process of modification and adaptation of beliefs followed: truth was being made continuously, the essential fact at any stage being the ability of the beliefs in question to satisfy the wishes of the holder in regard to his environment.

This interpretation sheds a light on the nature of syndicalism. Syndicalist ideas on a number of major issues (e.g. political neutrality, the nature of direct action, the general strike) changed over time. The analytic observer is bound to raise the question of consistency. Syndicalism, however, was essentially a pragmatic philosophy. It was, like science, a policy and not a creed, a policy which—given changing environment—was never complete and could never be completely true. A contemporary observer defined it as a doctrine evolved by men immersed in action in order to render their action more effective.[1] Seen thus, it was not surprising that the syndicalist militants should continuously modify their principles in the light of the unsatisfactory nature of their experience when they tried to apply them. It was the particular satisfaction demanded, perhaps, rather than the belief in how this could be achieved, that was the true constant. The syndicalist method, the changing policy, on the other hand, can be seen to have a different sort of consistency as a pattern of gradual adaptation. The Italian syndicalist theoretician Panunzio made this point very clearly: "It is facts which, by their external force of expansion, must alone determine the living process and the flux of ideas. If facts contradict the first ideas, they must not oppose them inflexibly but reformulate themselves, plunging into the melting-pot of new elements which will raise them to a new theoretical unity."[2]

W. Y. Elliott, in *The Pragmatic Revolt in Politics*, published in 1928, attributed the current political revolt against rationalism—and he included not only Sorel and Mussolini, but also Laski and Duguit—to the ideology of pragmatism. The evidence was not very convincing but it was true that the writers he considered all shared a pragmatic impatience with

[1] Challayé, 'Le syndicalisme révolutionnaire', in *Revue de Métaphysique et de Morale*, January/March 1908, p. 105.
[2] Panunzio in *Mouvement Socialiste*, 15 January 1906, p. 61.

truth that remained at the level of theory but did not work, was not even designed to work, in practice. They showed the same pragmatic inclination to favour action over discussion and to look to activity rather than speculation as a guide to further action.

If pragmatism meant that beliefs were true because they worked, and not that they worked because they were true, it was logical enough for the pragmatists to look to their own experience. Thus James: "A pragmatist turns away from abstraction, from verbal solutions, from bad *a priori* reasoning, from fixed principles, closed systems and pretended absolutes. He turns towards concreteness and adequacy, towards facts, towards action and towards power. That means the empiricist temper regnant and the rationalist temper sincerely given up." This attitude obviously corresponded closely to that of the militant syndicalists. Like James, they preferred 'the open air and possibilities of nature' to artificiality and dogma. They did so, however, for no very philosophical reason. Pragmatism was nevertheless very much in the air they breathed. Some of the theorists were probably subject to a more direct influence: the similarities of argument are striking, at very least. Lagardelle, for example, declared that within the broad, even elastic, frame set by its aims, the tactics of the labour movement should be determined not by reference to some pre-constructed system but in action, according to the needs of the moment and the lessons of experience. The class struggle would itself enlighten the workers. "Theory arises out of practice, action creates the idea."[1]

James said that there were two commands for the philosopher: 'Believe truth!' and 'Shun error!' These were not identical. One may regard the search for truth as paramount and the avoidance of error as secondary; or one can treat the avoidance of error as imperative and let truth take its chance. The sceptical attitude of the rationalist favoured the latter. For the pragmatist, on the other hand, theories were instruments rather than solutions; their ultimate truth was less important than the need for an immediate guide to action for unless something is believed, one is condemned to inactivity. One may therefore commit oneself, in fields other than science, to working hypotheses if by backing them one thinks one can live more happily or more effectively. James applied this to religion, thus justifying Pascal's famous wager: You must either believe in God or not; if you stake all on God's existence and win, you gain eternal salvation; if you lose, you lose nothing at all. There were other hypotheses which, if backed, could prove of more immediate, temporal value than Pascal's. What was important was that the backing of such a hypothesis could help to make it true. As James points out: "Who gains promotion, boons,

---

[1] Lagardelle in *Mouvement Socialiste*, September/October 1911, p. 174.

appointments, but the man in whose life they are seen to play the part of live hypotheses, who sacrifices other things for their sake before they have come and takes risks for them in advance. His faith acts on the powers above him as a claim and creates its own verification." This principle, could, of course, be transferred to the field of politics. There, it sounded very like the syndicalist slogan *vouloir, c'est pouvoir*.

The notion that faith in a fact can help to create that fact linked even more closely with the Sorelian myth of the general strike. The myth was an instrument in the class struggle which Sorel specifically defined as a means of acting on the present. It was true or false, therefore not at any abstract level of truth or falsity but to the extent that it worked, i.e. succeeded in sharpening the class struggle. And this, in turn, depended on the extent to which it was believed. If the militants had sufficient faith, they would commit themselves to action and thus validate the myth in practice. The same relationship could be shown to exist between the idea and the reality of the class war itself: the hypothesis became real when sufficient people accepted it. What else was syndicalist propaganda designed to achieve?

The revolt against democracy

The revolt against Reason burst the boundaries of philosophy and swept into the field of politics in the twentieth century. This was *The Great Betrayal*, the *trahison des clercs*, which Benda attacked in 1927. Until his day, men of thought and culture had generally remained strangers to political passions, saying with Goethe 'Let us leave politics to the diplomats and soldiers'. If, like Voltaire, they took such passions into account, they adopted a critical attitude towards them; if, like Rousseau, they actually took them to heart, they did so with a generalising of feeling and a disdain for immediate action which made the term inappropriate. Men like Mommsen, Treitschke, Barrès, Péguy, Maurras, d'Annunzio and Kipling, however, showed all the characteristics of passion: love of action, thirst for immediate results, preoccupation with ends, scorn for argument, excess, hatred, fixed ideas.[1] Social, economic and political conditions were such that these philosophers found a willing audience and ready-made allies.

The rule of Reason meant the rational conduct of public affairs. In practical terms: reliance on persuasion rather than force; persuasion by argument rather than emotion; argument based on observation rather than intuition. And it meant reasonableness in another sense: willingness to accept other points of view and to compromise one's own. This was a bourgeois attitude as well as an intellectual one. Whatever the hidden truth about the springs of thought and action, the bourgeoisie modelled its behaviour on assumptions of rationality and enshrined this belief in its institutions. Private enterprise assumed the rational and advantageous exchange of goods in the economic market; liberal democracy assumed a similar exchange in the political market. Parliamentary government—argument, persuasion and compromise—was a mode of conducting affairs favoured by the bourgeoisie. Did not Alain, the most quoted exponent of liberal democracy in France, write simply "est bourgeois ce qui vit de persuader" and was it not a commonplace to call parliament a talking-shop? This phrase, hostile in use, actually pointed to the heart of the democratic faith: that men were essentially rational; that they (or their delegates) were capable of reaching agreement through debate; that decisions so reached would reflect the best interests of the community.

It was not surprising, therefore, that the revolt against Reason should have expressed itself in political terms as a revolt against bourgeois intellectuals and the parliamentary democracy which enshrined their rule. Or, looked at the other way round: the revolt against bourgeois democracy

[1] J. Benda, *La trahison des clercs*, 1927, p. 33.

Revolt against democracy

(political, not philosophical, in origin) was bound also to express itself as a revolt against Reason. The direct, political causes of the revolt against democracy in France will be examined in the following chapter. Here two points are to be stressed.

First: the terms Reason, bourgeois and intellectual, parliament and democracy, were all closely linked and an attack on one usually implied an attack on others. The link between democracy and rationalism was particularly close in France. The men of 1789 had hoped to replace the aristocracy of blood by an aristocracy of the intellect; what survived was the prestige of the intellectual. The radical party, most deeply rooted in the life of the Third Republic, was also the party of the intellectual and the petit-bourgeois; the journalist, the schoolmaster and the lawyer were its typical figures. Thibaudet provided the label *République des professeurs*.

Second: historically, it was the apparent failure of democratic institutions which made so many people sympathetic to attacks on Reason in politics. It was their rejection of democracy and all it implied that brought syndicalism, fascism and nationalism into a common historical perspective. The divergence between these movements (and others of like nature) was obvious enough, but this itself reflected a characteristic common to them all. Lovejoy saw this in 1913: "The peculiarity of anti-intellectualism is that you cannot be sure where it will bring you out. What it leads from, the sober austerities and the hard slow achievements of the life of reason, you know. But it is a road that soon forks, and there is at the turning no plain guide-post to point in one direction rather than another; all the clearly decipherable guide-posts have been left behind in the place you came from. And the one branch if followed to its extreme brings you to a position diametrically opposite to that which lies at the end of the other."[1]

WIDER PERSPECTIVES OF REVOLT. The revolt against democracy was wider than the revolt against Reason. The rationalist, anti-parliamentary left ranged from communism to guild socialism. The revolt against Reason, for its part, did not always imply a rejection of democracy. Bergson and James both remained rational democrats. It is nevertheless significant that in other anti-intellectual movements, non-political in origin (in the field of art, for example) close parallels to the political revolt can be seen.

In 1909 *Figaro* published the first futurist manifesto of Italian writers and painters. They sang the love of danger and the beauty of struggle. An activist temper was coupled with an attack on bourgeois values and a call to destroy such bourgeois institutions as museums and libraries. In their

[1] Lovejoy, 'Practical Tendencies of Bergsonism' in *Journal of Ethics*, April/July 1913, p. 253.

place, they glorified the machine and the worker, symbols of the new age, describing lyrically the sounds and vibrations of the industrial plant, its bright lights and perpetual movement.[1] 'Plastic dynamism' was not, perhaps, a great success. Interesting was their cult of action and their cultivation of the workers. One critic, drawing the parallel, suggested that futurism represented syndicalism in art. More significant was the fact that many members of the group and especially its leader, Marinetti, counted among the first supporters of Mussolini, himself an activist on the road without guide-posts.

Dada was the absolute revolt against bourgeois values and outlook. The only consistent aim of the dadaists, indeed, appears to have been to shock the bourgeoisie. It was also a revolt against Reason chemically pure. The last words of one of its manifestos were 'don't know, don't know, don't know!'—the literally nonsensical was its only standard of value. Out of dada arose surrealism, the last romantic movements in art as Cyril Connolly once called them. Instead of the dynamism preached by the futurists and the absurd preached by the dadaists, surrealism came out as the champion of the irrational forces in man, of intuition and the unconscious. To Plato's recognition that the inspired poet must be out of his senses, the surrealists merely added a knowledge of Freudian psychology. Plato had also demanded the exclusion of the poets from the Republic and, to prove the truth of his foresight, surrealism became a revolutionary movement in France. It was necessary to overthrow the authority of Reason in order to set free the poetry stored in the darker recesses of the mind, and this, the surrealists argued, could not be separated from the overthrow of the bourgeois society which Reason had created to protect itself. *Le surréalisme au service de la révolution* was the title of their magazine. The service, though never gratefully acknowledged, was that of the communist revolution. Had surrealism flourished a decade earlier, however, it would have seen itself as the ally of the syndicalists.

CRITIQUE OF DEMOCRACY. Both right and left identified the Republic with their own enemies and laid the blame for its weakness at their door. The workers naturally saw capitalists and bourgeoisie as the source of all evil; the nationalists found their scapegoat in Jews, foreigners, protestants and freemasons. In less prejudiced moments, however, most critics agreed that the vices of democracy were inherent in the system itself. Reason stultified action and led to weakness. As Hamlet recognised, "conscience does make cowards of us all, and the native hue of resolution is sicklied o'er with the pale cast of thought". Too much Reason also undermined old

---

[1] *Le Figaro*, 20 February 1909.

virtues without creating new traditions to replace them. This fault lay not only in the rationalist spirit of the age but deep in the falsely rational structure of democratic society.

A passage in the *Communist Manifesto* is relevant here: "The bourgeoisie, wherever it has got the upper hand, has put an end to all feudal, patriarchal, idyllic relations. It has pitilessly torn asunder the motley feudal ties that bound man to his 'natural superiors' and has left no other nexus between man and man than naked self-interest, than callous 'cash payment'. It has drowned the most heavenly ecstasies of religious fervour of chivalrous enthusiasm, of philistine sentimentalism, in the icy waters of egoistic calculation. It has resolved personal worth into exchange value and in place of the numberless indefeasible chartered freedoms has set the single, unconscionable freedom—Free Trade." The triumph of capitalism, or the Great Revolution—the choice is according to taste—destroyed all bonds and all values; traditional morality was replaced by an abstract liberty that in fact meant self-interest and sordid commercialism; an integrated society gave way to an abstract equality that in fact meant individualism run riot and the ultimate domination of money. This development was reflected in the political system. "L'état s'est démystiqué" wrote Péguy. Parliament was merely an extension of Free Trade: "The world of politics had acquired the morality of the market place", declared Paul Louis, a syndicalist sympathiser.[1] Lagardelle found democracy a demoralising system, incapable of producing human values[2]—a sentiment that could have been attributed to the nationalist right as easily as to the syndicalist left. A new morality, the regeneration of society, seemed to require the rejection of the individualism and the materialism that went with democracy. Syndicalists, nationalists, fascists, all joined in the attack.

Democracy's concept of citizenship also meant the disintegration of society. If Free Trade had destroyed all bonds save the cash nexus, the Revolution of 1789 had, for its part, tried to destroy all social ties save those of the state. In Le Chapelier's words, no group loyalty could be allowed to intervene between the citizen and the state. The opponents of democracy could argue that it ignored the real man, with his real interests and his real groupings; the abstract citizen, counted and represented in parliament, was a figment of the theorists' imagination. This was the criticism the monarchists brought against the Republic: in place of the real man, participating in matters of immediate concern and within his competence through a variety of natural organisations (local, professional, religious or family), democracy had substituted the elector, whose only right it was to

---

[1] P. Louis, *Le syndicalisme contre l'Etat*, 1910, p. 56.
[2] Lagardelle in *Les documents du progrès*, 1908, p. 304.

pronounce at intervals on matters about which he knew nothing. The Revolution has been described as an expression of the *esprit géométrique*; with it the mechanistic rationalism of Descartes was transferred to the state. In Bergsonian terms, democracy was based upon analysis—*ordre géométrique*—and thus failed to grasp the reality of the *ordre vital*. The point was made by Pirou in 1910 when he said of the syndicalist theoreticians that they saw democracy as the political expression of intellectualism and universal suffrage as a philosophy of discontinuity, a misunderstanding of the deep, internal unity of social reality.[1] Proposals for a more real, more organic structure of society were advanced on all sides: social catholicism, guild socialism, solidarism and communism in the days when it still favoured government by soviets. Such proposals formed part of the same movement as the fascists' call for a corporate state, the monarchists' for a nation of estates and provinces, and the syndicalists' for a society based on trade unions. Alternatives to parliamentary democracy were very much in the air, before and after the first world war.

[1] G. Pirou, *Proudhonisme et syndicalisme révolutionnaire*, 1910, p. 307.

The discredit of French democracy

The Third Republic was but a poor thing compared with the monarchy of Louis Quatorze and the empire of Napoleon. Whatever its virtues, it was never glorious or inspiring. The sombre black of the civilian frockcoat proved dull after the splendours of King and Emperor. Its prestige was low abroad as well as at home. Militarily weak, nothing was done to avenge the loss of Alsace-Lorraine: the figure of Strasbourg in the Place de la Concorde was a perpetual reproach to the Republic in the eyes of men who valued honour above peace and prosperity. Although France had joined in the race for colonies, she was consistently rebuffed by the stronger power of England, her humiliation dramatised at Fashoda. The result was something like an inferiority complex, especially severe in the case of the nationalists. While few Frenchmen ever abandoned hope of reversing the Treaty of Frankfurt, the reconquest of the lost provinces gradually sank into the background as attention focussed on colonial expansion abroad and commercial activity at home. For the nationalists, however, *revanche* remained the question that dominated all others and they were soon brought together by Déroulède in the *Ligue des Patriotes*. After the death of Gambetta, whose slogan 'guerre à l'outrance!' had won Déroulède's confidence, they lost faith in the politicians of the Republic. The League, which had been non-partisan so long as the parties seemed united on reconquest, turned to attack the democratic regime, demanding strong government as a necessary step to the war of revenge. The parliamentary Republic was at the same time attacked by a wider front for its weakness in dealing with internal affairs.

FAILURE OF THE PARLIAMENTARY SYSTEM. The French democratic tradition differed from the English. It was based less on community feeling than on individualism, less on participation than on defence against government. The Radical Republicans, who set the tone, had an almost anarchic suspicion of authority. After their experience of strong executives, it was not surprising that the deputies of the Third Republic tried to keep power in their own hands. Parliament, distrusting the executives, would have liked to govern itself. Assembly government as tried at the French Revolution was hardly possible, but France got something nearer to parliamentary than cabinet government. Constitutional practice reinforced this. MacMahon's misuse of the power of dissolution in 1877 undermined the presidency. It also deprived the cabinet of what might have been a useful weapon against an irresponsible legislature: deputies were free to do what they liked for four years. The system of interpellations allowed a deputy to call on a minister to explain his policy on any issue, and necessitated a debate before the business of the day could continue. If defeated on this, no matter how trivial, the government was expected to resign. Ministerial stability was thus sacrificed to parliamentary control over policy. The committee system was another spoke in the wheel. The specialised committees, introduced in 1902, were used to control, even direct, the action of government.

The multi-party system in the assembly worked in the same direction. After Gambetta's failure to create a sufficiently wide and well-disciplined Republican party, it was clear that no prime minister could rely on a continuous majority of his own. France was to have weak premiers as well as weak presidents. Coalition government has its difficulties at the best of times; the weakness of party organisation, the instability of parliamentary groups and the large number of independents in the Chamber made the life of any coalition even more precarious. A game of politics was played in the Palais Bourbon, shifting groups conspiring to gain office, overturning ministries with light-hearted impunity in the process. The making, unmaking and remaking of cabinets was a favourite pastime of the Third Republic: its seventy years saw eighty-eight ministries and fifty prime ministers. Ministers were more often appointed as a reward for political intrigue than for administrative skill. The uncharitable said that this hardly mattered as they were so busy manoeuvring to keep their portfolios, in the next cabinet if not the present, that they hardly had time to visit their ministries. It was difficult to get agreement between coalition members of the cabinet, even more difficult to retain the support of the coalition parties outside. Policy often tended to vanish in the search for a common denominator.

None of the parties had very effective national organisations, the radicals virtually none at all. When single-member constituencies replaced the system of voting for party lists in larger constituencies, the nomination of candidates fell into the hands of self-appointed committees of local shopkeepers, schoolmasters, doctors, lawyers and journalists, primarily concerned with local issues. Their power led Halévy to speak of the *République des comités*. While candidates generally adopted a party label or subscribed to a national programme, they were often really standing as individuals or fighting on local issues. As a result, the *esprit de clocher* of the constituencies was introduced into parliament. Sectional interests confused national politics. Their personal following made many deputies free-lancers, socialists not excluded, and played havoc with parliamentary discipline. They could bargain, vote, realign as they pleased, owing only a final

Discredit of French democracy

allegiance to their electors. There were numerous national parties, numerous, and often distinct, parliamentary groups, and endless splinters, not to mention the band of independents. This kaleidoscopic confusion of views in the Chamber made agreement on any major issue difficult. Cabinets based on such shifting sands were bound to be unstable and weak.

The only counter-balance was the ever present threat to the Republican regime. This forced the parties of the centre to unite, after a fashion, in republican defence, in bloc and cartel. Republican defence, however, was a negative policy; there was no agreement on economic or social reform, little positive action, indeed, beyond anti-clerical legislation. *Débrouillage* was the motto of the Third Republic and that meant half-measures, usually too little and too late. The failure of legislative programmes, the weakness of governments in the face of crisis, their instability, the obvious need for reform in many sectors, the permanent intrigue in the corridors of parliament, the careerism of the deputies and their irresponsibility in overthrowing cabinets—all combined to undermine parliamentary democracy. R. K. Gooch wrote in 1927, and his comment was equally true of the prewar years: "There can be little if any doubt that the parliamentary system is today in discredit in France. The attitude of the people towards parliament and the parliamentary system may take the form of violent antipathy, supercilious disdain or regretfully admitted criticism; but enthusiasm or even mild popularity seems not to exist."[1]

THE CHARGE OF CORRUPTION. The first Republic, with its cult of the classical, placed high value on public morality. The scandals that were a feature of the Third made a mockery of that tradition. In 1887 a widespread traffic in honours and promotions came to light and the trial led directly to the Elysée Palace where the deputy Daniel Wilson was residing with his father-in-law, President Grévy. At the trial of the military commander of Paris, one of those implicated, it was found that the file of the case had been tampered with and documents exchanged. The regime itself became suspect. Grévy stood behind his son-in-law. Despite obviously sincere protestations of personal innocence, he could hardly escape the touch of suspicion and was eventually forced to resign. Sadi Carnot was chosen by the Assembly to replace him, reputedly on the principle 'vote for the stupidest', and this itself marked a further stage in the decline of the presidency. Wilson, aquitted on technical grounds after appeal against a two-year sentence, returned to the Chamber. The deputies ignored him

[1] Gooch, 'The Anti-parliamentary Movement in France' in *American Political Science Review*, August 1927, p. 553.

215

but, as an observer said, "It was the whores keeping clear of the woman taken in adultery."

Two years later came the failure of the Panama Canal company. It had been financed by thousands of small investors throughout the country, attracted by the name of de Lesseps, successful constructor of the Suez canal. De Lesseps, however, had badly underestimated the cost and this was aggravated by mismanagement in Panama. As more and more funds were required and investors grew scarce, money had to be spent bribing the press. Finally, when the public refused to subscribe to a lottery, work had to stop and the whole scheme collapsed. The investors raised an outcry; an enquiry followed and the officers of the company, including de Lesseps, were found guilty of obtaining money by false pretences and malversation of funds. The trial of the great Frenchman of Suez caused a stir but it was not until 1892 that the real scandal broke. The *Libre Parole*, an extreme anti-semitic paper recently founded by Drumont, accused the company of having used the Jewish financier Baron de Reinach to bribe members of parliament. Two days before the Chamber was to debate the question Reinach committed suicide. A story of blackmail and embezzlement emerged, involving another Jewish financier. It was then discovered that large sums of money had been distributed to members of parliament, largely to obtain their vote for the authorisation of a lottery to finance the company. Legal proceedings were instituted against a number of deputies and senators, including five former ministers. With one exception, they were later withdrawn: Baihaut insisted on confessing that he had accepted a large bribe when Minister of Public Works to pilot through the lottery legislation; he was convicted.

For the republicans all was saved but honour. The mud which had been stirred up did not settle again for many years, however, and those who were labelled *chéquards* found it difficult to regain the confidence of the public. In 1893 even Clemenceau was not re-elected while the socialists increased their seats from twelve to fifty. The atmosphere of suspicion lasted for many years. The scandal seemed to confirm vague suspicions that had existed before and seemed to make probable charges subsequently made. Thus Paul Louis, in his book on syndicalism, could speak of a much wider corruption in parliament, deputies generally in the pay of great industrialists and financiers, without his accusation sounding too implausible.[1]

THE DREYFUS AFFAIR. The tragedy of Captain Dreyfus is too well known to need retelling. The story dragged on for twelve years, from 1894 when the leakage of military information was discovered and Dreyfus

---

[1] P. Louis, *Le syndicalisme contre l'Etat*, 1910, p. 53.

sentenced to imprisonment on Devil's Island, until 1906 when he was finally rehabilitated by a resolution of the Chamber. With Zola's open letter to the president—'J'accuse!'—and Clemenceau's articles in *L'Aurore* in 1898, the personal destiny of Dreyfus became linked with that of the Republic and his case became *l'Affaire*. In the following years it resolved itself into a conflict between those loyal to the Republic and its principles, including justice, and its opponents: nationalists, traditionalists, militarists, monarchists and clericals.

The foreign posting of Colonel Picquart who had protested at the weakness of the evidence against Dreyfus; the discovery that the Chief of Military Intelligence, Colonel Henry, had been forging evidence in the dossier against Dreyfus; the refusal of the military authorities to revise their attitude after Major Esterhazy, on whom suspicion had originally fallen, fled the country—all went to undermine the honour of the army and the faith of the public first in the High Command, then in the conservative government of the time. The stubbornness of the anti-Dreyfusards seemed also to show the complete immorality of the conservative parties, ready to sacrifice an innocent man in order to preserve the good name of the army. The tone of their campaign, the virulence of their attack on republican opponents, the intolerance, the hatred of foreigners, the anti-semitism, the crudeness and dishonesty of their propaganda—these left a taste as unpleasant as anything Goebbels could later produce.

In time, however, the virtue of the Dreyfusards was also challenged. Originally appearing as the disinterested champions of honesty, decency and the rights of the individual, they turned out to be politicians. To Sorel and some others it appeared as if they were using the case as a spring-board, an electoral issue to advance their own party. Both sides drew what benefit they could from the affair: the anti-clericals used it against the church and the radicals against the right; the reactionaries used it against the Republic and the militarists against the parliamentarians. The Dreyfusards, once in power, suppressed their enemies. They could have done little else in the circumstances of the time. But it allowed Sorel to accuse them of rivalling the intolerance of their opponents by their own petty vengeance. Writing of Jaurès, he declared: "Experience has always shown that revolutionaries plead *raison d'état* as soon as they get into power, that they then employ police methods and look upon justice as a weapon which they may use unfairly against their enemies."[1]

It was the attack on the Church that gave some ground to Sorel's accusation. A law of 1901 provided for the dissolution of all religious

[1] G. Sorel, *Reflections on Violence*, 1916, p. 118.

orders not specifically authorised by parliament. Few requested authorisation and few requests were accepted. The majority were dissolved, particularly the teaching orders, whose members were forbidden to teach in France; unauthorised religious establishments and schools were closed by force. In 1904 the Concordat was denounced. A law of 1905 proclaimed the final separation of Church and state: all state subsidies to religious bodies were ended and all ecclesiastical property was transferred to the state. The confiscation of buildings and the expulsion of the orders were carried out with vigour. The laws themselves were harsh and they were further strained by Combes in their application. When churches were later handed back on loan, they bore—as they bear to this day—the stigma of the Republic on their walls: *Liberté, Egalité Fraternité*. To a large extent the Church reaped what it had sown. Its consistent hostility to republican principles, its open allegiance with the forces conspiring to overthrow the Republic, probably made the expulsion of certain orders and *laïcisation* of the schools inevitable. And it is hard to feel much sympathy for the priests behind the anti-semitic campaigns of *La Croix*. The radical revenge was nevertheless intolerant and often petty: *Clochemerle* was a satire, not a fantasy. While the anti-democratic right naturally saw only the faults of the radicals and republicans, Sorel concluded despairingly that all were corrupt but the workers.

THE CRITIQUE OF PARLIAMENTARY GOVERNMENT. The failures of parliamentary democracy in syndicalist eyes have been discussed earlier. Attention may nevertheless be drawn once more to two aspects which link syndicalism with two wider but distinct movements hostile to the parliamentary system.

At the turn of the century, at a time when the workers were becoming more vocal in their demands, it seemed as if the political system was wholly incapable of dealing with their demands. The fast moving forces of industrial development were quite beyond the slow-working machinery of the French parliament. The political capacity of democracy to organise the economic and social life of the nation was challenged. By its organisation and procedures parliament was obviously ill-suited to deal with the legislation required; it had neither the time nor the knowledge required. The situation was aggravated in France by its extreme reluctance to delegate powers to more competent bodies, notably the executive. At the same time, and this was another peculiar fault of the French parliament, it was invariably occupied with political questions and the defence of the Republic. The manoeuvres necessary for any legislative programme to succeed meant that it could only contain the common denominator of agreement—and as there were many groups that had to agree, that denominator was always low.

While this was sufficient to damn the whole democratic system in the eyes of hostile critics, the more friendly criticised the machinery while remaining attached to the spirit of democracy, of rationality and reasonableness in politics. The revolt against parliamentary democracy was thus wider than the revolt against Reason. It included all those groups which hoped to replace, or at least supplement, traditional political institutions by economic institutions designed to meet the needs of a complex industrial society. The Webbs' constitution for the socialist commonwealth of Great Britain was an example of this trend.

More important for the syndicalists than the incapacity of the parliamentary machine, itself something of an abstract notion, was probably the more emotional charge of corruption. The socialist deputies appeared to have betrayed the interests of those whom they were elected to represent. The ever more bourgeois character and republican policies of the socialist parties were noted. It was natural that the workers should resent the attempted leadership of another class. The French experience of *arrivistes* and turncoats was an added provocation. It led to bitter hostility towards politicians whose life and outlook stamped them as bourgeois or intellectuals, whatever political faith they professed, towards socialists as much, if not more, than others. This hostility was directed equally against the parliamentary government. Having corrupted the socialist deputies so that the socialist opposition appeared to merge into the bourgeois majority, the whole parliamentary system became identified with the interests of the capitalist class. It was thus rejected in its entirety. As Lagardelle said, syndicalism was born from the reaction of the proletariat against democracy. The workers, thrown on their own resources, relied on their own strength to achieve their demands. No more discussion, but action; no more compromise, but war. From the revolt against democracy to the revolt against Reason was but a step.

This aspect of the syndicalist revolt, based as it was on the bourgeois-intellectual character of parliamentary democracy, linked it to the anti-democratic movements of the right. Of course, there was an important difference. The syndicalist complaint was essentially material: for one reason or another—*embourgeoisement*, corruption or inefficiency—they had failed to obtain the advantages they hoped from the system. The right ostensibly based its attack on moral grounds: it condemned both the corruption and the weakness of the regime; democracy was undermining the prestige of France abroad and the good order of society at home.

Nationalism, monarchism and the right

The history of the anti-parliamentary right in France, from Bourbon legitimates to fascist leagues, was an endless stream of movements, parties and groups of thinkers, polemicists and doctrines, far more complex than French socialism. A right-wing movement ran parallel to the syndicalist left, forming part of the same revolt against democracy, linked by a common enemy, sometimes a common temperament, with an overlap of ideas, and brought together in the person of Georges Sorel.

THE BOULANGER CRISIS. In 1882 Déroulède founded the *Ligue des Patriotes* to press for the reconquest of the lost territories. To this aim another was soon added: revision of the constitution to establish a strong government capable of achieving this end. He found a potential leader in General Boulanger, the Minister of War, a popular hero who had earned the nickname *Général Revanche*. The radicals and moderate conservatives combined in alarm to keep the general out of future cabinets. Thwarted, he decided to seek direct, popular support in his plebiscitary campaign of 1888, when he won six by-elections in different parts of the country on the programme 'Dissolution, Constituente, Révision'. The climax came next year when he was elected in Paris amid scenes of great enthusiasm. Had he given the word that night, a *coup d'état* might well have succeeded. He hesitated and the government, shocked into action, decided to impeach him. Boulanger's nerve failed entirely; he fled to Belgium and shortly afterwards committed suicide.

Boulanger had become the focus for all those discontented with the regime, for those who longed for revenge against Germany, for those who wanted a revision of the constitution, for those who wanted to purify the state of its corruption, for monarchists and even for some of the extremists of the left who sought a transformation of the social order. If there was any positive agreement, it was the belief in strong, personal, but democratically elected, government. In that sense the movement was Bonapartist, though the attack was directed against the parliamentary system rather than the Republic itself. Déroulède demanded not the Empire but a *République plébiscitaire*. Boulanger was an ostentatiously republican general who had shown his hostility to the royalists by depriving the princes of their commissions and to the Church by not releasing candidates for the priesthood from military service. Much of his support, however, came from quite different quarters: he was financed by the ultra-royalist Duchesse d'Uzès and had the support of the Baron de Mackau, leader of the monarchists in the parliament; he was also financed by Baron Hirsch, a Jew, but supported at the same time by Drumont and his anti-semitic band; his campaign manager, Dillon, was a catholic while one of his main supporting newspapers was the violently anti-clerical *Intransigeant*, edited by Rochefort. Monarchists, imperialists, republicans, anti-semites and even *blanquistes*—the failure of *boulangisme* reflected not only the General's lack of nerve but also the lack of unity in the anti-parliamentary opposition.

One effect of the Boulanger affair was to show the royalists that the parliamentary monarchy of the Orleanist tradition was unlikely to attract many supporters. The Comte de Paris announced his conversion to the imperialist doctrine of the plebiscite and strong government without ministerial responsibility. The way was thus opened for the monarchy to become a rallying point for the anti-parliamentary forces.

THE DREYFUS CRISIS. The next crisis centred round the figure of Dreyfus. The former *boulangistes*, now simply *plébiscitaires* or nationalists, the anti-semites, the royalists and most of the clerical party again formed a common front. For many there appeared no choice. On the one hand there was a Jewish captain convicted of treason, not a true Frenchman and therefore probably guilty; even if he were not, what were abstract principles like truth and justice compared to the things they really loved: the army's honour, *la patrie* and the authority of the state? But the affair also provided an obvious opportunity for the rallying of forces. Rioting in the streets grew to dangerous proportions. The *Ligue des Patriotes* was revived and joined by the *camelots du roi*, the *jeunesse anti-sémite*, the *comités de la jeunesse royaliste* and other groups. But the anti-democratic forces again lacked cohesion. When Loubet, a Dreyfusard, was elected president in 1899, Déroulède planned a *coup d'état*, only to find that some of the other groups preferred to organise their own. Nor was there a leader available. General Pellieux, who was to lead the troops to the Elysée after President Faure's funeral was even less reliable than Boulanger. The curtain fell with Déroulède running alone after the troops as they marched home to their barracks, trying to persuade them to turn.

The formation of a ministry of republican concentration by Waldeck-Rousseau placed the moderates firmly in control of the government. A new *Ligue de la Patrie Française*, headed by Lemaître, turned to electoral activities. Though it had considerable membership, it was internally divided and had little success. The victory of the Dreyfusards was sealed when the president remitted Dreyfus' sentence of imprisonment. At the same time, the senate found Déroulède and others guilty of plotting to overthrow the Republic. In the face of their defeat, many made their peace with the Republic. The demoralisation of the anti-parliamentary forces was complete when royalists and nationalist republicans began to quarrel about the responsibility for their failure.

THE ACTION FRANÇAISE. This disintegration led Barrès to remark despairingly in 1899 that no progress was possible without a doctrine. Charles Maurras found the answer. The doctrine was monarchy and 'integral nationalism'. The organisation that rallied the anti-republican forces anew was the *Action Française*. This group, formed in 1898, was originally led by Henri Vaugeois who declared himself a sincere republican but a Frenchman first and foremost. He advocated a mixture of boulangiste strong government and Drumont's anti-semitic nationalism: a new, oligarchic Republic, where power would be personal and responsible. France was to be governed not by laws but by living heads, or even one head, though it might have to be cut off from time to time—so Maurras later summed up his programme. Maurras wrote for the group's magazine and used his polemical skills to obtain the support of those who remained firm anti-Dreyfusards even after the discovery of the Henry forgery. His defence of Colonel Henry, whom he painted as a martyr in the public cause and whose forgery he described as a work of the highest patriotism, coming at a time when less brazen minds were disconcerted, made him almost overnight the leader of the anti-democratic right. He soon won over Vaugeois to his way of thinking and, after him, many other prominent nationalists and *républicains plébiscitaires*.

In 1901 the *Action Française* formally adhered to the royalist cause. In Maurras it had a man whose power of argument and strength of conviction provided a framework of political doctrine within which most of the right wing opponents of democracy were to work, at least until the rise of the fascist leagues; which, indeed, was not without influence on some of its opponents on the left. The *Action Française* provided both the organisation and the philosophy which the *Ligue des Patriotes* and the *Ligue de la Patrie Française* had lacked. In many ways, however, the philosophy was more important: the *Action Française* was less of a party than an organ for the propagation of a doctrine to which the discontented could rally. In a very real sense the *Action Française* was Maurras himself.

The organisation nevertheless proved effective in carrying the fight against the Republic into the streets. Its main vehicle of propaganda was its paper which changed from a fortnightly review to a daily in 1908 and carried articles by Maurras, Daudet and Bainville. The work of propa-

Nationalism, monarchism and the right

ganda was also carried out through the publications of the *Nouvelle Librairie Nationale*, under Jean Rivain and Georges Valois, and by the *Institut d'Action Française*, a 'royalist Sorbonne' founded in 1906, which drew distinguished audiences to its lectures. The *Ligue de l'Action Française* was formed in 1907 to rally a wider circle of supporters under the slogan *France d'abord*. The fighting wing of the movement, led by Maurice Pujo, included the *Etudiants de l'Action Française* and the *Camelots du Roi* whose original purpose was to hawk the newspaper in the streets of Paris but who soon turned into a body of storm-troopers.

NATIONALISM AND THE REVOLT AGAINST REASON. In an article published in 1899 in the royalist *Gazette de France* Maurras showed that the contemporary anti-parliamentary movement was split into several groups, each pursuing different lines, but all opposed to what were in fact only different aspects of the doctrines of the Revolution.[1] Some, who wanted testamentary freedom and the reconstruction of the family, criticised the succession law. Some, who wanted the reconstruction of the communes, the restoration of the provinces and a measure of local independence, criticised the division of the country into artificial *départements* and the centralised state. Some wanted to strengthen the role of professional corporations and criticised economic liberalism. Some criticised the parliamentary system because they wanted strong government, directly answerable to the people but able, at the same time, to restore the authority of the state and make France a great power once more. If one added up these criticisms, one got the five natural powers which were the basis of the constitution of ancient France. Combine the family, the commune and the province, the corporation and stable political authority and you have the formula of the monarchy. In the following year Maurras published the *Enquête sur la monarchie* and drew his conclusion more clearly. Nationalism logically implied the monarchy, for that alone could integrate the diverse strands of nationalist thought into a consistent doctrine: the monarchy was integral nationalism. History, moreover, showed that monarchy alone could achieve the ends which nationalists had been trying to pursue by other means; it must therefore be their first objective. The monarchy was logically necessary. The argument was rationalist. Maurras was always a precise thinker, if often dishonest, and loved to exalt Reason. He spoke with contempt of the alien barbarous romanticism of Rousseau, which he saw as a perversion of the classical tradition on which French civilization was based. Indeed, he also spoke of the microbe of romanticism and revolution; on romanticism he blamed the Revolution, the cult of

[1] *Cit.* W. C. Buthman, *The Rise of Integral Nationalism in France*, 1939, p. 270.

223

democracy and individualism, the disorder of society and the destruction of morals.

It may seem difficult to fit this rationalist outlook into the revolt against Reason. The answer is to be found in the realism which lies at the root of his approach to politics. Edouard Berth, ardent disciple of Sorel and Bergson, but also of Maurras, showed—to his own satisfaction at least—how the gap could be bridged. He claimed that Bergson's intuition was in practice the same as the classical Reason which Maurras professed. Democratic rationalism—naturally to be despised—was really idealism, the attempt to base politics on speculation. The classical variant, on the other hand, was another way of saying realism, the derivation of policy from experience. The monarchist programme was based on the lessons of history: France had invariably benefited from the wars of the *ancien régime* while her emperors had left her smaller than they found her; Britain and Germany were flourishing under their monarchs while France was languishing under the Republic. "We judge an institution by its fruits" declared the *Action Française*, staking a claim to pragmatism similar to that of the syndicalists. Maurras called his method *empirisme organisateur* after Sainte-Beuve. His interpretation of history was always directed to a purpose: how to make France strong, great, prosperous and well-ordered. Having discovered in monarchy the social and political order which experience proved successful, he preached reorganisation on those lines.

Maurras' attitude to politics was almost machiavellian. He knew his goal and would use any practical means to attain it. Typical was his view of the Henry forgery: "The great fault, but the only fault, of Colonel Henry was that he let himself be found out. The irregularity, I will not say the crime, has one excuse in success. It must succeed. It ought to succeed." As typical was his attitude to catholicism. He supported the Church because he judged it a valuable force in promoting order in society and an essential part of the tradition he wished to restore, but at the same time he was too much of a rationalist to believe the doctrines for which it stood: "*Je suis catholique, pourtant athée.*" The validity of an 'ism', even traditionalism, lay in its ability to work. This was the pragmatic approach; it also came close to an acceptance of the myth as a means of acting on the present, thus forming another link with syndicalist ideas.

A very different approach can be seen in the writings of Maurice Barrès, the other great protagonist of nationalist thought at the time, also closely associated with the *Action Française*. His traditionalism, though it claimed also to be realistic and pragmatic, really fitted better into the romantic movement and showed similarities to the intuitive elements of syndicalism. He did not apply Reason to history in order to use its lessons but accepted history as his guide. "My enemies," wrote Barrès, "are those who would transform France according to their own ideas, whereas I want to preserve France." The Revolution had meant that the success of those enemies; the France he wished to preserve was in fact that which had ceased to exist a hundred years earlier. The syndicalists looked forward to the triumph of the working class while the nationalists looked back to the glories of the *ancien régime*. The syndicalists were guided by their experience in the class struggle; the nationalists preferred to consult the accumulated wisdom of the past—their pragmatism was that of Burke. The comparison was made in an article on pragmatism and democracy published in the *Revue des Sciences Politiques* in 1911.[1] Both syndicalists and nationalists declared themselves realists or positivists, but the latter saw 'positive reality' in tradition. From the sort of positivism in Barrès' dictum that nationalism was the acceptance of determinism, only an irrationalist philosophy could emerge. The determining forces he sought were tradition grasped intuitively by the true Frenchman in touch with the soil of France; it meant submission to the *suggestions de notre terre et de nos morts*. Traditionalism could be interpreted in purely intuitive terms: France was a living organism with its own infallible vital instincts which it was necessary to discover.

The parallel to syndicalism is clear. For France one need only substitute the proletariat; for the nationalist claim that the Revolution had falsified French traditions, the syndicalist claim that democracy falsified the class struggle and thus the true path of history. The nationalist corollary was that all developments since the Revolution should be ignored; for the syndicalists the same applied to the democratic system. It is also worth noting that monarchist traditionalism was highly selective, not only in its idealisation of the past but in its resolute blindness to a whole century of French experience. The fact, of course, was that their hatred of the democratic system far outweighed their professed political realism. In that, too, they stood on common ground with the syndicalists. When it came to the test, the real pragmatists were the conservative republicans and the reformist socialists who accepted the reality of the regime in the name of expedience, rather than the revolutionaries of left and right whose strategy (though not tactics) was determined less by a realistic analysis of the situation than by their overwhelming dislike of parliament.

THE NATIONALIST ALTERNATIVE TO DEMOCRACY. It is time to return to the conquering idea of Maurras. In 1900, after consultation with

[1] Combes de Patris, 'Pragmatisme et démocratie' in *Revue des Sciences Politiques*, September/October 1911, p. 797.

Ideological context

representatives of the Duc d'Orléans, he published his *Enquête sur la monarchie*. The question he posed was this: Does salvation lie in the traditional, hereditary, anti-parliamentary, decentralised monarchy? The traditionalist aspect has already been discussed with its distinction between a natural society and the artificial order imposed by democracy. The task of the monarch was simply to study forces at work in the country and to embody them in laws. According to the *Enquête*, nationalists had declared almost unanimously against the parliamentary system and in favour of personal, personally responsible, government. This was the real theme of many who were neither monarchists nor traditionalists at heart but who supported the *Action Française* because it seemed the only effective anti-parliamentary movement on the right and because they needed some political philosophy to make respectable their demand for authoritarian government. In the process, tradition had to be strained a little. Anti-parliamentary authoritarianism was associated with the plebiscitary empire, with *boulangisme* and Déroulède's republican nationalism, rather than with the monarchy of Orleans. All these, of course, the *Action Française* regarded as perversions, by-products of the democratic ideas of the Revolution. The king must be freed not only from the control of parliament, but from the electorate also, in order to act firmly in the national interest. Only the hereditary character of the office could ensure continuity and devotion to the long-term interests of the nation. With strong, unhampered government guarding the interests of France, glorious things might again be achieved.

Parallel to this centralisation of power in all matters affecting the national interest, particularly foreign affairs and defence, Maurras argued for an extensive decentralisation of powers to professional and regional bodies in all matters concerning professional and regional life. This included much of the economy. The artificial system of democracy was to be replaced by an organic structure based on natural units, representing not abstract electors but the real interests of a particular town or profession. Decentralisation thus meant the re-creation of semi-autonomous municipalities and provinces, with their own loyalties, each allowed to manage its own affairs. The picture was similar to that drawn by G. K. Chesterton in *The Napoleon of Notting Hill* and probably reflected the romantic mediaevalism common to many catholic thinkers of the time. It also meant the re-creation of the mediaeval system of semi-independent, self-regulating corporations: trade guilds, professional organisations, academies, inns of court, religious bodies and similar institutions. A parliament, with advisory functions, would be based upon them.

The differences to syndicalism are clear, but so are the similarities. The monarchists were devoted to a national, the syndicalists to a class interest; the monarchist corporations were based on class collaboration, not on class war. The monarchists wanted a powerful ruler at the head of the state, responsible for his actions but not responsible to anyone; the syndicalists wanted the abolition of the state. Common, however, was the concept of an organic society based on a double system of professional and regional organisations: the corporations, provinces and municipalities on the one hand, the *syndicats*, federations and *Bourses* on the other. A few monarchist writers, emphasising the functional corporation as an alternative to parliamentary government, tried to use syndicalist ideas to forge a link between the two movements (e.g. Valois' book *La Monarchie et la classe ouvrière*, published in 1909). From the other side, the syndicalist theoretician Panunzio emphasised the regional basis of syndicalist organisations and stressed the civic character of the *Bourses*, actually comparing them to mediaeval communes.[1] Both systems, moreover, would have excluded the professional politician in favour of the expert, in one sense or another. Both, by the same token, were hostile to the role of intellectuals in politics. Thus Berth could write approvingly of the Maurrasian monarchy that it would be "a non-intellectual state...no longer the prey of intellectuals and their instrument of government, the modern democratic state".[2]

THE NATIONALISTS AND DIRECT ACTION. In his original enquiry Maurras had answered the question "What is to be done?" by "Establish the monarchy." It was not until the edition of 1903 was published that he answered the question "How is it to be done?" His answer was simple: "As all other governments since time immemorial—by force." The first task, however, was propaganda. For a whole generation Maurras spoke as if the king was going to enter Paris any day. The picture of the triumphal return of the Duc d'Orléans filled the need for a myth, playing a role similar to that attributed by Sorel to the general strike, serving as a rallying point and as a spur to action.

Four groups were hostile to nationalist aims. The 'four confederate states' —Jews, protestants, freemasons and citizens of foreign origin—had gained control of the country according to Maurras, just as capitalists and bourgeoisie had for the syndicalists. Both considered it hopeless to try and defeat them by constitutional means as they had the parliamentary machine firmly in their hands. The evidence seen by syndicalists has already been traced; the nationalists found theirs in the reaction to Boulanger's electoral campaign. In any case, it was the republican constitution itself they wished

[1] Panunzio in *Mouvement Socialiste*, July/August 1912.
[2] E. Berth, *Les méfaits des intellectuels*, 1914, p. 57.

to overthrow. With the syndicalists, they echoed Proudhon's *vaincre le pouvoir sans lui demander rien*. Until 1914 the *Action Française* refused to participate in electoral campaigns or press for reforms through parliament. "The monarchists did not want to cap the Republic with the *fleur-de-lis* of the monarchy; they wanted to cut its throat."[1] Their revolutionary position was clear. So were their methods. Riot, conspiracy, *coup d'état*—all would serve. Blanqui was their unacknowledged master. As Brogan has pointed out: "The revolutionary doctrine of a conservative party backed by fighting squads of ardent young men was a French invention, destined to achieve great things outside the country of its birth."[2] The fighting squads were largely recruited from the students of Paris. How the *coup d'état* was to be achieved was left for events to determine. On joining the *Ligue de l'Action Française* members had to sign a declaration engaging them to employ all means to fight the Republic and serve the restoration. But it was not until 1934 that a serious attempt was made, not until 1940 that the republican regime collapsed, and then only through military defeat. Though many nationalists turned into collaborators, such was their hatred of the parliamentary system, it was the *Etat Français* that was established, headed by a marshal, not the monarchy. One may judge for oneself which part of such members' engagement reflected their true desires, which part was mere doctrine.

The importance of Maurras lay in the fact that he had a doctrine available when a doctrine was needed. Its content mattered little. The first words of the Enquiry were significant: "Those who are satisfied need not open his book; it is for the discontented." Many of the discontented took his word for the doctrine and followed the *Action Française* because it was the best outlet for their discontent. They had a wide range of dislikes: the Republic, parliament, democracy, freethinkers, Jews, pacifists, internationalists, the bourgeois parties, socialists—or just their own dull lives. It appealed to the activists whose social background made it unlikely that they would find an opportunity for action in the revolutionary left. "The strength of the *Action Française* was to be found in its opportunism rather than in its programme", wrote Dorothy Pickles.[3] The true character of the movement showed itself in the form taken by its revolutionary action: members restricted themselves to hostile demonstrations, more or less violent, directed much less against the Republic than against individuals they happened to find displeasing.

This can be illustrated by the two most notorious of the numerous

---

[1] D. Pickles, *The French Political Scene*, 1938, p. 63.
[2] D. W. Brogan, *The Development of Modern France*, 1940.
[3] D. Pickles, *The French Political Scene*, 1938, p. 63.

incidents mounted by the *Action Française* before 1914. In 1908 and 1909 a campaign was directed against Professor Thalamas of the Sorbonne, whose demythologisation of Joan of Arc was seen as an outrage against a national saint and against the honour of France. There were riots within the university and in the streets outside, violence to persons and battles with the police, the whole showing considerable evidence of conspiracy. Thalamas was prevented from lecturing and shortly afterwards the dean of the law faculty, Lyon-Caen, a Jew, was forced to resign. In 1911 royalist youth broke up the performance of a new play by Henry Bernstein, another Jew and a former deserter, at the *Comédie Française*. These attacks were doubtless seen as a romantic crusade. They were also an outlet for activist tempers. Such violence probably served its own purpose. As with other activist movements, the end was less important than the means. The means were direct action, fighting in the streets, assault, breaking up meetings, damage to property and the terrorisation of opponents. These practices bore some resemblance to the riots, violence and intimidation employed by the syndicalists to further their purpose. In both cases it reflected the same limited, immediate hostility to a specific group, whether Jews or blacklegs, and bore little relation either to the forms it was supposed to take (i.e. *coup d'état*, strike) or the ends it was supposed to serve (i.e. restoration of the monarchy, emancipation of the proletariat). Nationalist action was almost entirely an expression of this undirected spirit of revolt and was invariably violent. The direct action of the syndicalists, on the other hand, was more often directed to an end, was generally less personal and was frequently not violent at all.

Fascism: the alternative path

Fascism was the most acute expression of the revolt against Reason and democracy. By the time it took shape, well after the 1914–18 war, revolutionary syndicalism had virtually disappeared. Similarities nevertheless showed that both were part of the wider revolt of the time. Both were a reaction against liberal democracy, the parliamentary system, bourgeois society and the capitalist economy. The means they employed had something in common, as did the new social order they preached. More important, perhaps, were the direct personal links. Syndicalism was a movement of the working class, fascism, though the subject is still much debated, was essentially middle class. But there were those, particularly the theorists, intellectuals, *déracinés*, who turned from a movement that had failed to one that seemed to promise success, another outlet for revolutionary action, remaining true at least to their rejection of bourgeois democracy. A consideration of fascism makes clear this aspect of the romantic activist temper. While extreme right and extreme left were two ends of a spectrum, in the case of syndicalism and fascism it was a spectrum that met.

THE CASE OF MUSSOLINI. In the early days of the century the Italian socialists were split, like the French, into reformists and revolutionaries. Labriola's *Avanguardia Socialista* spoke for the latter. It stressed the proletarian basis of the socialist movement, advocated the general strike as a means of emancipation and criticised the *embourgeoisement* of the parliamentary socialists. Its policy closely resembled that of the *Mouvement Socialiste*, edited in Paris by Lagardelle. Mussolini was a contributor to the paper and, at the time, a revolutionary socialist with strong syndicalist sympathies. He attacked the reformists in parliament for their ministerial tendencies and their commitment to social legislation, both of which diverted socialists from their real aim, the abolition of the capitalist system. The bourgeois government had succeeded in domesticating them without offering any real concessions in return. Following the slippery road of opportunism, the party had become respectable and was no longer a threat to the system; the danger was that it would also undermine the revolutionary spirit of the workers. Mussolini preferred direct action, the general strike. During the great strike of 1904 he wrote: "I hope this will be the strategic prelude to the coming and supreme battle."[1]

In the decade before the war, then, Mussolini was an active revolutionary socialist, a successful agitator and an effective journalist. In

[1] *Cit.* G. Megaro, *Mussolini in the Making*, 1938, p. 105.

1912, when the revolutionary wing gained control of the party, he became one of its leading spokesmen. The years that followed brought rapid changes of front. As editor of the *Lotta di Classe* he had preached antipatriotism and antimilitarism with a fervour equal to Hervé in France, making his own the latter's dictum that the national flag was a rag to be planted on a dunghill. In 1914, like Hervé and the French syndicalists, he was converted to patriotism and—expelled from the socialist party—urged Italy's entry into the war. In 1919 he organised his *fascio de combattimento*, battle groups, with a very heterogeneous programme, more or less democratic: electoral reform, anti-clerical legislation and workers' control of industry. Finding the parliamentary approach a failure—not a single fascist was elected—he moved back towards the revolutionary left. In 1920 he supported the occupation of factories in northern Italy by strikers and the policy of direct action then propagated by the communists. The failure of this revolt, and a realisation that support for his fascist bands was coming largely from the middle class, caused him to veer sharply to the right again. In 1921 the fascists fought the election as members of the anti-socialist constitutional bloc. The March on Rome came in 1922. Mussolini headed a government of fascists, nationalists and conservatives; made his peace with the monarchy and the Church; declared himself in favour of economic liberalism and parliamentary government. A final switch came in 1925 when he felt strong enough to dissolve all parties except his own: state control of industry and the abolition of parliamentary government followed.

How can one explain such instability? It has been said that fascism was no more than Mussolini's own biography. He said himself: "Having created the fascist party, I have always dominated it."[1] Was Mussolini simply an adventurer, a twentieth century *condottiere* consumed by the lust for power and willing to follow whatever course served that overriding purpose? The worker's inability to maintain control of the factories showed him in 1920 that he could not step to power on their shoulders. He turned, therefore, to exploit the very bourgeoisie in whom his own earlier, syndicalist tactics had aroused such fear of revolution that they were now ready to welcome a strong man and a firm hand in the defence of property and order. He dropped syndicalist, and emphasised nationalist, ideas in recognition of the changing clientèle for his bands: as the workers and ex-servicemen drifted towards communism, they were replaced by middle-class youths and student admirers of the adventurer-poet Gabriele d'Annunzio.

But this was not the whole explanation. The constant was Mussolini's

---

[1] B. Mussolini, *My Autobiography*, 1936, p. 296.

activist temper, a temper which declared that the movement was all, the end nothing. He cared more for passionate political combat than for the ultimate social object of such combat. Much of the same was true of his earlier followers. The fascist movement was *azione e sentimente*; it found joy in action for action's sake, in action without preconceived ideas or much racking of brains, determined by the opportunities of the moment and shaped by the ever changing experience of life. The activist temper sought its outlets where it could and it was the changing opportunities, outside its own control, which explained the shifts of direction. The opportunities open to Mussolini were, in turn, syndicalist agitation, war, and the fighting bands of anti-socialist youth. Finally, when he had attained power and there was no one left to fight at home, he turned outwards to military expansion, which he pursued in a spirit no less bellicose than that of his revolutionary youth. The first step was also taken by the militant syndicalists of France, the second by many of the theoreticians who had supported the movement.

PRAGMATISM, INTUITION, ACTION AND MYTH. There was nevertheless a rationale for this sort of activism. In his preface to Rocco's *Political Doctrine of Fascism* Mussolini claimed that "fascism has a doctrine or, if you will, a particular philosophy with regard to all questions which beset the human mind today". This book—the first official statement of such a philosophy—was not published until after the fascist conquest of power, however, and by then the fascist party had become identified with the state. There was thus considerable difference between the philosophy elaborated by Rocco and Gentile, with its Hegelian trappings, its emphasis on the state, order and tradition, and the unwritten philosophy of Mussolini's days as an outsider, which lacked both the metaphysical and the *étatiste* paraphernalia. The ideology of fascism was in some ways a fusion of syndicalist and nationalist ideas, but the former gradually receded into the background and the latter came to dominate. The present concern is with the earlier period.

Mussolini made a remark that has often been quoted: "The sanctity of an 'ism' is not in the 'ism'; it has no sanctity beyond its power to do, to work, to succeed in practice. It may have succeeded yesterday and fail tomorrow, failed yesterday and succeed tomorrow", and he added: "The machine must first of all run."[1] The machine was the movement. He made no secret of his anti-intellectual bias, his dislike of abstract thought and his practical attitude to all questions. He condemned marxism on the same grounds as the syndicalists. "Fascism is based on reality, bolshevism

[1] B. Mussolini, *My Autobiography*, 1936, p. xiv.

Fascism: the alternative path

on theory. We want to be definite and real, we want to come out of the clouds of discussion and theory."[1] This was the pragmatic approach to politics. Mussolini was equally attached to the intuitive approach. "Before all I trust my insight. What I call my insight—it is indefinable."[2] The result was a striking combination of realism and mysticism. Both were characteristic of the revolt against Reason.

Another constant in Mussolini's philosophy was the demand for action for its own sake, as a value in itself, typical of the romantic movement. "Fascism desires man to be active and engaged in action with all his energies. It wants him to be virilely conscious of existing difficulties and ready to meet them. It considers life a struggle, thinking that it is man's task to conquer for himself that which is really worthy of him...So for the individual, so for the nation, so for humanity." And again: "Above all fascism believes neither in the possibility nor in the utility of perpetual peace. It thus repudiates the doctrine of pacifism, born of a renunciation of the struggle and an act of cowardice in the face of sacrifice. War alone can bring up to its highest tension all human energy and puts the stamp of nobility upon the people who have the courage to meet it."[3] Earlier, Mussolini would have substituted class for nation and class struggle for war, but there was no doubt that this Nietzschean hymn also represented, perhaps more truly indeed, his attitude in the years before success.

As Lovejoy said, the peculiarity of anti-intellectualism is that one can never see where it will lead. It was impossible to understand Mussolini without realising that the core of his philosophy, in socialist as well as fascist days, was his belief in the need for violence as an instrument of social change. He has been described as a voluptuary of activism whose entire life was a hymn to the nobility of violence.[4] In syndicalist days he declared that the final triumph of the workers would involve 'a bloody duel—an insurrectional tempest'.[5] But he was really more of a *blanquiste* then, believing in propaganda by the deed, minority leadership, insurrection, *coup d'état* (even the general strike was seen in political terms) and transitional dictatorship. This explains why he was really more interested in the organisation of revolutionary élites than in trade union organisation as such. To an extent, of course, the same was true of the militant syndicalists. Some were followers of Blanqui, or anarchists, who had come to the labour movement because they saw there the best opportunity for revolutionary action. They too believed in minority leadership; they too wanted

---

[1] Cit. F. W. Coker, *Recent Political Thought*, 1935, p. 473.
[2] Cit. E. Ludwig, *Talks with Mussolini*, 1932, p. 109.
[3] Cf. 'Political and Social Doctrines of Fascism' in *Enciclopedia Italiana*.
[4] G. Megaro, *Mussolini in the Making*, 1938, p. 104.
[5] Cit. G. Megaro, *Mussolini in the Making*, 1938.

233

to keep the unions as a fighting force. In time, however, as the labour movement grew stronger and more effective, they adapted their philosophy to possibilities of reform; Mussolini, like Sorel, sought the revolutionary spirit elsewhere.

There are other similarities, though with Sorel rather than the syndicalist workers. Fascism was action and sentiment. "Were it otherwise," wrote Rocco, "it could not keep up the immense driving force, that renovating power which it now possesses, and would merely be the solitary meditation of a chosen few."[1] For Sorel it was the action and sentiment (*élan*) of the workers, not any theory they held, that would save the world from moral degradation. Mussolini also believed that it was faith that moved mountains, not reason. He endorsed Sorel's doctrine of the myth. Though his myth was not the general strike—by the time he had digested Sorel it was no longer opportune—his exposition was that of the master: "We have created our myth. The myth is a faith, a passion. It is not necessary that it shall be a reality. It is a reality by the fact that it is a goal, a faith, that it is courage. Our myth is the nation, our myth is the grandeur of the nation. And to this myth we subordinate all the rest."[2]

THE CORPORATE STATE. In 1926 the fascist Labour Charter set up a system of parallel *syndicats* and national federations for workers and employers whose purpose was to establish collective agreements, settle disputes and ensure collaboration between capital and labour (though without derogating from the managerial responsibility of the employer). In 1928 the composition of the Chamber of Deputies was altered and the electors were presented with a single slate of candidates chosen—ostensibly at least—by an elaborate procedure involving a large number of organisations including local authorities, economic organisations and cultural institutions. In 1934 employers and workers were brought together in national corporations, co-ordinated by a National Council of Corporations. Although they were supposed to determine wages and prices, production standards, plant management and labour relations, they were in practice little more than a façade for control by the Ministry of Corporations. It was not until 1939, finally, that the corporate state itself was created. The Chamber of Deputies was replaced by a Chamber of *Fasces* and Corporations. There were no elections: councillors were selected from the Fascist Grand Council and the National Council of Corporations. The Senate remained unchanged, its composition according well with fascist ideas. Senators were appointed from specified groups such as dignitaries

[1] A. Rocco, *The Political Doctrine of Fascism*, 1926, p. 10.
[2] *Cit*. H. Finer, *Mussolini's Italy*, 1935, p. 218.

234

of the Church, ambassadors, judges and senior civil servants, distinguished scientists and academicians. Neither assembly had any power. The party's Grand Council was recognised as the highest organ of government and legislation.

The attempt was thus made to build some semblance of an organic, or corporate, structure into an authoritarian system. It clearly bore little resemblance to the sort of society the syndicalists had envisaged. The only common element was the notion that society should be organised on a functional basis. Radically opposed was the enforced collaboration of capital and labour as well as the supremacy of the state. Significant, however, was the fact that it was an attempt to find an institutional alternative to the hated system of parliamentary democracy with its abstract electors, its conflicting parties, its power in the hands of professional politicians. That power was concentrated instead in the hands of a dictator was another matter. Significant too was that the fascist state did not pursue bourgeois-material values. It was true that capitalists did well, but the pursuit of national glory did even better. War was the result. The syndicalist utopia was never tried. The fascist alternative, when achieved, proved to have only a shadowy resemblance to the original ideals of the right-wing opponents of democracy.

INTELLECTUALS AT THE FORK WITHOUT SIGNPOSTS. Mussolini's own discontent he himself also ascribed to Nietzsche: "the *tedium vitae* of our life, of life as it goes on in contemporary civilized societies where irremediable mediocrity triumphs".[1] It was bourgeois life he disliked. In Italy, as in France, the revolt against bourgeois values was a characteristic of the nationalist right as of the syndicalist left. The causes were different, so were the ostensible goals, but the two seemingly opposite poles were linked by their hostility to the centre, clarified in an attack on the democratic order. They shared a common temper in the cult of action. The intellectuals in both camps soon lost themselves in an orgy of anti-bourgeois heroics which quite overshadowed the original differences between them. As the effective centre of action shifted to the right, syndicalist intellectuals, disappointed as the syndicalist revolution did not materialise, drifted steadily and without much thought to the camp of reaction, speaking of revolution all the while. Instability was characteristic of the revolt against Reason and democracy. On the whole, Lovejoy was right when he claimed that experience semed to show that the tendency of anti-intellectual movements was to issue in traditionalism. To that extent, Ramsay MacDonald was justified when he declared that "the answer to

[1] *Cit.* G. Megaro, *Mussolini in the Making*, 1938, p. 107.

syndicalism is Fascismo".[1] It must be remembered, however, that this applied to the syndicalist theoreticians who were not tied to reality by the pressure of material interests as were the syndicalist workers.

The case of Georges Sorel will be discussed later but is also relevant here. As a theoretician of syndicalism he was probably better known in Italy, where the *Reflections on Violence* were first published, than in France itself. After 1908 he gradually disassociated himself from the syndicalists and turned his interest to the *Action Française*. Mussolini, as editor of the *Lotta di Classe*, bitterly attacked this somersault in 1911: "The parabola of Georges Sorel is highly significant. The man has passed, almost with impunity, from the theory of syndicalism to that of the *camelots du roi*."[2] The association of Sorel, and the even closer association of his disciple Edouard Berth, with the royalists was indeed significant, for it symbolised a similar and wider movement that was taking place in Italy, where other syndicalist theoreticians were flirting with the nationalism of Corradini. Mussolini might well castigate the intellectual politicians of syndicalism, oscillating between Sorel and Corradini, but in 1914 he followed the same parabola. One could thus say that in Sorel's own flirtation lay the seeds of the marriage between revolutionary syndicalism and revolutionary nationalism, the child of which, Italian fascism, was born in 1925. It is also worth noting that in 1912 Sorel himself professed to admire Mussolini as a *condottiere* who would redress the feebleness of Italian governments. That did not last, however, and in 1919 it was Lenin he welcomed as yet another possible force of regeneration.

Georges Valois was another link. Son of the working class, at eighteen an anarcho-syndicalist, pupil of the organiser of the *Bourses du Travail*, Pelloutier, then briefly a disciple of Sorel, he crossed in 1906 to the *Action Française*. For a while there was a meeting. Followers of Maurras and Sorel joined to form the *Cercle Proudhon* and published their own review. After the war he again tried to influence the *Action Française* in a syndicalist direction, conducting there an anti-bourgeois campaign greatly to the dislike of Maurras—a campaign which he himself called the fascism of the moment. Frustrated, he left the monarchists and organised his own *Faisceau* in 1925, the first fascist group in France. Then he swung back from right to left, rallying to the Republic in the process and forming in 1927 the *Parti républicain syndicaliste*. He thus moved in the opposite direction from Mussolini and, as he said afterwards, for a while their paths appeared to cross.[3]

[1] R. MacDonald, *Syndicalism*, 1912.
[2] *Cit.* G. Megaro, *Mussolini in the Making*, 1938, p. 235.
[3] G. Valois, *Technique de la révolution syndicale*, 1935, pp. 23–110.

Fascism: the alternative path

The career of Gustave Hervé showed even greater instability. In his youth he had been a *boulangiste* and a follower of Déroulède. Then, as a member of the socialist party, editor of the *Piou Piou de la Yonne* and *Guerre Sociale*, he became the most virulent of the antimilitarists and anti-patriots in France, the scandal of his party and the object of numerous prosecutions by the state. He lost his job as a history teacher and was imprisoned several times. With the outbreak of war, he became an ardent patriot: *Guerre Sociale*, which had been favourable to syndicalism after its fashion, turned into *La Victoire* and supported the Clemenceau government. After the war he left the socialist party, trying in 1919 to find a link between left and right in his own *Parti socialiste national*. By 1925, in his *Lettre aux ouvriers*, he was preaching the authoritarian Republic, a mixture of *boulangisme*, collaboration of the classes and the corporate state. Ten years later came his pamphlet with the prophetic title *C'est Pétain qu'il nous faut*. In 1936 he was converted to the Roman Catholic church.

Finally, and perhaps most interesting, there was the case of the syndicalist theoretician, Hubert Lagardelle (1875–1958). As editor of the intellectual review *Mouvement Socialiste* he brought together labour militants, Sorel and his disciples, and other socialists. While Sorel was primarily interested in the moral problems of democracy, Lagardelle, like Valois, was more concerned with the institutional. He described syndicalism as a socialism of institutions. His move to the right was less a reflection of Sorel's search for moral heroism or Mussolini's search for action than a search for new, organic institutions to replace democracy. He came to realise that syndicalism could only be effective if it passed beyond the boundaries of the labour movement: the industrial workers, after all, were a minority in France while the crisis of democracy affected the whole nation.[1] After the war Lagardelle spent some time in Italy, finding his organic order in the authoritarian corporate state which, he claimed, he had helped Mussolini to create. These links led the French government to appoint him a councillor at their Rome embassy from 1933–40. Finally he moved the whole circle, coming in one sense at least back to his point of departure: having supported the *C.G.T.*'s unsuccessful campaign against the parliamentary Republic in his youth, he associated himself with Pétain's more successful attack in his old age. At the age of sixty-seven he became Vichy Secretary of State for Labour in 1942 and 1943 and it was during his period of office that the *Charte du Travail* was introduced. In practice inoperative, though intended as one of the constitutional laws of the new French State, the charter was actually a synthesis of fascist corporatism and the nazi Labour Front, its slogan 'Solidarity, Duty,

[1] Lagardelle, preface to J. Gaumont, *L'Etat contre la nation*, 1911.

Sacrifice'. Lagardelle preferred to see it as the foundations of an organised society, based on the institutions of natural groups, part of an organic state that was replacing the individualistic structure of the democratic Republic. He proclaimed it a truly revolutionary step in which he had rediscovered a dream linking his whole career.[1] Such confusion was inherent in the dream. The awakening came when, in 1946, he was sentenced to life imprisonment as one of those responsible for the deportation of French workers to Germany.

[1] H. Lagardelle, pamphlet, *La Charte du Travail*, a speech made on 23 September 1942.

Sorel: a moralist in search of action

At the age of forty-five Georges Sorel (1847–1922) resigned from the civil service—he was a member of the elite corps of civil engineers—to devote the rest of his life to study. He spent much of it in the *Bibliothèque Nationale*, reading voraciously, almost indiscriminately, whatever came his way, filling page after page with angry exclamations as he read. These exclamations he rushed into print in a host of small journals, occasionally re-editing those that pleased him most in book form. As he said, "I am a self-taught man exhibiting to others the notes which have served for my own instruction."[1] The results were encyclopedic: interpretations of the bible, the metaphysics of Aristotle, ancient and modern science, the history of technology, the origins of mathematics, Renan, Vico, Proudhon and Bergson—all were considered. Syndicalism formed but a small part but the notoriety of the *Reflections on Violence* stamped him in the public mind as its philosopher. In fact, he was a philosopher who wrote about syndicalism. An eternal student, he wrote to Croce: "I have never asked myself what would be the synthesis of my various writings; I wrote from day to day, according to the needs of the moment."[2] He produced no system nor, indeed, was he consistent. His was an endless search. "The wandering Jew may be taken as a symbol of the highest aspiration of mankind, condemned as it is never to know rest."[3] It is hard to find the pattern even in a single work. Sorel was a conversationalist rather than a writer, stringing together unexplored allusions and half-developed ideas, omitting from the chain of argument what failed to interest him, little concerned with the logical organisation of his material. There was a Bergsonian justification for this approach—"We must beware of too much strictness in our language because it would be at odds with the fluid character of reality"[4]—ingenious but not always helpful.

A certain unity can nevertheless be found in his thought, common themes that ran through his articles and books. Much has been written about Sorel and this is not the place for another assessment. It will simply be shown that a certain approach, an unchanging hope, lay behind all his changes of political front. This temper dominated theory. Sorel, the wandering Jew, sought a movement as much as a philosophy.

[1] G. Sorel, *Reflections on Violence*, 1916, p. 3.
[2] *Cit.* V. Sartre, *Georges Sorel*, 1937, p. 17.
[3] G. Sorel, *Reflections on Violence*, 1916, p. 5.
[4] G. Sorel, *Matériaux d'une théorie du prolétariat*, 1919, p. 58.

Ideological context

THE UNCHANGED TEMPER. Sorel was first and last what the French call a *moraliste*. As deeply concerned as Nietzsche with the decadence of the society in which he lived, his life's work was an unbroken search for the means of regeneration. He was a pragmatist, seeking not truth for its own sake but a moral principle that would work, interested in parties and programmes not for their own sake but as the troops and tactics in a moral cause. *Morale d'abord*—but what sort of morality did Sorel hope to see? The answer lay in a single word, heroism. All Sorel's thought turned on the question of how to restore the heroic virtues of older days.

A recent editor of the *Reflections* put it thus: underlying all is a common theme, that the highest good is the heroic, aggressive, action performed with a sense of impersonal consecration to the ends of a group bound together in fervent solidarity and impelled by a passionate confidence in its ultimate triumph in some cataclysmic encounter.[1] One can point, as in Nietzsche, to passages glorifying war, discipline, dedication and sacrifice. It was Proudhon who declared "La France a perdu ses moeurs", the Proudhon *belliciste* of *La Guerre et la Paix*, who was his favourite model. Sometimes he wrote of the possibilities of a European war as an antidote to the demoralising social harmony favoured by the bourgeoisie,[2] but more often it was the class war he sang—a means by which the nations, at present stupified by humanitarianism, could recover their former energy.[3] Heroism and the sense of the sublime were essentially military virtues. The proletarian acts of violence, incidents in the class struggle, he saw as 'purely and simply acts of war', as such 'carried out without hatred, without spirit of revenge'.[4] By their unity, their disciplined resolution, their personal courage in the pursuit of an impersonal end, the workers showed a high level of morality. What mattered for Sorel was not the material gains the workers might reap from the class war, whether in the short term (e.g. wage increases) or in the long (i.e. expropriation of the capitalists), but the immediate, social value of war as such. It was not unfair to say that it was pure action, action for its own sake, that concerned him; in such action alone was true nobility to be found; through it alone could the world be saved.

His was the activist temper. In 1908 he wrote: "I do not hesitate to declare that socialism can no longer exist without an apologia for violence."[5] But it was Sorel, rather than socialism, who felt the need for this rationalisation. His activism, of course, was purely intellectual, for his own life was one of quiet routine, spent among books and in conversation. He wore

[1] E. A. Shils (ed.), *Reflections on Violence*, 1950, p. 18.
[2] G. Sorel, *Insegnamenti sociali della economia contemporanea*, 1906.
[3] G. Sorel, *Reflections on Violence*, 1916, p. 90.
[4] G. Sorel, *Reflections on Violence*, 1916, p. 21.
[5] G. Sorel in *Le Matin*, 18 May 1908.

Sorel: a moralist in search of action

the rosette of the *Légion d'Honneur* with pride and did nothing to disgrace it; no life could have been more respectably bourgeois than that of the apostle of violence. The thrill could nevertheless be experienced at second hand. One critic spoke aptly of his nostalgia for heroism. He identified with it when he thought he had found it. He did, however, play his part in the battle with the pen. Thus Wyndham Lewis' accusation: "Of all the apostles of dangerous living, pure action, heroism, blood and iron, Sorel was the worst—the most shrewd and the most dangerous."[1] Like Nietzsche, he really desired a sublimated form of war, but even that left him without a compass at the crossroads. Any cause interested him that looked as if it might serve his purpose. And he was likely to drop it on finding that it could not live up to his high expectations. It has been said that he valued means more highly than ends but, in fact, the means were the end: it mattered less who was heroic and to what end that someone should be heroic to some end. Such a morality was empty of content and could be applied to many social movements. He admitted this frankly: "It is hardly worth while to know what is the best morality but only to determine if there is a mechanism in existence capable of guaranteeing the development of morality."[2]

Another aspect of Sorel's character must, however, be taken into account. His make up had a very strong puritan strand. With Proudhon, again, he declared that the world would only become better as it became more chaste. Chastity, loyalty, duty, discipline, family life, pride in work—these were the virtues he cultivated and the virtues he praised. Another interpretation of Sorel's instabilty could be based on this side of his character. He has been seen as an old-fashioned conservative, in the tradition of Renan, Le Play and Taine, whose world had vanished; he was left seeking for something to fill the gap. More realistic than the traditionalists, influenced by Marx, he saw that history could not be turned back. The restoration of an older bourgeois morality was impossible; the bourgeoisie, indeed, had become the very symbol of present degeneration. Another and more vigorous class, one with the forces of history on its side, might, however, achieve the same end by overthrowing the existing society. He could thus be called a revolutionary conservative.[3] It was something of a paradox that Sorel should have seen the proletariat as the class capable of saving the best of the bourgeois tradition and the only truly conservative force in society; he had an equally paradoxical forerunner in Proudhon.

[1] Wyndham Lewis, *Rude Assignment*, 1950, p. 33.
[2] G. Sorel, *Matériaux d'une théorie du prolétariat*, 1919, p. 127.
[3] Cf. M. Freund, *Georges Sorel, der revolutionäre Konservatismus*, 1932.

Ideological context

There was, of course, on the level of theory at least, a link between these two aspects of his character. The key lay in Sorel's pessimistic view of the nature of man and society. A high level of morality could only be maintained by great effort. Times of peace were times of decadence because they did not inspire such efforts. Without the stimulus of war, man sank into complacency and self-interest, society tended to disintegrate. Sorel compared the morality of militant Sparta with the immorality of civilized Athens. He preached war as the creator of heroes and of puritans also.

This moralism explained the greater part of his sympathies and his antipathies. While his sympathies changed, his antipathies remained constant. His enemy was the bourgeoisie, its values and its institutions. He saw bourgeois society through Nietzschean eyes as the triumph of the slaves. R. H. Soltau summed up his accusations for him. "You dare not take any risks for your children and therefore bring them up as mollycoddles with a safe government post and a pension, or with a dowry as an insurance against possible disaster. You dare not take any risks for your country: economically you are incapable of far-seeing schemes which involve the barest possibility of financial loss; politically you dare not consider any change that might disturb the fixed balance of political forces in the country; militarily you try to obtain security by colossal expensive armaments which as likely as not will lead to another war, or by preaching a pacifism which is only another form of cowardice or a shrinking from reality: you sometimes try and combine both methods, and proclaim with equal ardour the need for national defence and the terror of war. You are afraid for your skins, afraid for your class, afraid for what you call European civilization."[1] Fear had led the bourgeoisie to the unheroic doctrine of class solidarity and social peace; fear had led it to forsake action for talk. Democracy embodied both vices. What linked the extremes of right and left was their common attack on bourgeoisie, Reason and democracy. Sorel's significance for modern political thought was that he stood at its most important crossroads. His *Plaidoyer pour Lénine* ended with these words: "I am only an old man whose life is at the mercy of trifling accidents; but may I, before descending into the tomb, see the humiliation of the arrogant bourgeois democracies, today shamelessly triumphant." This, his life-long ambition, led him to explore many paths.

THE CHANGING POLITICS. Sorel's earliest writings were in the conservative tradition; some could have come from the pen of Burke. In his first book he studies the Scriptures from a pragmatic-traditionalist point of

---

[1] R. H. Soltau, *French Political Thought in the Nineteenth Century*, 1931, p. 454.

view, as powerful literature, a moralising and conserving force in society that might prevent the spread of utilitarian and revolutionary ideas which threatened old values, inspiring men at the same time with a sense of the heroic and the sublime. In the same year, 1889, came his *Trial of Socrates*, a traditionalist attack on the intellectual approach to politics with a Nietzschean flavour, though he had then not yet read Nietzsche. Socrates, the first rationalist, had committed the sin to which all rationalists in politics aspire, breaking the chain that bound man to society in the name of an abstract idea. Captivated by the theory of the Absolute, refusing to acknowledge the value of historical laws, he was a revolutionary of the worst sort. The book was really a trial of the intellectuals in contemporary government. The theme was to appear in the *Reflections*.

Sorel's retirement in 1892 coincided with the discovery of Karl Marx, previously little read in France, by a group of younger intellectuals. Marxism appealed to him immediately. This may have been because he was by training and outlook a technician and liked Marx's emphasis on the role of technique (i.e. the methods of production) in determining the economic system and, with it, the superstructure of ideas. Other factors were a grow-ing dislike of the bourgeoisie, so colourfully attacked by Marx, and a new vision of working-class morality brought to him by his wife, herself of working-class stock. Disappointed in the former, he found in Marx reasons to pin his hopes on the latter. For a few years he contributed regularly to marxist reviews. He managed to find the link between morals and classes, morality and class war. Edward Shils explained: "He re-garded political separatism as the morally most appropriate form of social and political organisation. Only when one group drew sharply defined boundary lines around itself could it lead a moral life. Only when it regarded itself as bound by no moral obligation to other sections of the population could it perform its moral duty. For moral duty entails hostility to those outside one's own group. The very content of moral action lay for him in the aggressive affirmation of the group's integrity and solidarity against an outside group."[1] To the slave morality of the bourgeoisie, Sorel opposed the master morality of the emergent proletariat. He followed Marx and Nietzsche simultaneously, discovering, more by instinct than reflection, a way of reconciling the two. Nietzsche saw the slaves' revolt in socialism. Sorel answered by distinguishing between the eternal rebellion of the envious masses and socialism proper—the battle waged by a courageous, dedicated elite of skilled producers, capable of creating a new civilization to replace the one they wished to destroy. This, he claimed, was Marx's distinction between proletariat and *Lumpenproletariat*. He

[1] E. A. Shils (ed.), *Reflections on Violence*, 1950, p. 17.

16-2

emphasised that Marx had not only preached the class war but also the historic mission of the proletariat, essentially moral.[1] Temperamentally unsuited to the rigidities of Marxist doctrine as interpreted in France by Guesde and his followers, he soon revolted against the new clericalism of the marxist doctors. The death of his wife in 1897 left an emptiness in his life and he turned, as he said, to a deeper study of the working class in order to create a monument worthy of her memory. Inspired also by Pelloutier, he laid even more emphasis on the autonomy of the working class. In two articles published the following year and in an introduction of Pelloutier's history of the *Bourses du Travail* (1902) he endorsed the *syndicat* as basis for the reconstruction of society and declared with Proudhon that the proletariat must discover its own capacity: education through action was the key to the progress of socialism.[2] His position, however, was broadly reformist; he defined socialism as a labour movement within democracy.[3] He contributed, in his own style, to the revisionist movement represented in Germany by Bernstein and by Croce in Italy. He was a Dreyfusard and supported Millerand's entry into the Waldeck-Rousseau cabinet, a step he called the passage from the sectarian spirit to the political.[4] The disillusion was swift. The Dreyfusards, Jaurès included, turned out no better than their opponents, intolerant, petty and dishonest once in power.

Disgust with the present led him to reject parliament, democracy and socialism even more decisively than his earlier historical studies. His loyalty to the working class remained. This was the moment for revolutionary syndicalism. He urged the labour movement to break completely with bourgeois democracy, isolating itself to prevent the corruption from spreading. A sharpening of the class war was the best barrier. The concept of proletarian violence—revolutionary direct action—was increasingly emphasised. The *Reflections on Violence*, written between 1906 and 1908, concentrate his ideas at this stage. The dominant theme remained the search for heroism and a new morality. For a moment his hopes were pinned entirely on the proletariat, whom he saluted as the Greeks saluted the Spartan heroes who defended the Thermopyles and helped to preserve the ancient world. Hardly had the *Reflections* been published, however, than his enthusiasm began to wane. He discovered that the militant syndicalists were not heroic lovers of battle but imbued with the same utilitarian spirit as the bourgeoisie; the class struggle was about material things.

---

[1] *Cit.* Dolléans, 'Le visage de Georges Sorel' in *Revue d'Histoire Economique et Sociale*, vol. 26, No. 2, p. 102.
[2] G. Sorel, preface to F. L. E. Pelloutier, *Histoire des Bourses de Travail*, 1902.
[3] G. Sorel, *Matériaux d'une théorie du prolétariat*, 1919, p. 179.
[4] G. Sorel, preface to N. Colajanni, *Il socialismo*, 1898.

Sorel: a moralist in search of action

Worse, the unions were turning reformist, seeking immediate concessions, often through parliament; the revolutionary general strike was fading into the background.

In 1908 Lagardelle tried to form a syndicalist group within the socialist party. The first number of a new paper, *Action Directe*, carried a statement trying to reconcile the two. The role of the party in the grand strategy of the labour movement remained limited: the emancipation of the proletariat could only be achieved by the direct action of the proletariat itself. The party's task was to extend political liberties, thus assuring a democratic environment more favourable to the autonomous development of the labour movement.[1] It allowed the workers to join with other classes in parliamentary politics for this purpose without thereby compromising the class character of their own unions. As a result Sorel broke not only with Lagardelle but with his *Mouvement Socialiste*. He wrote to Delesalle that he was retiring into his hole so as not to compromise himself, though he retained his faith in the working class.[2] By his action he broke up the small group of syndicalist theoreticians who had gathered in the review's office. As they constituted his only real link with the syndicalist movement, he could thereafter be little more than a well-wishing observer. Even that did not last long. The drift towards reformism was as strong in the *C.G.T.* as in the editorial offices of the *Mouvement Socialiste*. By 1907, before the *Reflections* had even been published in their final shape, syndicalism had already passed its heroic age. "The bourgeoisie may find resources to defend itself for a long time to come", he noted.[3] In 1910 he lost patience. As syndicalism had failed to follow the path he had mapped out for it, he would write no more on the subject but devote himself to other matters. "I am too old to wait for distant hopes to come true, so I have decided to use the few years I have left to study more closely other questions in which French youth takes a lively interest today."[4] It was typical of Sorel that this statement, published in Italian, should have been omitted in the French edition which appeared after his reconversion to syndicalism.

Sorel's remark was a little disingenuous. The problems which interested French youth were those of nationalism. Nationalist youth was also anti-bourgeois. It was not merely enthusiastic for action but appeared idealistic also—student violence was not directed to sordid economic gain but pursued for its own sake. The nationalist movement had as its explicit

[1] *Action Directe*, 30 September 1908.
[2] G. Sorel, *Lettres à Paul Delesalle*, 1947, letter of 2 November 1908, p. 108.
[3] G. Sorel in *Mouvement Socialiste*, July 1907, p. 36.
[4] G. Sorel, *Confessioni*, 1910, introduction.

Ideological context

aim the moral regeneration of France, an aim which Sorel had merely been able to impute (and impute wrongly) to the syndicalists. Here were new tactics to combat the decadence of bourgeois society, a new army to lead against the Republic. The fact that Sorel's admirers were already almost entirely drawn from the right no doubt also influenced him. Having contributed an article to a royalist review, he wrote to Croce: "These youngsters are very intelligent; since they cite my books all the time, I could not well refuse them a collaboration of this sort." Perhaps he thought he had more chance of influencing them than the workers; perhaps he was happy to find an attentive audience; above all, there was a new outlet for his energies.

In 1910 plans were drawn up for a new review, *La Cité Française*, to be edited by Sorel, his *alter ego* Berth, the royalist Variot, for a time his Boswell, and Valois, an earlier disciple who had realised some years before that his master had misinterpreted the syndicalist movement and who had thereupon joined the *Action Française*. It was never published as the editors could not agree on its policy. In a prospectus they had sent out, however, they spoke of a need to re-awaken the classes to the self-awareness that democracy had stifled—a need to inspire them with a sense of their own peculiar virtues, without which none could accomplish its own historic mission. By its lack of discrimination between the classes, this statement made clear what was already implied in Sorel's earlier work: the virtues he sought were not specific to one class but could be found in several at the same time. Certain bourgeois writers soon discovered this fact. In the work of their *frère-ennemi* they found argument for the bourgeois counter-revolution. In his *Eloge du bourgeois français* Johannet wrote that Sorel was the best introduction to the bourgeois idea. Of Bourget, whose play *La Barricade*, which Pirou described as the transposition of Sorelian ideas for the edification of the middle class,[1] Sorel himself said: "I would be happy if his great talent determines the bourgeoisie to defend itself, to abandon its inglorious resignation in the face of a courageous enemy."[2] Small wonder that Wyndham Lewis should exclaim: "Sorel's masterpiece of incitement to violence was directed to providing the maximum of class hatred. It was a matter of complete indifference to him which class got charged with hatred first. The bourgeoisie was all right, provided it loathed the pro-letariat so much that it increased the natural dislike of the poor class for the rich class. There was a beautiful detachment about Sorel."[3]

Sorel then joined with Variot to found another review, *l'Indépendence*.

[1] G. Pirou, *Georges Sorel*, 1924, p. 40.
[2] *Cit.* G. Pirou, *Georges Sorel*, 1924.
[3] Wyndham Lewis, *Rude Assignment*, 1950, p. 34.

Sorel: a moralist in search of action

Its committee listed many distinguished names of the right, including Barrès and Bourget. The tone was nationalist, traditionalist, authoritarian and anti-semitic. A possible explanation of his collaboration was the breach that had occurred between Sorel and Péguy, at the office of whose *Cahiers de la Quinzaine* he had held court for more than a decade; at the new editorial office he tried for a moment to fool his hunger. He resigned brusquely in 1914, however, when he saw that he could no more direct the policy of the nationalists than that of the syndicalists. His relations with the *Action Française* during this period were more distant. He remained hostile to Maurras, whom he paradoxically accused of being too much of a democrat, by which he meant too much of a rationalist—and the hostility was mutual. Berth, always a step ahead of his master, was converted to the monarchy; in *Les méfaits des intellectuels* he saluted both as the two masters of French regeneration. In 1911 the *Cercle Proudhon* was founded under their dual protection but was never much more than a small group of monarchists who admired Sorel. "Despite the efforts of Berth and Valois, monarcho-syndicalism never melled. It remained the brainchild of a coterie, still-born."[1]

Sorel was now disillusioned with nationalist youth. In 1914, glossing over his temporary infidelity, he dedicated to his wife and to Delesalle of the C.G.T. a collection of essays, the *Matériaux d'une théorie du prolétariat*— "this book written by an old man who insists, as did Proudhon, on remaining a disinterested servant of the working class". But he expected little of it. When the war, which he had once hoped would rouse Europe from her lethargy, actually came, he was too sunk in pessimism to see any good in it. It was the sordid conflict of plutocracies; the democratic war aims of the Allies just another step in the wrong direction.

After the war two heroic figures appeared on the European scene. One was Mussolini. Sorel had told Variot as far back as 1912 that he would one day see Mussolini, no ordinary socialist but a *condottiere* of the fifteenth century, salute the flag of Italy at the head of a consecrated army.[2] This time Sorel appeared to have picked a winner; fascism was a successful movement. Croce, for one, thought that he approved it; in answer to an enquiry, he wrote: "Being the impressionable man he was, he was in principle favourable to Mussolini; he hated professional politicos, and saw mistakenly in Mussolini a spontaneous and beneficial force."[3] But Sorel was a shrewd enough observer of Italian affairs to realise his own mistake. In one of his last letters to Delesalle he confessed to having suggested that the Italian

---

[1] J. H. Meisel, *The Genesis of Georges Sorel*, 1951, p. 241.
[2] *Cit.* G. Pirou, *Georges Sorel*, 1924, pp. 55.
[3] *Cit.* J. H. Meisel, *The Genesis of Georges Sorel*, 1951, p. 225.

247

Ideological context

socialists should come to an agreement with the government in order to defend the institutions of the labour movement against fascism.[1] That concession to democracy must have cost him dear; it showed it was the workers to whom his loyalty returned in the end.

The second heroic figure was Lenin. It was the Russian revolution of 1917 that aroused Sorel from his pessimism. In 1919 he added a post-script—*Pour Lénine*—to his *Reflections*. He was impressed by the *élan* of the revolutionaries. The bolshevists had overthrown bourgeois civiliza-tion in its entirety, destroyed the democratic state, ousted politicians and intellectuals. They had created a spontaneous new order based on producers' soviets. Sorel hailed Moscow as the Rome of the proletariat. "Lenin may with good right be proud of what his comrades have done; the Russian workers have to their eternal glory begun to realise what was hitherto only an abstract idea." While Mussolini paid him unsolicited tribute, Lenin, whom Sorel admired to the last, repudiated the philosopher who had taken up his cause. He dismissed Sorel in one sentence: "There are people who can give thought to absurdity; to that class belongs the notorious muddlehead, Georges Sorel."[2] Had Sorel lived longer, he would doubtless have found the bolshevist contribution to the noble and the sublime even more illusory than that of the other movements which had aroused his hope. His last loyalty was doubly tragic.

[1] G. Sorel, *Lettres à Paul Delesalle*, letter of 13 July 1921, p. 236.
[2] V. I. Lenin, *Materialism and Empirio-Criticism*, 1947.

The philosopher and the labour movement

It would probably be true to say that whatever interest exists in revolutionary syndicalism outside France today is the result of the attention drawn to it by Georges Sorel. The *Reflections on Violence* has become one of the classics of political science. It is in his terms that syndicalism is usually discussed, not only in the histories of political thought but even in the histories of the social movement. Posthumously at least, Sorel has monopolised syndicalism. This is a false identification. He was never an active member of the labour movement, not did he have any real influence on its militants. His interpretation of their ideas, moreover, was very much his own. Two facts remain: his insights contribute to an understanding of the syndicalist movement; his ideas add depth to the philosophy of syndicalism, if such a philosophy is allowed to exist independently of the movement.

SOREL AND THE SYNDICALISTS. Sorel had no contact with the labour movement as such. He never set foot in the offices of the *C.G.T.* and played no part, however small, in its affairs. His world consisted of his home, the *Bibliothèque Nationale*, the editorial offices of whatever review he was associated with at the time and the bookshops of Marcel Rivière and Paul Delesalle. His contact with the militant theorists of the *C.G.T.* was hardly greater. Delesalle was a personal—probably the last—friend; they corresponded regularly after 1917 and he was sufficiently interested in Sorel's work to compile an excellent bibliography which was published in 1939. But this contact came after Delesalle had left the *C.G.T.* Griffuelhes and Pouget told a historian of the movement that they had never read a single line of Sorel's work.[1] He probably met some of the militants during the brief period when both contributed to the *Mouvement Socialiste* although there is no record of any discussion between them. The style of some of the militants was occasionally reminiscent of Sorel, especially Griffuelhes, who claimed, however, to read nothing but Dumas. The ideas of Pouget and Delesalle were shaped by the anarchist tradition from which they came; Yvetot and Sorel were poles apart. It was unlikely that the rank and file had even heard of the *Reflections*; had they read it, they would probably not have understood; had they understood, they would certainly not have agreed. Sorel the *causeur* was usually the centre of a group of young bourgeois intellectuals; Sorel the syndicalist was an isolated figure. His connection

[1] M. Leroy, *Les tendances du pouvoir et de la liberté en France au XXe siècle*, 1937, p. 89.

249

with the *Mouvement Socialiste* was itself short lived, lasting from 1898 to 1901 and again from 1906 to 1908. Lagardelle was for a time under his spell but remained a political creature at heart, a fact which led to their break. The syndicalist *nouvelle école*, of which he liked to write, consisted in the last analysis of himself and Edouard Berth.

It could of course be said that Sorel never claimed, nor even wished, to influence the labour movement; he wanted merely to understand and clarify the tendencies working themselves out within it. He saw himself as a historian and remained constantly aloof despite the polemics that filled his work. Sorel certainly stressed his own detachment in the *Reflections*: "One does not need a great knowledge of history to perceive that the mystery of historical development is only intelligible to men who are far removed from superficial disturbances; the chroniclers and the actors of the drama do not see at all what, later on, will be regarded as fundamental; so one might formulate this apparently paradoxical rule: it is necessary to be outside in order to see the inside."[1] But this view was not entirely consistent with the Bergsonian theory of knowledge he professed. By standing outside the drama, he risked seeing a play which had no existence in reality; falling into the rationalist-utopian trap he so often condemned, he could people the stage with imaginary characters. That, of course, accounted for his subsequent disappointment.

Nor can one easily accept the claim that Sorel remained aloof from current strife. If one takes into account the whole tenor of his work, one is likely to see not the disinterested historian but a man passionately concerned that syndicalism should succeed in the task he had set it. His repeated demands for an intensification of the class struggle were not the revelations of historical inevitability nor, presumably, were they thrown out without an audience in mind. For a decade at least he tried to influence the men of action, to convert socialists and urge on syndicalists, by the only means open to an intellectual: polemical articles in left-wing reviews. He has been more justly described as a Commander of the Faithful proclaiming the Holy War against the infidel, incessantly preaching the virtues of violence to the workers.[2] But he preached from his bourgeois retreat and they barely heard him.

Questions of influence aside, how much did the syndicalism of the militants have in common with Sorel's syndicalist philosophy? There were undoubted similarities but there were also fundamental differences. The workers saw the class struggle not as a tactic of moral regeneration but as a way of improving the material conditions of their life; this was as true of the

---

[1] G. Sorel, *Reflections on Violence*, 1916, p. 49.
[2] P. Perrin, *Les idées sociales de Georges Sorel*, 1925, p. 104.

The philosopher and the labour movement

revolutionary phase (the emancipation of the proletariat meant the material expropriation of the expropriators) as it was of the reformist. For such ends Sorel showed no sympathy. As a rule he simply ignored the fact that immediate, material improvements might be achieved by strike action. Sometimes he even opposed the workers' immediate demands: the eight-hour day, a fundamental issue for the *C.G.T.*, he rejected as an element of decadence.[1] He was not even entirely committed to the ultimate triumph of the proletariat. The movement was all; merit lay in the battle rather than in victory. Even if the general strike never occurred and the proletariat remained unemancipated, the idea of the strike would have served its purpose if it had rendered socialism more heroic. Another point: the militants, optimists of anarchist extraction, looked forward to a utopian era of peace and plenty; this the pessimist Sorel saw as a bourgeois ideal of the worst sort. His utopia meant discipline, morality and hard work which, in Proudhon's phrase, would be the moral equivalent of war. It is only fair to add, though it would have been little consolation to the workers had they grasped it, that he was almost consistently devoted to their interests as he saw them.

Sorel professed to see in the emerging class of skilled industrial workers the development of a new morality to replace the threadbare morality of the bourgeoisie. He rediscovered the virtues of the mediaeval craftsmen in the modern producer: integrity and pride in work, discipline and solidarity. But, while craftsmen contributed to the development of syndicalist ideas, it was often the unskilled labourers who formed the revolutionary—or at least violent—rank and file. It was unlikely that many syndicalists found pleasure in work for its own sake; it was, on the contrary, something they hoped to reduce to a minimum after the revolution. Their practice of sabotage was an obvious offence against the principle of pride in work, a fact which Sorel realised. Nor did they share his code of morals, summed up in the phrase that the world would only become more just as it became more chaste. He opposed syndicalist propaganda for birth control for this reason.

Sorel's writing about violence, though it referred to syndicalist direct action, also showed little appreciation of reality. He contrasted the 'jacobin violence' of the bourgeoisie with the 'pure violence' of the proletariat. The latter he saw as a form of war as it might have been practised in some distant age of chivalry: its motives were neither hatred nor vengeance, nor selfish interest, but only devotion to a higher cause. The violent methods used by the syndicalists have been discussed under the headings of strike, boycott, sabotage, intimidation and political pressure. These were neither disciplined nor disinterested; they were not war at all in Sorel's sense but often outbursts of hatred, directed to no other purpose than revenge.

[1] G. Sorel, *Insegnamenti sociali della economia contemporanea*, 1906, p. 252.

Ideological context

Sorel looked at the syndicalist movement through the spectacles of his own morality. His account was not an objective description but a subjective interpretation charged with value judgements; his anti-intellectualism notwithstanding, it was really a utopian construction. Syndicalism developed without Sorel and Sorel without syndicalism. What, then, was their relationship? Allowance must be made for his natural and sustained sympathy for the workers, and for the fact that his support of the proletariat found some logical justification in the marxist doctrine that it was the class of the future. In the last resort, however, his espousal of the proletariat was an accident of history. Sorel turned to syndicalism because it appeared to reflect his temper and because the forces of history appeared to be on its side. As Schumpeter said, to those who at the time hated not so much the economic arrangements of capitalist society as its democratic rationalism, syndicalism could well have appeared as the complement of their own need in the world of the masses.[1] His syndicalist philosophy was a superstructure built to justify this utilitarian alliance.

The first decade of the present century saw the dominance of syndicalist ideas in the labour movement. Syndicalism soon gave way to reformism and the movement developed along orthodox lines of co-operation with party and state. This remained true even with the subsequent development of a communist wing. The aim—the welfare of the working class—remained unchanged; what changed was the temper and with it, the strategy. Syndicalism was the anti-democratic, anti-intellectual, activist moment in the history of the French trade-union movement. During this period Sorel called himself a syndicalist. It was the trade-union moment in the history of the revolt against Reason and democracy in France. For a short while the two movements crossed one another. Sorel stood at the crossroads.

THE CONTRIBUTION OF GEORGES SOREL. According to Sorel, the official marxists of his day had entirely failed to grasp the inner meaning of their master's work and were simply repeating in a pedantic manner the more trivial, and dubious, of his formulae. Their blind devotion had led all but Bernstein to ignore the failure of his prediction that the class war would become ever more acute. Starting with Bernstein at this point of criticism, Sorel followed a revisionist path of his own to reinterpret Marx in terms of his own theory of the myth. Marx's theory of the class struggle, he wrote, was not objective but subjective, not a scientific observation but an abstraction, a happy symbolic formula—a sort of social poetry, designed to inspire the workers, urging them forward in the best interests of mankind.[2]

[1] J. A. Schumpeter, *Capitalism, Socialism, Democracy*, 1943, p. 340.
[2] G. Sorel, *Matériaux d'une théorie du prolétariat*, 1919.

252

The philosopher and the labour movement

Another way of putting it was that he reinterpreted historical materialism in terms of the new philosophy of pragmatism. The class war was not necessarily a social fact already but thinking could make it so: the myth might validate itself. "The philosophers have only interpreted the world, in various ways; the point, however, is to change it." That—Marx's concluding thesis on Feuerbach—Sorel felt deserved more weight than the marxists gave it. For the militants, concerned with action, ideas only mattered as motors of action. The idea of class war simplified the complexities of the social order and created a class awareness that itself made the conflict a reality. Sorel's interpretation of the doctrine of the class war as myth rather than law of history, of the class war itself as something to be achieved rather than a fact of existence, was a view not entirely dissimilar from that of the syndicalist leaders. They recognised the material conflict of interests, but saw the need to stimulate awareness of that conflict in the minds of the rank and file, on the whole by the propaganda of action.

Scientific socialism, with its claim to the knowledge of social causation and its deterministic view of history, was repugnant to Sorel's temper. He reinterpreted what he still claimed to be historical materialism in psychological terms, injecting at the same time a large measure of free will into history. Class consciousness was not determined by objective production relations but subjectively by a myth which was more than a marxist superstructure of ideas. Sorel used Bergson's philosophy of creative evolution. The orderly process of social change was periodically broken by spontaneous mass movements, similar to mutations in biology. History moved forward by revolutionary surges, when a new force suddenly burst on the world. Dialectical materialism recognised similar revolutions, when quantitative change gave way to qualitative, but these were part of a unilinear process (even if the line moved dialectically) and were historically determined. The Sorelian revolution was the result of an almost self-generated force of ideas and largely unpredictable. Twisting the marxist phrase, he saw those moments as leaps from the realm of necessity to the realm of freedom.

Sorel complained that the doctrinaire marxists of his time were ignoring the first half of the sentence: "Man makes his own history, but in determined conditions." Berth took up this theme in his *Du 'Capital' aux 'Réflexions'*: it was necessary to adopt a less mechanistic philosophy than the vulgar marxism which taught the workers that history would serve them their emancipation on a platter; the workers must realise that revolution depended on them, not on events—it was the human factor, free will, that counted in the end.[1] The syndicalists shared this view. Rejecting the fatalism

---

[1] E. Berth, *Du 'Capital' aux 'Réflexions'*, 1933, pp. 39, 43, 48.

of Guesde and his marxist colleagues, they saw the revolution as a poten-
tiality, not as the iron law of necessity; it could only become actuality by the
workers' own conscious efforts. *Vouloir, c'est pouvoir* was the militants'
slogan.

The class war, far from becoming sufficiently acute to create a revolutionary situation, was actually being smothered by the spread of democratic
ideas. According to Sorel, the intellectual theorists of democracy had
diverted the capitalist bourgeoisie from the unadulterated pursuit of its
own interests, which naturally clashed with those of the workers, to a
timid policy of compromise that went under the name of social peace. The
socialist parties had done nothing to prevent the resulting confusion of
classes; indeed, they had been the first to fall under the spell of the intellectuals. It was the task of syndicalism to reassert socialist independence.
Both Sorel and the militants preached the complete breach between proletariat and the bourgeois order, its institutions as well as its parties. Only
thus could the struggle acquire clarity, the proletariat its identity, and the
myth its content.

Sorel's interpretation of the idea of the general strike has already been
discussed. He argued in the *Matériaux* that it contained all the essentials
of the syndicalist stand: it proved that the proletariat could emancipate
itself without resort to political revolutions; it showed the futility of reforms,
expressing in concrete terms Kautsky's thesis that capitalism could not be
abolished piecemeal; it was born of everyday experience, learnt in the
everyday strike by a simple association of ideas, without any need to study
the philosophy of history.[1] In this respect the general strike was as much
the centre-piece of Sorelian doctrine as of syndicalist theory. The truth of
the myth was a question without meaning; it was a useful formula for
influencing the present. This was something of an esoteric doctrine; one
which would have lost all potency had it been shared by the workers. And
what of the picture itself that he wanted them to grasp without reflection?
To the critical observer he seemed to be preaching a new mysticism, a new
religion almost, with its own believers. The myth of the general strike was
intended as a stimulant; it could be seen more negatively as a new opium
of the working class.

"The whole future of socialism lies in the autonomous development of
the *syndicats*", wrote Sorel.[2] The unions were to be the basis of the new
society as well as the ranks in which the battle was to be fought. A conservative at heart, he saw the unions as a modern alternative to Le Play's
autorités sociales. He quoted Durkheim to the effect that corporations,

---

[1] G. Sorel, *Matériaux d'une théorie du prolétariat*, 1919, p. 59.
[2] G. Sorel, *Matériaux d'une théorie du prolétariat*, 1919, p. 59.

composed of persons doing the same work and with the same interests, were the best foundation for the growth of a social spirit. Wisely, he refused to commit himself on details of the new order. He asked a critic who complained about this whether he thought that the socialists were students sitting an examination: the working class had entered the struggle without waiting for the permission of schoolmasters; they were making a siege, not a critique.[1] One thing could however be said of the *syndicats*. Exclusively working class in membership, they isolated the workers from bourgeois ideas and bourgeois values. A society based on the unions would be a producers' society. Socialists should look with suspicion on those who live on the margin of production—and what he meant by production was quite clear: there were not a hundred ways of producing but only one, and that was in the workshop. There would be place neither for the business men of capitalism nor for the intellectuals of democracy. His hostility to the non-productive professions was absolute: apropos the expulsion of managers from industry, he declared that they were as useless as members of the Academy, sociologists and heroes of national defence.[2] It was an attitude shared by the militants of the *C.G.T.* In Sorel's case it may have reflected the hostility of the engineer to the administrator, but it came oddly from a man who spent the last twenty-five years of his life as a professional thinker—scribbler, the militants themselves might have said.

[1] G. Sorel, *La décomposition du marxisme*, 1908, p. 4.
[2] G. Sorel, *Les illusions du progrès*, 1908, p. 358.

The militants and the
activist temper

Syndicalism, defined as the ideas and practice of the French labour movement, could not be understood simply by looking at books expounding
syndicalist theory: it is necessary to consider what actually happened, to
impute, as best one can, a theory into behaviour. Even the ideas of the
leaders of the movement cannot be presented as straightforward theory. It
was not just that they wrote occasional propaganda rather than texts for
the history of political thought. Syndicalism was primarily an attitude of
mind, an approach to politics—more basically still, a temper. This was
even truer of the leaders than the rank and file. Their philosophy was a
superstructure, not of marxist production relations but of their own spirit
of revolt; the policies they advocated were part rationalisations, the form in
which their personality could find expression at a given time, in a given
place. The activist temper was the real core of syndicalism, just as it was the
underlying core of the wider revolt against Reason and democracy. This
motivating force was directed into the channels it took by the objective
conditions in which the militants found themselves and was, to that extent,
not divorced from economic realities. But there was another side. The
activist temper, undirected in origin, sometimes translated itself into undirected practice. The syndicalist movement contained a measure of pure
action, action for its own sake. Schumpeter commented. "Why should we
refuse to recognise the truth which life teaches us every day—that there is
such a thing as pugnacity in the abstract that neither needs nor heeds any
argument?".[1]

It is difficult in the analysis of any social movement to strike a balance
between the part played by men and the conditioning scene. Earlier chapters considered the background, the various factors—social, economic,
political, ideological—which together made revolutionary syndicalism
possible, even likely. In the last resort, however, such historical 'causes' are
insufficient to explain more than the possibility. Movements finally depend
upon action; thus upon the motives for action; the motives are individual,
not social, phenomena. This is the more true of movements in which the
leadership plays an important role. The role of the hero in history can
obviously not be discussed here. The fact remains—and the point has been
made earlier—that a few militants led the syndicalist movement and put its
ideas into words; it seemed fairly clear that they also shaped those ideas and

[1] J. A. Schumpeter, *Capitalism, Socialism, Democracy*, 1943, p. 340.

256

influenced the direction the movement took. At some point, therefore, a psychological element must enter any explanation.[1] Clearly, not every person with an activist temper is driven to political revolt. Many find other outlets—on the battlefield, in the sports-field or even at the desk, in journalism or philosophy. The form their action takes is a secondary matter, however, because it depends on external circumstances, to that extent on chance. It is a secondary matter, furthermore, because in itself it contributes little to their satisfaction compared to the fact of action, of revolt as such.

THE MILITANTS OF THE LABOUR MOVEMENT. It is not hard to find in the writings of the militants statements which go far beyond the expression of any rational discontent with, for example, the economic system (a dissatisfaction that one might legitimately expect of workers in a capitalist system) but which point to a more fundamental conflict. Pelloutier, when he called himself a '*révolté de toutes heures*', gave no economic form to the object of his revolt; he added significantly that he was an irreconcilable enemy of all forms of despotism, not only material but moral. 'Moral despotism' sounds very much like 'social order'; Pelloutier was in revolt, not against the capitalist system or the political regime of his time but against society as such and its demands on the individual. Indeed, in another passage, he specifically praised the free man who placed himself outside the laws, however liberal they might be, in order to destroy them.[2] Pouget also expressed this sentiment of absolute revolt. The *révolté*, the revolutionary, he declared, was the man who denied the legitimacy of existing society and worked for its destruction; his attitude was one of permanent insurrection, permanent refusal to adapt himself to the existing order.[3] The tone was such that for 'existing order' one could almost certainly have substituted 'any order'. Both, of course, came from anarchism and had more than a touch of Bakunin in their make-up.

Not enough is known about the early life of the syndicalist leaders to explain their character. In several cases, however, one can point to the sort of conflicts that might give rise to a sense of frustration. In many cases the spirit of revolt preceded their allegiance to syndicalism. Nor were all the leaders born into the working class: they were not natural syndicalists (i.e. by force of circumstance).

Fernand Pelloutier (1867–1901) came from a bourgeois family which was, with the exception of a republican grandfather, of legitimist leanings. His

---

[1] Cf. R. Behrendt, *Der politische Aktivismus*, 1932.
[2] Pelloutier, *Lettre aux anarchistes*, cit. H. Montreuil, *Histoire du mouvement ouvrier en France des origines à nos jours*, 1947, p. 162.
[3] E. Pouget, *Le parti du travail*, 1905.

first education was in a seminary. At the age of nineteen he failed the *baccalauréat*, a necessary qualification for the sort of career normally followed by one of his class and education. He turned, as a result, to the typical profession of the dissatisfied intellectual—radical journalism; and from radical politics he turned to anarchism.

Emile Pouget (1860–1931) also came from a bourgeois background; he was the son of a notary. In his case the spirit of revolt can be traced back to his schooldays: at the age of fourteen he edited a manuscript newsletter in the radical cause, the *Lycéen Républicain*. He was preparing for the *baccalauréat* when the death of his stepfather forced him to leave school at fifteen and seek employment as a shop-assistant. Thereafter he was a professional revolutionary: at nineteen he organised the first union of Paris shop-assistants: at twenty-three he was arrested together with Louise Michel on a charge of riot and pillage; released from prison after serving part of an eight-years sentence, he edited the anarchist paper *Père Peinard*; his support of the anarchist outrages of Ravachol, Vaillant and Emile Henry (themselves examples of revolt without content) forced him to flee the country and he lived as an exile in England until the next amnesty.

Georges Yvetot (1868–1942) came from a humbler but respectable family. His father was a guardsman and he was born in the barracks of the Paris *gendarmerie*. The background was military and religious. When he was seven his mother died and he was sent to the Christian Brothers to be educated; soon in conflict with the school authorities, he was sent home again. Then his father died and he received the remainder of his schooling in a catholic orphanage. His vehement antimilitarism, it may be guessed, had its roots in family history.

Paul Delesalle (1870–1948), like Pouget, was from early youth a professional revolutionary and figured regularly as such in the police records of the time. He was a leading member of the anarchist *Groupe des étudiants socialistes révolutionnaires internationalistes* from its foundation in 1891 and of other anarchist groups. According to one historian, though his evidence is not convincing, Delesalle himself confessed many years after the event that he was responsible for one of the anarchist outrages of the time, a bomb thrown in the Restaurant Foyat in April 1894.[1]

The leaders of the *C.G.T.*, far from being manual workers, in many cases led a white-collar life similar to that of a less prosperous bourgeois intellectual. Pelloutier was a journalist and at one time edited the *Démocratie de l'Ouest*. As secretary of the *Fédération des Bourses* from 1895 until his death in 1901, he also edited, and in large part wrote, the review

---

[1] A. Zévaès in *Ordre*, 13 and 29 April 1948.

The militants and the activist temper

L'Ouvrier des Deux Mondes. For a time he held a post as temporary civil servant in addition, doing research in labour statistics. Pouget was another journalist. Having edited the *Père Peinard* and *La Sociale*, his main function in the *C.G.T.* was the *Voix du Peuple*. Delesalle was a skilled craftsman, a precision mechanic who, in his youth, had received a medal for draughtsmanship at evening classes. He also took the first opportunity, at twenty-five, to turn to journalism and after 1897 assisted Grave with the anarchist paper *Temps Nouveaux*. In 1908 he acquired a secondhand bookshop and to all intents retired from the labour movement. Yvetot was a typographer, a trade that has always been noted for the intellectual character of its members (Proudhon was a forerunner). Victor Griffuelhes (1874–1923) alone had a genuinely working-class background, starting life as a shoemaker. But even he became a permanent union official in early youth, secretary in turn of his local *syndicat*, of the leatherworkers federation, the trades council for the Seine and the *C.G.T.* He spent most of his life as an organiser, speaker and pamphleteer.

It is an old fact that revolutionary movements have been led by uprooted members of the very class against which they were directed. There is hardly a great name that escapes this rule, from Marx, author of a thesis on Greek philosophy, down to Stalin, the Tiflis seminarist. It may be argued that socialism was largely the product—and the instrument—of activist-minded intellectuals.[1] Before such a generalisation is applied to syndicalism, its character as a popular movement must be remembered. So, however, must the fact that the principles adopted by the *C.G.T.* owed a good deal to a small group of leaders. A syndicalist historian of the *C.G.T.* called Pouget its grey eminence: "Il fit triompher ses convictions et ses procédés par la souplesse de son esprit, son opiniâtreté d'auvergnat, sa puissance de travail, sa logique de dialectique, son expérience de tous les instants."[2] Another historian saw the energy of Griffuelhes as the decisive factor in the growth of the *C.G.T.*: "Il possède les vertus d'un chef: courage, force agressive, rapidité de vision et décision."[3]

In any case, the question here is not whether a revolutionary-minded group of militants created the syndicalist movement but why they themselves turned to syndicalism as an outlet for their energy. Activism, according to Karl Jaspers, finds its direction by the chance of the situation in which it occurs.[4] One must distinguish between the activist temper as such (i.e. the motive for action) and the form in which it is expressed (i.e. the politics it pursues). Allegiance to a movement depends on the possi-

[1] Cf. R. Behrendt, *Der politische Aktivismus*, 1932.
[2] A. Pawlowski, *La C.G.T.*, 1910, p. 102.
[3] E. Dolléans, *Histoire du mouvement ouvrier*, 1936–9, vol. 2, p. 118.
[4] K. Kaspers, *Psychologie der Weltanschauungen*, 1919.

17-2

bilities of the time, involving not a rational decision but a rationalisation. At this point, of course, economic factors enter the picture. The conflict between the individual and society may actually have an economic cause: career frustration rather than frustration in earlier youth; even if that is not the cause, it may still be that the economic structures prevent him from finding an adequate outlet for his energies. More important, his politics, his language and way of thinking, will certainly reflect a class background and class interest. This is good marxist doctrine and hardly needs elaboration. Griffuelhes may be cited as an example. Before he became a syndicalist he was a *blanquiste*—and *blanquisme* was essentially a matter of temperament, a mode of action, rather than a political doctrine; it was clearly the economic environment, however, that determined the direction he took.

On the other hand, it is not so simple to explain the adherence to syndicalism of such militant anarchists as Pouget and Delesalle. The development of Pouget's ideas was nevertheless instructive. Although his revolutionary activity went back at least to 1883, the year he was arrested with Louise Michel, he did not turn to syndicalism until 1894 when, a refugee in London, he finally saw the futility of the anarchist tactics of the time, mainly individual action, propaganda by the deed (in other words, bomb-throwing). As he wrote in the *Almanach du Père Peinard*: "I am an anarchist; I want to spread my ideas; I already have the *bistro*; I want something better."[1] He discovered the *syndicat* as the best place for revolutionary propaganda. The same argument was put forward by Delesalle in a later pamphlet advising the anarchists to take over the *syndicats* as the ideal basis of revolt.[2] Both came to syndicalism because they saw there the best chance of revolutionary action; individual action having failed, they turned to collective action and, making a virtue of necessity, translated their old anarchist doctrines into the new theory of syndicalism.

Equally significant was the extent to which Pouget remained an individualist at heart even as leader of the *C.G.T.* In a revealing passage he proclaimed the right of the individual to act as he thought fit regardless of the sentiments of his fellows: he had the right to revolt against oppression even if he was in a minority of one; the mass of men, indeed, he contemptuously described as 'human zeros' who could be safely ignored by the militant. That Pouget should have allowed himself so open a glorification of the individual, despite the theory that syndicalism expressed the will of the movement (and that in a pamphlet entitled *Les Bases du syndicalisme*), showed the nature of his conversion to syndicalism and the primary character of the activist temper.

[1] E. Pouget, *Almanach du Père Peinard*, 1897.
[2] P. Delesalle, *L'action syndicaliste et les anarchistes*, 1901.

The militants and the activist temper

There were other times when this primary temper broke through rationalised syndicalist doctrine and the militants affirmed the virtue of action as such, regardless of content. Thus Pouget again, in his pamphlet *Action directe*: "Action is the spice of life, the creative element in human societies. Outside action there is nothing but inertia, weakness, passive acceptance of servitude. In such periods men are reduced to the level of beasts in the field, drudges without hope, their minds empty, their horizon closed. But let action come! Their torpor is shaken, their tongue-tied minds function, radiant energy transforms the human mass." Even the more sober Griffuelhes wrote that syndicalism called the workers to action and thus showed itself as the force capable of regenerating the world.[1] This was the spirit of the romantic movement. The militant syndicalists could take their place beside Nietzsche and Sorel.

On the other hand, the four militants of the *C.G.T.* never showed the instability of the adventurer Mussolini or the theoretician Lagardelle. Griffuelhes, secretary of the *C.G.T.* from 1902 to 1909, played no role in union affairs thereafter, though he did sympathise with the communists after the war. Pouget, assistant secretary from 1901 to 1908, tried to start another paper but soon withdrew. Delesalle, assistant secretary of the *Section des Bourses* from 1898 to 1908, turned to his bookshop. Yvetot, secretary of that section from 1901 to 1918, disappeared until 1939 when he signed an appeal for immediate peace. Consistent in his pacifism, unlike Hervé, though perhaps confused by age, he allowed himself to be appointed president of a collaborationist committee for workers' aid and it was a representative of the German embassy who spoke at his funeral. None of the four sought alternative outlets for action; discouraged but loyal, they preferred retirement once the heroic age of syndicalism had passed.

[1] V. Griffuelhes, *Le syndicalisme révolutionnaire*, 1909.

Syndicalism as a philosophy of action

Syndicalism has sometimes been called a philosophy of action. This description was apt because it covered in a single phrase the twofold character of the revolt against Reason. First, distrust of theory as a proper guide to conduct: syndicalism derived from action, drawing its principles from the lessons of life rather than ivory-tower speculation; it was concerned with action, a strategy to achieve material aims, rather than the solution of philosophical problems. Second, the glorification of action itself: instead of rational, democratic modes of conduct such as discussion, compromise and reform, it preached the tactics of direct action. Syndicalist hostility to Reason thus reflected on the one hand an approach to problems that was part intuitive, part pragmatic, and on the other the spirit of revolution and the activist temper. The purpose of this chapter is to illuminate further the anti-intellectual aspects of syndicalist doctrine. It is necessary to emphasise once more that the syndicalism considered here is that of the leaders and, to that extent, is something rather different from the principles and practice of the *C.G.T.* as discussed earlier. The philosophy of action is found, or, better perhaps, implied, in the ideas of the militants. The point has already been made, of course, that these were themselves something of a rationalisation and could not be taken entirely on their face value. This, however, no more invalidates their philosophy than any other.

THE INTUITIVE ELEMENT. The phrase 'philosophy of action' has sometimes been used as if to imply that there was no consciously held syndicalist theory at all, as if syndicalist action was a philosophy in itself. The syndicalists, so the argument ran, did not philosophise about their actions but acted more or less spontaneously; in their case, therefore, the way they acted could be considered as the equivalent of the philosophies found in other social movements. An example of this view: "Syndicalism is a mode of action rather than a doctrine, and it is in the activity of the workers rather than in any books that its expression is to be found."[1] Seen thus, syndicalism was a mode of conduct, unreflected upon beforehand and not reflected upon afterwards, given its 'ism' merely to bring it into line with other social movements.

A similar definition, but one that raises other problems: "Created by the daily action of the militants, syndicalism is a practice rather than a theory; for them, it could not resemble a theory which one might adopt or reject—

---

[1] R. H. Soltau, *French Political Thought in the Nineteenth Century*, 1931, p. 465.

Syndicalism as a philosophy of action

it grew out of them and was identified with them."[1] Clearly, the militant theorists of the movement could not themselves have believed that syndicalism was simply a form of action, for that would have contradicted their own activity as writers and thinkers. Nor could they have believed that it simply grew out of them, without the possibility of choice between theories; as writers and thinkers they were, after all, self-conscious. They nevertheless maintained that syndicalism was characterised by spontaneous action and this view was not untypical. Such remarks, taken more literally than they deserved, would force one to conclude that syndicalism really existed on two levels: as a spontaneous form of action in the case of the rank and file; and as a theory about such action in the case of the pamphleteers. It is a nice point whether the theorists were simply putting practice into words or producing something rather different: the syndicalist theory that syndicalism was action is not the same as syndicalist action. It looks a bit like language and meta-language and perhaps one should talk of syndicalism and meta-syndicalism. In practice, however, it is enough to remember that the theorists were making two points: that syndicalist action ought to be largely spontaneous and that syndicalist principles in fact emerged more or less spontaneously from the experience of action.

According to Pouget, the grouping of workers into *syndicats* took place spontaneously and without the intervention of preconceived ideas.[2] This was confirmed by Griffuelhes: it was economic need and the sense of exploitation that drove him, as a worker, to his union. There, he learnt the lessons of action one by one, his vision widened, the implications of the class struggle became clear and his ideas began to define themselves.[3] A composite picture of ends and means gradually took shape. This syndicalist picture—the principles and practice of the *C.G.T.*—grew out of experience and impressed itself on the mind in the same natural fashion, intuitively, without the intervention of thought. Socialist theory, by contrast, was the result of reflection in the abstract—about life, perhaps, but in a study—and was accepted intellectually. Lagardelle, as usual, took the argument to its extreme. Experience was the school of syndicalism; life would reveal to the working class what it must do; the class struggle would enlighten the workers; practice would shape their ideas; *l'action crée l'idée*.[4] This brought one directly to the romantic movement: life was the true guide; the barren leaves scattered by intellectuals could only divert the workers from their true path.

---

[1] J. Maitron, *Le syndicalisme révolutionnaire: Paul Delesalle*, 1952, p. 34.
[2] E. Pouget, *La C.G.T.*, 1908.
[3] V. Griffuelhes, *L'action syndicaliste*, 1908.
[4] Lagardelle in *Mouvement Socialiste*, 1/15 October 1905, p. 263, and September/October 1911, p. 174.

Ideological context

The intuitive and the pragmatic approach were inseparable here. Practical experience was a better guide than any theory, so was the common-sense of the ordinary working man. This double point was made by Pouget in a less mystical version of the experience-is-the-school-of-life argument. The revolutionary could learn the most useful lessons from a study of the tactics working themselves out within the proletariat; when they did not allow themselves to be diverted by outsiders, the good sense of the workers nearly always showed them the best direction to take.[1] The task of the theorist of syndicalism was thus to study the existing practice of the working class and its sentiments. He should clarify, formulate and explain. As a propagandist, he should make the workers aware of the nature of their hitherto spontaneous action, the significance of their hitherto unexpressed feelings. The theorists were to be interpreters, not original thinkers, explaining the workers to themselves, not teaching them their own philosophy. This duty was laid down by Griffuelhes: "It is not a question of teaching a strategy of action but of exposing its *raison d'être* (i.e. its origin) and its justification (i.e. its use)—thereby giving syndicalist action the clarity and authority it requires."[2] The role of the propagandist, in other words, was to enable the rank and file to act more effectively and to stimulate it to further action.

THE PRAGMATIC ELEMENT. The term 'philosophy of action' could be defined in another way—as "a doctrine evolved by men immersed in action in order to render their action more effective".[3] This was another way of saying that principles were adopted because they were useful, because they worked. The syndicalists were much less concerned with elaborating a closed social philosophy, an internally consistent doctrine, even a programme consistent over time, than with solutions to the immediate, practical questions facing them in their everyday struggle against employers and state—questions of strategy and tactics. The ends of this strategy, the sense in which it was to be effective, could be taken as self-evident, hardly requiring discussion: in the short run the improvement of the workers' position, in the long run the emancipation of the proletariat. The answers did not need to form a systematically organised body of ideas, nor did they have to remain unchanged. Individual problems, altered circumstances, even changing demands—all could be accommodated.

The syndicalists made this pragmatic, essentially non-theoretical,

---

[1] Pouget in *Mouvement Socialiste*, June/July 1904, p. 166.
[2] V. Griffuelhes, *L'action syndicaliste*, 1908.
[3] Challayé, 'Le syndicalisme révolutionnaire' in *Revue de Métaphysique et de Morale*, January/March 1908, p. 114.

approach part of their theory. It was expressed most clearly in the writings of Griffuelhes. In an important passage (from which the remark that syndicalism was characterised by the spontaneity of its action has already been quoted) he said that syndicalist action was the result of practical experience, reflecting the needs of the moment, rather than the expression of a previously worked out theory or even a previously defined plan. He added that as syndicalism sprang from practice, and as this practice was created by events, by life that changed and modified every day, so, for that reason, it was incoherent and full of contradictions.[1] Ideas were held, in other words, so long as they served a purpose. Such ideas did not need to be consistent as their logical underpinning was hardly relevant to their usefulness.

The pamphlet in question, however, was written at a time when he had moved towards a more realistic interpretation of the tasks of the labour movement, slightly different from his earlier and purer revolutionary ardour. In the following year, in 1908, he commented approvingly on an increase in trade-union activity which, by filling the militants' time, had detached the movement from its earlier revolutionary romanticism and bound it to actuality, to the ordinary everyday issues of unionism.[2] Unless one remembers the underlying revolutionary temperament, as well as the pragmatic approach, one is likely to miss the true character of the syndicalist movement.

THE ACTIVIST ELEMENT. Yet another commentator said of syndicalism that it represented a renaissance of revolutionary volontarism.[3] Elie Halévy declared that, having awoken the taste for violence in the working class, it had led to the reappearance of a romantic ideal.[4] The syndicalists' taste for revolutionary action was indisputable. Certain of the militants made a cult of action that went well beyond the merely practical. Action, wrote Pouget, was the spice of life—or, more simply, action was life itself.[5] To an extent, such remarks reflected a particular temperament, one for which the mere fact of action was as important as the ends to which it was directed. But the cult of action also formed an integral part of syndicalist doctrines. This was dramatically expressed in the key slogan of the movement—*action directe!* That sober arguments were advanced in support of direct action has been shown in the earlier discussion. The failure of the workers to achieve their demands through parliamentary (i.e. indirect) action threw them back on their own resources (i.e. direct action). Support

---

[1] V. Griffuelhes, *L'action syndicaliste*, 1908.
[2] Griffuelhes in *Action Directe*, 23 April 1908.
[3] M. Raléa, *L'idée de révolution dans les doctrines socialistes*, 1923.
[4] E. Halévy, *Histoire du socialisme européen*, 1948, p. 234.
[5] E. Pouget, *L'action directe*, 1910.

could also be found in the truth recognised by the *Communist Manifesto*: the emancipation of the proletariat must be the work of the proletariat itself. Good fortune was not a gift, wrote Griffuelhes, it had to be conquered; syndicalism proclaimed the duty of every worker to act for himself.[1]

The communists, when it suited their purpose, also preached direct action to the workers, but their understanding of the term was very different. This difference highlights the activist character of syndicalism. A marxist historian of the labour movement stigmatised syndicalism as anarchistic on the not entirely unfair grounds that it involved the exaltation of the individual, the rejection of discipline, the reliance on an active minority—as compared to the massive action of the proletariat.[2] The only thing odd about his interpretation was that it was written after Lenin's elitist revolution. The syndicalist concept of direct action was certainly marked by three notions: emphasis on the individual rather than the mass; acceptance of spontaneity rather than planned, disciplined policies; belief in the creative possibilities of action regardless of historical laws.

Of all the syndicalists, Pouget advanced the elite theory in its most extreme form. The rule of the slumbering, unrevolutionary majority, so many zeros, he contemptuously labelled *démocratisme*. For him, the strength of syndicalism lay in its giving the class-conscious minority the right to act as it thought fit. He relied on the impulse of the elite to spur the movement forward.[3] *Vouloir, c'est pouvoir* was another favourite slogan of the syndicalists. Given the will to act, all can be achieved, The revolutionary task of the proletariat was thus far greater, and far nobler, than the mere midwifery ascribed to it by Marx and Engels. It would create the revolution by its own power and of its own free will. This volontarist doctrine, in the words of Lagardelle, taught the workers that there was no fatality, that man made his own history, that syndicalism needed only to call upon *ardeurs combatives, appétits d'héroïsme, enthousiasme, besoin de combat* and *soif de conquête* to triumph against all odds.[4] Spontaneity was the third characteristic. Griffuelhes claimed that the French worker, once aroused, passed immediately to action. It was this that distinguished him from his German brother, stolid, prudent and overburdened by marxist theory. The syndicalist did not allow himself to be distracted by too much reflection; he did not waste his time on unproductive arguments. Carried forward by his impulsive spirit, he acted—*et voilà tout!*[5] Griffuelhes might well have quoted Hamlet on the dangers of thought: enterprises of great pith and

---

[1] V. Griffuelhes and L. Niel, *Les objectifs de nos luttes de classe*, 1908.
[2] R. Garmy, *Histoire du mouvement syndical en France*, 1933, p. 276.
[3] E. Pouget, *La C.G.T.*, 1908.
[4] Lagardelle in H. Lagardelle *et al.*, *Le parti socialiste et la C.G.T.*, 1910, p. 31.
[5] Griffuelhes in H. Lagardelle *et al.*, *Syndicalisme et socialisme*, 1908, pp. 56–8.

Syndicalism as a philosophy of action

moment by this regard their currents turn awry and lose the name of action. There was much to be said, in practical, revolutionary terms, for the Latin temperament.

THE ANTI-INTELLECTUAL ELEMENT. Schumpeter maintained that syndicalism differed from all other forms of socialism in being anti-intellectual, both in the sense that it despised constructive programmes with theories behind them and in the sense that it despised the intellectuals' leadership.[1] He might have made a partial exception for British socialism, but that is by the way. Historically seen, hostility to the intellectuals could be explained by the betrayal of the bourgeois socialists in parliament. It was also the result of a natural antipathy to those who, as members of another class, had not experienced the privations of the workers and who led an entirely different life—a point made by Yvetot.[2] Intellectuals have theoretical programmes, moreover, and these also the less well educated workers were likely to regard with impatience: they often had little capacity, and even less taste, for theoretical discussions which led to no immediate results. But the double hostility to which Schumpeter drew attention was also a corollary of activism, The attitude of the militants was a common one, found in all walks of life—that of the practical man or the man of action towards mere theory and the armchair critic. It was expressed by Pelloutier when he likened socialist theory to the predictions of the astrologer's almanac; the unions preferred the more practical approach of the workers.[3]

The refusal to philosophise Pouget called the sobriety of syndicalism.[4] He saw in it, like Schumpeter, the mark that distinguished syndicalism from all other forms of socialism, but he also saw in it its superiority—*on philosophe peu; on agit!* The reports of the first labour congress of 1876 already had warnings against the infiltration of bourgeois intellectuals into the labour movement. The ineffective socialist utopias of earlier years could all be attributed to socialist thinkers who were quite out of touch with the realities of working class life, however well intentioned they might have been. To prevent such system-makers from leading the movement along another blind alley, the congress decided to admit only working-class delegates. In similar fashion, Pouget warned the proletariat against allowing itself to be deflected from the path indicated by its own good sense by those who would set themselves up as its directors of conscience. For this

[1] J. A. Schumpeter, *Capitalism, Socialism, Democracy*, 1943, p. 339.
[2] G. Yvetot, *Les intellectuels et la C.G.T.*, n.d.
[3] F. L. E. Pelloutier, *Histoire des Bourses du Travail*, 1902, p. 155.
[4] E. Pouget, *Le parti du travail*, 1905.

reason the syndicalist contribution to socialism, the idea of the general strike, could boast no proud genealogy; it emerged from the everyday practice of the labour movement: this explained both its discredit in orthodox circles and its superiority as a weapon in the hands of the proletariat.[1]

The rejection of intellectuals had deeper roots than this. Hostility to the bourgeoisie as a whole was deeply ingrained in the syndicalist movement. Syndicalism, in this respect more marxist than Marx, preached class war in its purest form, the absolute breach between proletariat and the rest of society. Pouget defined syndicalism quite simply as the autonomous organisation of the working class.[2] The proletariat was sufficient unto itself. It tended to see any member of another class, and such the intellectual necessarily was, as an irreconcilable enemy, however ardent his protestations of good will. In a pamphlet on the intellectuals and the *C.G.T.* Yvetot drove the doctrine to its ultimate conclusions. *Chacun chez soi!*— leave us in peace!—was his slogan. The proletariat could manage its own affairs; it alone understood what needed to be done, the goals to be achieved and the strategy to be followed; it neither required, nor desired, assistance from another class—be it moral or material. Sympathetic members of the bourgeoisie and well-intentioned intellectuals had no role to play in the strategy of syndicalism. The general strike would not involve any action on the part of professors, lawyers, doctors, journalists or parliamentarians. Nor, it appeared, would intellectuals have much of a role to play in the new society that the syndicalists hoped to establish. Literature and art were secondary professions at best; the workers could in any case write the novels and sing the songs themselves that society might legitimately require. The proletariat alone would inherit the future: then, said Pouget, all parasites will be eliminated and only the working class will survive.[3]

[1] Pouget in *Mouvement Socialiste*, June/July 1904, p. 166.
[2] E. Pouget, *Le parti du travail*, 1905.
[3] E. Pouget, *Le parti du travail*, 1905.

Conclusion

There were many similarities between the ideas of syndicalism and those of the wider revolt against Reason and democracy. Similar factors influenced both; both were a reaction against bourgeoisie, parliament and intellectuals. This double relationship—at once ideological and historical—suggests that syndicalism was itself part, the extreme left wing, of that revolt. There were also many similarities between the temper of the militants of the labour movement and the militants of the extreme right. This suggests another—psychological—relationship: not only a common enemy, but a common activist spirit, finding different outlets. The two can be linked. Activism was bound to mean revolt against the centre, partly because the centre was in power, partly because it stood for discussion, compromise and social peace. Syndicalism was not the last romantic movement of the left, any more than fascism was of the right. The revolt against Reason and democracy continues—and it continues for much the same reasons as those which influenced the syndicalists.

Until recently, syndicalism seemed to have been almost forgotten. The historians of political thought have usually treated it as a minor by-way of socialism, not part of any mainstream leading to the present, a curious, almost eccentric, episode, short-lived and several decades extinct. The syndicalists, it seemed, had explored a dead-end path. Even if this were all there was to the movement, it was more than a curiosity. The historical importance of syndicalism should not be underrated. It dominated the French labour movement for two decades and had its echoes elsewhere. Nor should it be underrated ideologically. Despite its apparent lack of coherence and its self-avowed dislike of theory, it offered, properly understood, a coherent, self-contained theory of socialism which could hold up its head amongst others, not as scientific as marxism perhaps, but no less scientific than fabianism. And it is no longer clear that it is entirely dead, that the path it followed was entirely false. True, there is no syndicalist labour movement today, but many of its ideas are in the air once more. Until recently, two socialisms dominated the scene: the reformist and the marxist, social democracy and communism. There was a tendency to write off most other socialisms as irrelevant, most other socialists as slightly odd. Tito, Mao and Castro, changed that. Socialist thought is richer for them. It is richer also for syndicalism which, it is now clear, also has something to contribute to the debate. Some may find its goal, the producers' society based on trade unions, too simple for the present day. Others may find its strategy of the general strike no longer plausible. Neither need invalidate

Conclusion

what it had to say about bourgeois democracy, the parliamentary system, party politics and reformist socialism. Nor need it invalidate what it had to say about the marxist alternative. The syndicalists, indeed, were they alive today would have found much in the intervening decades to prove them right. It is in its critique, perhaps, that syndicalism is most effective. That, unfortunately, it shares with many social philosophies. Unfortunately, there may be no practical alternatives that avoid the vices the syndicalists saw in the rival socialisms of their time. The direct-action socialisms of our own day may suffer the same fate.

Bibliography

TRADE-UNION CONGRESS REPORTS

Fédération nationale des syndicats (1886–95) and *Fédération nationale des Bourses du Travail* (1892–1902). *Confédération Générale du Travail: comptes rendus des congrès confédéraux de la C.G.T. avec les rapports morals et financiers des comités confédéraux et commissions pour l'exercice* (1895–).

JOURNALS

The official paper of the C.G.T., *La Voix du Peuple* (1900–), edited by Pouget. Two papers published for short periods by revolutionary syndicalists: *Action Directe* (1903–4) and *Bataille Syndicaliste* (1911–15). The anarchist *Temps Nouveaux* (1895–1914), edited by Grave with the assistance of Delesalle, and the antimilitarist *Guerre Sociale* (1906–15), edited by Hervé with contributions by Yvetot. Two reviews to which theoreticians and militants contributed: *Mouvement Socialiste* (1899–1914), edited by Lagardelle, and *La Vie Ouvrière* (1909–14), edited by Monatte.

SYNDICALIST PAMPHLETS

C.G.T., Commission des grèves et de la grève générale. *Grève générale réformiste et grève générale révolutionnaire*, 1903
Delesalle, P. *Aux Travailleurs—la Grève!* 1900
   L'action syndicaliste et les anarchistes, 1901
   Les deux méthodes du syndicalisme, 1903
   La C.G.T.—historique, constitution, but, moyens, 1907
   Les Bourses du Travail et la C.G.T., 1909
Griffuelhes, V. *L'action syndicaliste*, 1908
   Le syndicalisme révolutionnaire, 1909
   Voyage révolutionnaire—impressions d'un propagandiste, 1910
Griffuelhes, V. and Jouhaux, L. *L'encyclopédie du mouvement syndicaliste* (vol. A only), 1912
Griffuelhes, V. and Niel, L. *Les objectifs de nos luttes de classe*, 1908
Groupe des étudiants socialistes révolutionnaires internationalistes, *Les anarchistes et les syndicats*, 1901
   La grève générale, n.d.
Pataud, E. and Pouget, E. *Comment nous ferons la révolution*, 1909
Pouget, E. *Le parti du travail*, 1905
   Les bases du syndicalisme, 1906
   Le syndicat, 1907

Bibliography

Pouget (*cont.*)
  La C.G.T., 1908
  Le sabotage, 1910
Yvetot, G. *Le nouveau manuel du soldat*, 1903
  A.B.C. syndicaliste, 1906
  Les intellectuels et la C.G.T., n.d.

BOOKS ON SYNDICALISM AND THE FRENCH LABOUR MOVEMENT

Acht, A. *Der moderne französische Syndikalismus* (Dissertation, Jena), 1911
Blum, L. *Les congrès ouvriers et socialistes français*, 1901
Bothereau, R. *Histoire du syndicalisme français*, 1945
Bouglé, G. *Syndicalisme et démocratie*, 1908
Briand, A. *La grève générale et la C.G.T.*, 1900
Brisson, H. *Histoire du travail*, 1906
Buisson, E. *La grève générale*, 1905
C.G.T. *La C.G.T. et le mouvement syndical*, 1925
Cazalis, E. *Positions sociales du syndicalisme ouvrier en France*, 1923
  Syndicalisme ouvrier et évolution sociale, 1925
Challayé, F. *Syndicalisme révolutionnaire et syndicalisme réformiste*, 1908
Clark, M. R. *History of the French Labour Movement, 1910–1928*, 1930
Courtès-Lapeyrat, F. *La C.G.T.* (Thèse, Grenoble), 1914
David, J. *The Labour Movement in Postwar France*, 1931
Diligent, V. *L'action syndicale ouvrière* (Thèse, Caen), 1908
  Les orientations syndicales, 1910
Dolléans, E. *Histoire du mouvement ouvrier*, 3 vols. 1936–9
Dubuif, H. *Le syndicalisme révolutionnaire* (textes choisis), 1969
Estey, J. A. *Revolutionary Syndicalism*, 1913
Franck, C. *Les Bourses du Travail et la C.G.T.*, 1910
Garmy, R. *Histoire du mouvement syndical en France des origines à 1914*, 1933
Goetz-Girey, R. *La pensée française syndicaliste: militants et théoreticiens*, 1948
Gottsched, W. *Die sozialen und theoretischen Grundlagen des französischen revolutionären Syndikalismus* (Dissertation, Basel), 1917
Guy-Grand, G. *La philosophie syndicaliste*, 1911
Halévy, D. *Essais sur le mouvement ouvrier en France*, 1910
Humbert, S. *Le mouvement syndical*, 1912
Jouhaux, L. *Le syndicalisme et la C.G.T.*, 1920
  La C.G.T.—ce qu'elle est, ce qu'elle veut, 1937
Keufer, A. *L'éducation syndicaliste*, 1910
Kritsky, Mlle. *L'évolution du syndicalisme en France*, 1908

Bibliography

Lagardelle, H. *L'évolution des syndicats ouvriers en France* (Thèse, Paris), 1901
Le socialisme ouvrier, 1911
Lagardelle, H. (ed.), *La grève générale et le socialisme: enquête*, 1905
Syndicalisme et socialisme, 1908
Le parti socialiste et la C.G.T., 1910
Lefranc, G. *Histoire du mouvement syndical français*, 1937
Leclercq, M. and Girod de Fléaux, E. *Ces messieurs de la C.G.T.*, 1908
Le Gouellec, H. S. *De l'idée syndicaliste* (Thèse, Rennes), 1907
Leroy, M. *La coutume ouvrière*, 1913
Les techniques nouvelles du syndicalisme, 1921
Levine, L. *The Labour Movement in France*, 1912
Leyret, H. *De Waldeck-Rousseau à la C.G.T.*, 1921
Louis, P. *Histoire du mouvement syndical en France 1789–1906*, 1907
Le syndicalisme contre l'Etat, 1910
Le syndicalisme français 1906–1922, 1924
Histoire de la classe ouvrière en France, 1925
Histoire du mouvement syndical en France 1789–1948, 2 vols. 1947–8
MacDonald, R. *Syndicalism*, 1912
Maitron, J. *Le syndicalisme révolutionnaire: Paul Delesalle*, 1952
Ravachol et les anarchistes, 1964
Marchal, A. *Le mouvement syndical en France*, 1945
May, A. *Les origines du syndicalisme révolutionnaire* (Thèse, Paris), 1913
Mermeix (pseud. G. Tarrail), *Le syndicalisme contre le socialisme*, 1907
Montreuil, H. (pseud. G. Lefranc), *Histoire du mouvement ouvrier en France des origines à nos jours*, 1947
Pawlowski, A. *La C.G.T.*, 1910
Pelloutier, F. L. E. *Histoire des Bourses du Travail*, 1902
Lettre aux anarchistes, 1906
Pelloutier, M. *Fernand Pelloutier, sa vie, son oeuvre*, 1911
Petit, A. *Formation et esprit du syndicalisme* (Thèse, Rennes), 1911
Pierrot, M. *Syndicalisme et révolution*, 1905
Philip, A. *Trade-unionisme et syndicalisme*, 1936
Russell, B. *Paths to Freedom: Socialism, Anarchism, Syndicalism*, 1918
de Seilhac, L. *Les congrès ouvriers en France, 1876–1897*, 1899
Syndicats, fédérations, Bourses du Travail, 1902
Les congrès ouvriers en France 1893–1906, 1909
Serbos, G. *Une philosophie de la production, le néo-marxisme syndicaliste* (Thèse, Aix), 1913
Spargo, J. *Syndicalism, Industrial Unionism and Socialism*, 1913
Stoddard, J. T. *The New Socialism*, 1910

Bibliography

Tobler, M. *Der revolutionäre Syndikalismus*, 1919
Tridon, A. *The New Unionism*, 1917
Webb, S. and B. *What Syndicalism Means*, 1912
Weill, G. *Histoire du mouvement social en France 1852–1924*, 1925
Wirz, J. P. *Der revolutionäre Syndikalismus in Frankreich* (Dissertation, Zurich), 1931
Zacherl, C. *Entwicklung und Tendenzen der französischen Gewerkschaftsbewegung* (Dissertation, Erlangen), 1912
Zévaès, A. *Le syndicalisme contemporain*, 1912
    La C.G.T.—aperçu historique, 1939

BACKGROUND

Andreu, P. *Notre maître, M. Sorel*, 1953
Angel, P. *Essais sur Georges Sorel: de la notion de classe à la doctrine de la violence*, 1936
Antonelli, E. *La démocratie sociale devant les idées présentes*, 1911
Ascoli, M. *Georges Sorel*, 1921
Benda, J. *Le trahison des clercs*, 1927
Bergson, H. *L'évolution créatrice*, 1907
Berth, E. *Dialogues socialistes*, 1901
    Les méfaits des intellectuels, 1914
    Les derniers aspects du socialisme, 1923
    Du 'Capital' aux 'Réflexions', 1933
Biétry, P. *Le socialisme et les Jaunes*, 1906
Blanqui, A. *Critique sociale*, 2 vols. 1885
Bouglé, G. *Proudhon*, 1930
Bouglé, G. (ed.), *Proudhon et notre temps*, 1920
Buthman, W. C. *The Rise of Integral Nationalism in France*, 1939
Charnay, M. *Les allemanistes*, 1912
Cheydleur, F. D. *Essai sur l'évolution des doctrines de Georges Sorel*, 1914
Cole, G. D. H. *The World of Labour*, 1928
    History of Socialist Thought, vols. 1–3, 1953–6
da Costa, C. *Les blanquistes*, 1912
Crook, W. H. *The General Strike*, 1931
Curtis, M. *Three Against the Third Republic: Sorel, Barrès Maurras*, 1959
de Man, H. *The Psychology of Socialism*, 1928
Deroo, J. *Le renversement du matéralisme historique: l'expérience de Georges Sorel*, 1933
Dolléans, E. *Proudhon*, 1948
Droz, E. *Proudhon*, 1909
Elliott, W. Y. *The Pragmatic Revolt in Politics*, 1928

Bibliography

Esquerré, A. *Le néo-syndicalisme et le mythe de la grève générale* (Thèse, Bordeaux), 1913

Fouillée, A. *La pensée et les nouvelles écoles anti-intellectualistes*, 1911

Freund, M. *Georges Sorel: der revolutionäre Konservatismus*, 1932

Gray, A. *The Socialist Tradition*, 1946

Guy-Grand, G. *Le procès de la démocratie*, 1911
  Le conflit des idées dans la France d'aujourd'hui, 1921

Halévy, E. *Histoire du socialisme européen*, 1948

Horowitz, I. L. *Radicalism and the Revolt Against Reason: The Social Theories of Georges Sorel*, 1961

Humbert, S. *Les possibilistes*, 1912

Humphrey, R. *Georges Sorel: Prophet Without Honour*, 1951

Johannet, R. *Itinéraires d'intellectuels*, 1921

Joll, J. *The Anarchists*, 1964

Lasserre, P. *Georges Sorel, théoricien de l'impérialisme*, 1928

Le Bon, G. *Psychologie du socialisme*, 1898

Leroy, M. *Les tendances du Pouvoir et de la Liberté en France au XXe siècle*, 1937

Louis, P. *Histoire du socialisme en France de la Révolution à nos jours*, 1925

Maitron, J. *Histoire du mouvement anarchiste en France, 1880–1914*, 1952

Maurras, C. *Enquête sur la monarchie*, 1901

Mayer, J. P. *Political Thought in France from the Revolution to the Fourth Republic*, 1949

Meisel, J. H. *The Genesis of Georges Sorel*, 1951

Orry, A. *Les indépendants*, 1911

Pareto, V. *Mind and Society*, 1935

Parodi, D. *La philosophie contemporaine en France*, 1919

Perrin, P. *Les idées sociales de Georges Sorel* (Thèse, Alger), 1925

Perroux, F. *Georges Sorel et la grève générale*, 1928

Pipkin, C. W. *The Idea of Social Justice: A Study of Legislation, Administration and the Labour Movement in England and France*, 1927

Pirou, G. *Proudhonisme et syndicalisme révolutionnaire*, 1910
  Georges Sorel, 1924

Prolo, J. *Les anarchistes*, 1912

Prouhdon, P.-J. *Qu'est que la propriété?*, 1840
  Les confessions d'un révolutionnaire, 1849
  De la capacité politique des classes ouvrières, 1865

Raléa, M. *L'idée de révolution dans les doctrines socialistes*, 1923

Rennes, J. *Georges Sorel et le syndicalisme révolutionnaire*, 1936

Rocker, R. *Anarcho-Syndicalism*, 1938

Rossignol, F. *La pensée de Georges Sorel*, 1948

Bibliography

Sartre, V. *Georges Sorel: élites syndicalistes et révolution prolétarienne*, 1937
Saulière, A. *La grève générale: de Robert Owen à la doctrine syndicaliste* (Thèse, Paris), 1913
Schumpeter, J. A. *Capitalism, Socialism, Democracy*, 1943
Scott, J. W. *Syndicalism and Contemporary Realism*, 1919
de Seilhac, L. *Le monde socialiste*, 1896
Siegfried, A. *France, A Study in Nationality*, 1930
Sombart, W. *Socialism and the Social Movement*, 1919
Sorel, G. *L'avenir socialiste des syndicats*, 1901
    Introduction à l'économie moderne, 1903
    La décomposition du marxisme, 1908
    Réflexions sur la violence, 1908
    Matériaux d'une théorie du prolétariat, 1919
    Lettres à Paul Delesalle, 1947
Tannenbaum, E. R. *The Action Française*, 1962
Thibaudet, A. *Les Idées de Charles Maurras*, 1920
Valois, G. *La monarchie et la classe ouvrière*, 1909
    D'un siècle à l'autre: chronique d'une génération, 1922
    Techniques de la révolution syndicale, 1935
Variot, J. *Propos de Georges Sorel*, 1933
Vignaux, P. *Traditionalisme et syndicalisme*, 1943
Wanner, J. *Georges Sorel et la décadence* (Thèse, Lausanne), 1943
Weber, E. *Action Française: Royalism and Reaction in Twentieth Century France*, 1962
Woodcock, G. *Anarchism*, 1963
Zévaès, A. *Le socialisme en France depuis 1871*, 1908
    Les guesdistes, 1911
    Histoire du socialisme et du communisme en France de 1871 à 1947, 1947

Index

Alain, E. A. Chartier, 208
Allemane, J., 47, 67, 142
Andler, C., 199
d'Annunzio, G. 208, 231

Baihaut, M., 216
Bainville, J., 222
Bakunin, M., 30, 38–44, 150, 165, 257
Barberet, J., 63
Barrès, M., 208, 222, 224, 225, 247
Beauregard, Comte de, 133
Bebel, A., 50
Benbow, W., 148
Benda, J., 191, 208
Bergson, H., 6, 7, 8, 108, 191, 195, 200–3, 204, 209, 224, 239, 253
Bernstein, E., 35, 50, 103, 112, 244, 252
Bernstein, H., 229
Berth, E., 202, 224, 227, 236, 246, 247, 250, 253
Blanc, L., 21
Blanqui, A., 6, 33–7, 38, 41, 42, 48, 55, 100, 150, 165, 228, 233
Blum, L., 67, 144
Bodwitch, J., 18
Boncour, P., 32
Borgia, C., 198
Boulanger, Gen. G., 56, 220, 227
Boulé, 142
Bourchet, 166, 167
Bourgeois, L., 32, 57
Bourget, P., 246, 247
Bousquet, 116, 130
Breton, A., 196
Briand, A., 49, 59, 60, 65, 67, 141, 142, 143
Brogan, D. W., 25, 228
Brousse, P., 46, 47, 54
Buber, M., 103
Buisson, E., 110
Burke, E., 193, 195, 225, 242

Carnot, S., 43, 215
Carr, E. H., 38, 39, 42, 199
Cassirer, E., 162
Castro, F., 269
Cato, 13
Chesterton, G. K., 226
Clemenceau, G., 34, 59, 133, 216, 217
Clément, 118
Cole, G. D. H., 2
Combes, E., 57, 218

Comte, A., 191
Connolly, C., 210
Corradini, E., 236
Croce, B., 239, 244, 246, 247

Darwin, C., 197
Daudet, J., 222
Delesalle, P., 5, 43, 44, 76, 99, 120, 121, 125, 129, 130, 146, 148, 179, 181, 182, 245, 247, 249, 258, 259, 260, 261
De Man, H., 156, 157, 160, 162, 196
Déroulède, P., 213, 220, 221, 222, 226
Descartes, R., 191, 192, 212
Dillon, A. M., 221
Dolléans, E., 23, 182, 183
Dreyfus, A., 49, 57, 93, 128, 129, 216, 217, 221
Drumont, E., 216, 221, 222
Duguit, L., 205
Durkheim, E., 195, 254

Elliott, W. Y., 205
Engels, F., 54, 202, 266
Esterhazy, Major M., 217

Faure, E., 221
Feuerbach, L., 253
Frazer, Sir J., 195
Freud, S., 195
Fribourg, E. E., 29

Gallifet, General G. de, 49, 58
Gambetta, L., 213, 214
Gentile, G., 232
Girard, 143
Girardin, E. de, 140, 148
Goebbels, J., 217
Goethe, J. W., 7, 201, 204, 208
Gooch, R. K., 215
Grave, J., 259
Gray, A., 13, 18, 38, 103
Grévy, J., 215
Griffuelhes, V., 5, 69, 84, 85, 89, 93, 96, 101, 112, 128, 133, 137, 138, 149, 151, 154, 157, 163, 179, 181, 182, 186, 187, 249, 259, 260, 261, 263, 264, 265, 266.
Guérard, E., 90, 93, 113, 144, 150, 151, 152, 181
Guesde, J., 45, 46, 47, 50, 51, 53, 54, 55, 56, 57, 63, 64, 65, 66, 67, 93, 142, 149, 191, 244, 254

Index

Halévy, D., 214
Halévy, E., 42, 265
Hamelin, 144
Hegel, G. W. F., 28, 194, 196
Henry, E., 258
Henry, Col. H. J., 217, 222, 224
Hervé, G., 50, 55, 138, 181, 231, 237, 261
Hirsch, Baron, 221
Hitler, A., 191
Hume, D., 194

James, W., 8, 195, 204–7, 209
Jaspers, K., 259
Jaurès, J., 48, 49, 50, 55, 58, 217, 244
Joan of Arc, 229
Johannet, R., 246
Jouhaux, L., 4, 22, 89, 138, 181, 185
Jouvenel, R. de, 53

Kant, I., 194
Kautsky, K., 254
Keufer, A., 179, 180, 181
Kipling, R., 208
Kohn, H., 193, 196
Kropotkin, P., 43
Kugelmann, L., 29

Labriola, A., 230
Lafargue, P., 54, 65
Lagailse, 68, 69
Lagardelle, H., 39, 49, 62, 85, 100, 104, 155, 167, 206, 211, 219, 230, 237, 238, 245, 250, 263, 266
Laski, H., 205
Latapie, 90, 92
Le Bon, G., 131, 157, 159, 195
Le Chapelier, 20, 21, 22, 211
Legien, K., 138
Lemaître, J., 221
Lenin, V. I., 236, 248, 266
Le Play, P. G. F., 241, 254
Le Roy, E., 202
Leroy, M., 79, 91, 107, 129, 161
Lesseps, F. de, 216
Levine, L., 85, 133
Lévy, 133, 181
Lewis, Wyndham, 241, 246
Liebknecht, W., 65
Limousin, C., 29
Lorwin, V., 43
Loubet, E., 221
Louis XIV, 213
Louis, P., 211
Lovejoy, A. O., 202, 209, 233, 235
Lowell, A. L., 13
Luther, M., 191
Lyon-Caen, Prof., 229

MacDonald, J. Ramsay, 171, 235
Mackau, Baron de, 221
MacMahon, Marshall P. M. de, 213
Malatesta, E., 43
Mao Tse-tung, 269
Marinetti, F. T., 210
Maritain, J., 191
Marx, K., 25, 27, 29, 30, 36, 38, 40, 41, 42, 44, 45, 46, 92, 100, 101, 103, 105, 135, 137, 160, 165, 172, 195, 197, 198, 200, 202, 241, 243, 252, 253, 259, 266, 268
Maurras, G., 208, 222, 228, 236, 247
McGovern, W. M., 194
Merrheim, A., 181, 185
Mesureur, 74
Michel, L., 43, 258, 260
Michels, R., 167
Mill, J. S., 11
Millerand, A., 48, 49, 57, 58, 59, 60, 244
Mirabeau, G., 140
Mommsen, T., 208
Monatte, P., 115
Montesquieu, C. de S., 195
Mussolini, B., 8, 162, 205, 210, 230–8, 247, 248, 261

Napoleon, 213
Napoleon III, 21, 140, 141, 148
Niel, L., 69, 70, 90, 91, 92, 118, 149, 181
Nietzsche, F., 8, 194, 197–9, 235, 240, 241, 243, 261
Nomad, M., 36, 38

d'Orléans, Duc, 226, 227

Panunzio, S., 205, 227
Pareto, V., 161, 162, 163
Paris, Comte de, 221
Pascal, B., 191, 193, 206
Pataud, E., 87, 115, 150, 152, 160
Pavlov, I., 195
Pawlowski, A., 130
Péguy, C., 208, 211, 247
Pellieux, Gen. G. de, 221
Pelloutier, F. L. E., 30, 44, 65, 67, 68, 69, 75, 113, 142, 143, 149, 244, 257, 258, 267
Pétain, Marshall P., 237
Philip, A., 109
Pickles, D., 228
Picquart, Col. G., 217
Pirou, G., 61, 212
Plato, 162, 210
Pouget, E., 5, 43, 84, 85, 91, 97, 101, 105, 120, 121, 122, 124, 128, 132, 182, 183, 184, 249, 257, 258, 259, 260, 261, 263, 265, 266, 267, 268

Index

Proudhon, P. J., 7, 25–32, 36, 40, 42, 61, 91, 95, 100, 131, 166, 228, 239, 240, 241, 244, 247, 251, 259
Pujo, M., 223

Raléa, M., 104
Ramelin, 143
Ravachol, F. C., 258
Read, H., 195
Reinach, Baron de, 216
Renan, E., 239, 241
Renard, V., 179, 180, 181
Rist, C., 111
Rivain, J., 223
Rivière, M., 249
Rocco, A., 232, 234
Rochefort, H., 221
Rousseau, J. J., 39, 108, 191, 193, 194, 208, 223
Russell, B., 194, 200

Sade, Marquis de, 197
Saint-Simon, C. H. de, 191
Sartre, J. P., 191, 201
Schneider, 58
Schopenhauer, A., 194, 197, 198
Schumpeter, J. A., 6, 7, 13, 192, 252, 256, 267
Shils, E., 243
Siegfried, A., 16
Socrates, 197, 243
Soltau, R. H., 242
Sombart, W., 11, 108
Sorel, G., 2, 4, 5, 6, 8, 40, 62, 104, 108, 114, 140, 158–64, 192, 196, 197, 198, 199, 201, 202, 203, 205, 207, 217, 218, 220, 224, 227, 234, 236, 237, 239–55, 261
Spies, A., 184
Stalin, J., 259

Taine, H., 241
Tarde, G., 195
Thalamas, Prof., 229
Thibaudet, H., 209
Thiers, L. A., 23, 34
Thomson, D., 13
Tillich, P., 196
Tito, J., 269
Tolain, H., 29, 167
Tortelier, J., 43, 142
Treitschke, H. von., 208
Tridon, A., 123

d'Uzès, Duchesse, 221

Vaillant, E., 48, 50, 55, 57, 258
Valois, G., 223, 227, 236, 237, 246, 247
Variot, J., 246, 247
Vaugeois, H., 222
Vico, G., 239
Viviani, R., 59, 60
Voivin, 136
Voltaire, F. M. A. de, 191, 208

Waldeck-Rousseau, R., 22, 49, 57, 58, 64, 221, 244
Wallas, G., 195
Webb, S. & B., 219
Wilson, D., 215
Wordsworth, W., 193

Yvetot, G., 5, 44, 58, 70, 111, 113, 123, 136, 138, 179, 180, 181, 182, 242, 258, 259, 261, 267, 268

Zévaès, A., 134, 137
Zola, E., 217

279